BELOVED

Lisa Arnoux-Brown

WestBow
PRESS
A DIVISION OF THOMAS NELSON

WestBow Press books may be ordered through booksellers or by contacting:

WestBow Press
A Division of Thomas Nelson
1663 Liberty Drive
Bloomington, IN 47403
www.westbowpress.com
1-(866) 928-1240

ISBN: 978-1-4497-8570-3 (sc)
ISBN: 978-1-4497-8572-7 (hc)
ISBN: 978-1-4497-8571-0 (e)

Library of Congress Control Number: 2013904085

Printed in the United States of America

Scripture taken from the King James Version of the Bible.

Other books by Lisa Arnoux-Brown are the In the Line of Duty series.
In the line of Duty, Vendetta, Endgame and The Ezekiel Code

WestBow Press rev. date: 3/29/2013

INTRODUCTION

I have always enjoyed reading about Christian courtships. I have found them to be refreshing and have longed to experience them. Growing up in the church as I did, I have witnessed countless relationships begin and end. Some were godly while others followed in the worldly tradition.

It would be ideal to have courtships in the church modeled after Christ's example. We as a group are His intended and He treats us with the purest love and kindness. He never wavers in his devotion to us and He never conforms to the world.

The story unfolding in this book is a glimpse of what a godly courtship (I believe) should be. The couple is more mature but they face the same temptations everyone faces and yet they overcome it with prayer and temperance. The near misses are as teaching tools for future reference. Pastor D. Farmer and Evangelist D. Hollis were instrumental in helping me understand the mechanics of Godly courtship and Christian walk. Their impartation has proven to be invaluable.

I would like to see more godly courtship seminars in our churches. Perhaps it is because there aren't that many godly courtships in the church to use as examples to our youth that we find that even in churches across the country, there are young single parents. We have become too used to having our hearts broken and having our dreams fall apart that we don't teach our young boys and girls the proper way to a long, happy and successful courtship and marriage.

I hope the story is pleasing, entertaining and raises your awareness of what a godly courtship is and that you deserve it. May the Father that surpasses all things bless you and keep you!

CHAPTER ONE

Nina pulled the door closed behind her and then she walked down the three steps onto the lawn. Caving in, she turned around to look once more at the house she lived in for most of her life. She experienced a lot of good times and bad times in that house. Three months ago, she embraced her new status. She was on her own and was master of her destiny. With her forefinger and thumb, she flicked the For Sale sign planted on the lawn as she walked past it and stepped into the waiting limousine at the end of the curving driveway.

As an entertainer, Nina worked in show business for as long as she could remember. She was an acclaimed actor and award-winning singer. Her parents, who met at the famed Julliard School of Music in New York City, paved the way for her as talented musicians also. Her mother and father decided that California was the best place for them to make their fortunes in the music industry, and they married as soon as their careers took off. Her father was one of the best jazz musicians in the industry and her mother graced numerous stages singing chart-topping songs her dad wrote for her. Catalina and Charles Bennett were an unbeatable duo.

When Nina was just eight years old her mother died tragically in a car accident coming home from a performance in Chicago, leaving her dad sad and a single parent. Nina's father was a great parent in spite of how busy he was. She traveled with him wherever he performed until he discovered that she could sing too. Then he began to write music just for her and she often performed with him.

Nina and her father were a team until she was thirteen years old. Disney beckoned and the rest is history as they say. She was an instant sensation and as she got older, her star rose and soared.

Charles Bennett did not allow Hollywood to spoil his daughter. She hadn't fallen victim to the classic child star catastrophes that plagued her famous friends. She didn't drink or smoke and her father warned her long ago what drugs would do to her if she indulged in them. Now at twenty-five years of age, she was alone. Charles Bennett died a year ago of lung cancer. Apart from her career, he had been her world and she found that without him applauding her, her acting and recording career were not as satisfying as it once was. Feeling lost and alone, she decided that she was going home to her aunt her father's sister. She was going to New York.

Richard Feldman her longtime friend, agent and manager rode in the Limo with Nina as it ate up the road to the airport. He was the one person besides her father who really appreciated her abilities. He managed her career from the age of thirteen to the present. He was instrumental in helping her transition from singing with her father to acting in Disney's wholesome movies.

As she watched the scenery pass by, Nina found that she didn't feel sad.

"Nina there is still time to reconsider you don't have to do this," Richard said trying to reason with her.

Nina turned from the window to smile at him. She realized that she would miss him.

"Richard we've discussed this before. I know you feel that I should just take some time to regroup, but it really isn't about regrouping. It's about what I need right now. I'm no longer happy doing this," she tried to explain.

"I'm just saying that it doesn't have to be permanent. I could keep some doors open for you. All I ask is that you think about it while you're out there living the mundane life." Richard gestured with his hands as he spoke. He usually did that when he was upset.

Nina looked at the man who's managed her career ever since she was a very young girl and shook her head sadly.

"If I say I'll think about it you will run with it and before I know it, I'll be back doing the same old thing over and over again."

"No." Richard said shaking his head, "I'm giving you the chance to think about it and if you change your mind and want to come back, we can start slow until you're comfortable again. Okay?"

"Trust me to know what I want just this once Richard, please just this once." Nina begged him.

Because he cared about her and because it was hard to refuse her anything when she fixed those sea green eyes at him, he nodded and reached over to pat her hand. "Fine, but do me one favor while you're out there. Call me every now and then, I worry about you sometimes," he replied finally.

"I'm going to miss you too," Nina murmured and she reached over to hug her friend.

They didn't speak the rest of the ride to LAX. The driver parked as close as he could to the terminal doors while Richard helped Nina with her luggage. It took over an hour to check in with all the security precautions. The fact that she was a celebrity made every step longer. Nina felt frazzled by the time she boarded the plane to New York.

The flight was uneventful and since she wasn't the only celebrity on board the plane, celebrity hounds didn't bother her too much. After the inflight meal, Nina slid her sunglasses on like a diva and slept. The flight attendant shook her gently to wake her and to let her know that the plane had landed. Nina thanked her and stood up to grab her carry-on bag.

Following the signs, she arrived at the luggage bay to watch out for her suitcases. She had three big ones plus the carry-on.

She tipped the airport attendant handsomely for loading the cab for her and even waved at him as it took off. Nina promised her aunt that she would see her the following day and booked herself into a hotel. Richard almost had a stroke when she told him she was staying at a hotel in Queens. Nina reasoned that since her aunt lived in Queens she didn't want to travel very far to get to her. They planned to meet in church the following morning.

The hotel wasn't a four star but it was clean and it was close enough to the church. She even lucked out with the timing; it was late and the staff didn't recognize her.

Her first Sunday morning in Jamaica Queens dawned clear, sunny and cold. She accounted for March weather and dressed accordingly. Her plan was to check out early and to arrange for a rental car. When she stepped off the elevator, she made it to the front desk without recognition. Unfortunately, the desk clerk recognized her right away and Nina had to sign her autograph before she could obtain information about the rental.

Guests and staff alike crowded around her as she waited for the car. After what felt like hours, Nina took possession of a black Cadillac Escalade and once her luggage was stored in the back, she took off. She could hear Richard's voice in her head telling her that she should have rented the car when she booked her hotel room. Sunday school was out of the question now.

Nina drove the half mile or so it took to get to the church. It was ten o'clock and if she remembered correctly, the worship service would be just starting. The church was located in a secluded area behind a row of townhomes. The stain glass windows gleamed brightly in the harsh winter sunlight. Taking a deep breath, Nina parked in the church parking lot and stepped out pulling her scarf firmer around her neck. As she reached the door, people who were arriving just as she was were pointing and whispering. Nina paid them no mind and walked right in.

Nina was sure that her aunt had already arrived and was about to walk through the double doors that separated the vestibule and the sanctuary when a woman dressed in black and white stopped her.

"Praise the Lord, sister. Welcome to Christ Tabernacle," and she handed Nina a program. Nina thanked her and inquired about Sister Elaine Bennett-Hughes. The usher nodded and opened the doors to the sanctuary for her and pointed.

Her aunt it seemed sat very nearly to the front. The usher noted her hesitation and took her arm to lead her to her aunt. If the usher was waiting for a commotion, she was disappointed as Sister Elaine merely smiled and grabbed Nina's hand to pull her close. Afterwards she went right on singing and clapping her hands.

Aunt Elaine was a tall brown-skinned woman in her sixties. She was a little on the plump side with laugh lines on her smooth face. Nina's aunt and her father resembled each other a lot, which brought a small lump to her throat. Nina smiled back at her aunt and then turned her attention to the front of the church.

Again, some people recognized her and stared while others acknowledged her then returned to worshipping. Nina realized that she arrived at the very beginning of the service. It was praise and worship time.

Praise and worship was where a group of men and women led the congregation in song and worship until it was time for the Word part of the service.

After a moment of prayer and reading of the Scriptures, an elder introduced the pastor. He came up to the pulpit to welcome everyone. The elder whispered in his ear and immediately the pastor's eyes strayed to where Nina sat.

"Sister Bennett-Hughes has her niece visiting with us all the way from California this morning. Welcome to Christ Tabernacle Miss Nina Bennett," he said. All eyes turned to Nina and with the urging of her aunt, she stood up to modestly wave at those around her then she sat back down.

The sermon the pastor preached was very moving and Nina sat riveted in her seat. She was no stranger to the Word, but Nina had never heard it delivered so powerfully before and found herself shouting Halleluiah or Amen along with everybody else. Filled with power as the pastor spoke, Nina couldn't stop smiling. This was what she had been searching for she realized suddenly, this was what had been missing in her life.

Her father and she attended services in L.A but it was never like this. The power behind the words and the sincerity in the man who delivered it was authoritative and compelling. By the end, Nina had tears in her eyes and her aunt urged her to go to the altar for prayer, but she couldn't and shook her head. For the first time in her life, Nina felt shy. She felt that what she wanted was too personal for others to witness. Maybe when she was settled she would go, but for now it was enough that she could listen.

After service, she tried to be as inconspicuous as she could but didn't quite pull it off. The older people merely stared or smiled at her, but the younger set walked right up to her to shake her hand. Finally, at the insistence of her aunt, Nina approached the pastor.

"Sister Bennett, it was a pleasure having you worship with us," he said as he took her hand in his.

"Thank you. I am really glad I had the opportunity, I was really moved by your sermon." Nina told him honestly.

"Praise the Lord, that's what it is all about, sister." He pumped her hand once again and released it.

Next, her aunt introduced Nina to two of her friends, Sister Dorothea Jackson and Sister Rachel Winston. They smiled graciously at her but Nina recognized the phoniness in it. They had that look her father once described to her. It was a look that meant (you aren't all that).

Once they were outside, those who were waiting for her to come out flanked Nina. Nina shook her head and smiled apologetically at them then led her aunt to the rental.

"You don't expect me to ride in this monstrosity do you?" she asked.

The SUV was fully loaded with heated leather seats; power everything to name a few. Nina explained that she needed it because of her bulky luggage and further explained that she normally drove an SUV. She was having her Lincoln Navigator shipped later.

After making sure that her aunt buckled her seatbelt, Nina walked over to the driver's side and hopped in much to the amusement of the men eyeing her from the church's steps. Nina was only five feet five inches tall.

She flipped her reddish brown hair out of the way and started the car. Following her aunt's directions, they were soon parking in the driveway. Sister Elaine lived in Cambria Heights in a modest one family A-frame house. She has lived in that house forever and it hadn't changed one bit. Nina felt comforted by that.

Sunday brunch was a tradition in the Bennett family and her dad kept the custom in California too. She tried not to feel sad, but Aunt Elaine saw her shiny eyes and reached across the table to pat her hand.

"I miss him too baby," she confided to her.

"It's been a year but it still feels like yesterday. Almost everything reminds me of him," Nina explained.

"One day it will get better but for now we have to take it one day at a time. Now eat your food before it gets cold. Then we need to have a little talk. Go on eat," Aunt Elaine said gesturing with the hand holding her fork.

After eating the first real meal since she made up her mind to leave California, Nina was glad to help her aunt do the dishes. If she continued to eat this way, she would have to start going to the gym again, she thought.

Once the dishes were in the drainer, Aunt Elaine took her by the hand to lead her to the rooms upstairs. The house contained three bedrooms and she had a choice of the remaining two. The few times she came to New York were work related and if her dad accompanied her, she stayed in hotel in the city while her dad stayed with his sister. Nina asked for the room her father used when he visited and claimed it as hers. Side by side, they unpacked the suitcases and when they finished, Nina heaved a huge sigh.

"What was that for?" her aunt asked her.

"Unpacking makes it final. It's real and I'm here not there." Nina explained.

"That's something we have to discuss but if you're too tired from your flight, we can talk about it tomorrow or whenever you feel like talking," her aunt told her.

"We can talk now Auntie and as a matter of fact, I would prefer we do it now because once we are through, I can move on." Nina sat on the bed next to her to wait.

Her aunt shook her head, "Well I don't know about all that, but I wanted to make sure you knew what you were doing," she began.

"Did Richard call you?" Nina asked quickly.

"Who's he?" asked Aunt Elaine.

"He was my agent. He's been trying to change my mind ever since I told him that I wanted to quit. He couldn't understand why I needed to do this," Nina replied.

"Why *are* you doing this? You were living this wonderful life, having a ball from what I read in those magazines and a career that was making you a fortune," her aunt elaborated. Nina noted that her aunt's expression was one of concern.

This time it was Nina's turn to shake her head. "Auntie I wasn't happy. The money and the fame, none of it was worthwhile anymore if I wasn't happy in here," Nina said placing a hand to where her heart beat. "After Dad passed, it hit me. He was gone and I was alone. I realized that I did what I did because I could share it him. I enjoyed it but it was more for him than anything else because it made him happy and proud."

"What about your husband?" Aunt Elaine asked.

"What husband?" Nina countered. "You would know if I was married."

Aunt Elaine tapped a finger into the palm of her other hand. "I've kept every magazine that mentions you and in one of them it said that you had secretly married. Why would they print something like that if it weren't true?"

Nina got up to pace the length of her father's old bedroom. She was flabbergasted that her aunt believed the tabloids. Nina remembered the one to which she referred.

Richard advised her to ignore it because everyone would soon realize that it was not true when no husband materialized. There had been a lot of things printed about her that Richard advised her to ignore and now she was beginning to understand that he was using them for publicity. It might even be possible that he was planting those stories himself. To him, if she was in print then she was popular.

"I've never been married and there is no boyfriend either. It was just Dad and me. We didn't live as most celebrities did. We lived in a big house of course because that was what was available, and I had a nanny and a private tutor when I was younger. After I grew up, Dad and I took care of each other. We shared the housework and cooking." Nina's posture had taken on a proud stance as she spoke.

"I have magazines with pictures of you at parties and such. They have you dancing and drinking and carrying on; those pictures made me so sad Baby." Aunt Elaine said.

"There were pictures of me at parties and while there, I networked as Richard wanted me to. There was no drinking or carrying on. If there was a picture of me with a drink in my hand, you had better believe that it was Ginger Ale. You see Richard thought that if I were associated with the right people having fun, then I was what they called 'in'. Nina gestured quotation marks with her fingers.

"So you did all those movies to please your dad? What about the albums, did you sing to please him too?" Aunt Elaine had a frown on her face.

Nina thought for a minute and then shook her head. "No. I enjoyed making the movies they were fun. The singing was too but it seemed that after Dad died, the fun was gone."

"Wasn't there anything you did that you did for yourself?" asked her aunt.

"I didn't mean to make it sound like that. I didn't do anything I didn't want to do. I made movies and sang because I wanted to. Dad didn't force me and neither did Richard. I had a choice. It's just that one day I woke up and I didn't want to do them anymore." She told her aunt.

"So you just told everybody that you quit?"

"That wasn't easy either. I had to break my contracts, which cost a lot of money. Richard was upset about that. He'd been with me a long time and I truly believe that it wasn't about his percentage anymore, that he really cared about me. Still I had to fight to be free."

"So there's not going to be strange people knocking on my door looking for you?" Aunt Elaine asked pointing a finger at her.

"No. I severed all ties. I'm a New Yorker now. I'm going to stay with you for as long as you can stand me and maybe I'll find someone to marry and make you a great-aunt. What do you think of that?" Nina asked with a smile.

"That's right you are 25 years old now. Why aren't you married yet? You aren't one of those male/female types are you?"

Nina threw back her head to laugh long and hard. When she laughed herself out, she dried her eyes then hugged her aunt. "Auntie, what can I do for you, now that I'm here?"

"I don't need anything Baby."

Nina looked around the room taking in the peeling paint and old furniture.

"I know exactly what I'm going to do for you."

"What are you going to do for me?" Aunt Elaine asked her with a suspicious tone to her voice.

"I am going to wait until my belongings arrive and then I'm going to give this house a make-over." Nina told her with a gleam in her green eyes.

"Does that mean that you are going to fix this old place up?"

Nina nodded and her aunt hugged her tight. Then she told her to lie down and get some rest even if she didn't feel like it, her body had traveled a lot.

CHAPTER TWO

The following couple of months were busy ones for Elaine and her niece. Nina got her aunt excited about the renovations and she gave Nina free reign. While painters worked on the outside, Nina had the kitchen, bathrooms and all the bedrooms redone. Elaine wouldn't part with her old bedroom furniture though. She insisted that it was still good. She and her husband bought the furniture just before they moved into the house. Nina didn't push the issue anymore because there were a few pieces of furniture she had shipped to her that she couldn't part with either. There were things that she and her father shared like the baby grand piano and all of their awards. She arranged them in the room off the living room. Her aunt insisted the room was just a room she used to do her crafts. Nina couldn't find any crafts in the room and suggested that she use the other spare bedroom upstairs for her crafts since it was closer to her bedroom. Her aunt agreed.

Spring was giving way to summer and Nina continued to go to church with her aunt. The congregation had finally settled down to accepting her presence as status quo. She didn't have to rush to her car anymore and only worried about shopping. She figured that if she didn't visit the bigger store chains that she would do fine, but word does get around. Most times, she signed more autographs than she shopped.

It's been three months and Nina was finally starting to feel good about her choices when she found out that Richard had one more trick up his sleeve. He had been trying to get her to release a greatest hits CD. At the time, she agreed only to get him off her back, but didn't really intend on doing any recordings. She was feeling lost and just wanted to wallow in self-pity and sadness. She now realized that Richard ignored her and went ahead to commit her to several engagements. Perhaps he hoped to snap his client out of her funk.

She hadn't been able to pull out of an appearance he'd booked two weeks later, nor could she back out of a tribute to her father one month after that either.

The greatest hits CD must've been the other thing he had in mind for her. Richard didn't need her to record the CD. The record company just pulled a collection of all her more popular releases and placed them on two CDs.

When Nina called to speak with him, he very succinctly reminded her that she had agreed to it and signed a release form.

"Richard is there anything else I agreed to that I don't remember?" she asked him. She was being magnanimous because she honestly could not recall whether she signed a release or not.

"No. You turned down the cameo on that Bond movie. I was hoping that you had gotten bored by this time, but you even sound happy." Richard answered her.

"I am happy Richard and I'd like to think that you are glad for me," Nina told him not bothering to hide the annoyance in her voice.

"I am glad this is working out for you, really I am. I just think that we should keep in touch just in case you want to come back. I'll give you a ring next week."

The release generated another few weeks of autograph and CD signing after service, that even Nina felt a little uncomfortable. Her aunt's friends smiled their smiles and this time her aunt caught the look and commented on it.

It was late summer and the church was getting ready to have revival services. Her aunt explained that they did it every year after which they would have a picnic to end the summer season. The service and picnic was for the last two weeks in August with invited speakers and choirs from neighboring churches.

Christ Tabernacle had a great choir and Nina enjoyed listening to them sing. The choir director was young and he had vision. She thought that he could take the choir far if he wanted to. Elaine asked her about joining the choir and Nina answered that maybe someday she would.

It wasn't that she didn't want to sing, she did very much. She felt that if she sang with the choir, the director would feel obligated to have her sing lead. She didn't want that. The lead singer they had was fine with a powerful voice.

Just before the first service, Nina was home in the award room as her aunt had dubbed it, playing the piano. She displayed awards of every description and size on shelves and stands in the room. Before long, she lost herself in the music and didn't realize that she had been singing as well. She was singing one of her favorite Yolanda Adams songs. At the end of the song, the applause startled her. Elaine and the choir director were standing in the doorway clapping. Her aunt had tears in her eyes and the choir director stared at her with a gleam in his.

"Sister Nina that was absolutely wonderful," he said walking further into the room.

"Baby girl that was some mighty fine singing," Aunt Elaine agreed. She walked around the piano to sit next to her. She pointed to the choir director to introduce him.

"This is Brother Jonas our choir director."

"Hello Brother Jonas. Did you give my aunt a ride home from bible study?" Nina asked. Her heart was beating fast because she recognized the look in the man's eyes. She knew that he was going to ask her to sing.

"Yes I did. Sister Nina, I was wondering if you had any thoughts of joining our choir and if so I wanted to give you the schedule for our rehearsals." He was already sifting through a folder he held in his hand.

Nina pulled the piano lid down to rest her elbows on it. She regarded the man facing her with suspicion.

"I was under the impression that one had to be a member of the church before they could join the choir, is that not so?" Brother Jonas sputtered and nodded.

"Well yes that's right. I attended this months' administration meeting and Pastor mentioned that he had gotten your request to transfer from your old church in Los Angeles. I took it as an affirmative that you would become a member of Christ Tabernacle soon." Brother Jonas explained.

Nina nodded. "I haven't heard that it was granted yet Brother Jonas, but please don't take this the wrong way. I am very interested in joining the choir but I want to be comfortable as a member first before doing so."

Brother Jonas was clearly disappointed. He looked to Sister Elaine and shrugged. "Please be assured that when you decide to join the choir that you will be welcomed warmly. Goodnight Sister Nina." He turned to leave and Elaine got up to escort him out.

When she returned, Nina was still sitting at the piano and her aunt sat beside her once again. "You know Nina this isn't one of your shows where you make them wait. You are giving everyone the impression that you are a diva and unapproachable. We can't have those in our church," she said quietly.

"You told him that I would join the choir didn't you?"

"Of course I did. I remembered you mentioning just the other day how you wanted to join. I had the man give me a lift from the church just so he could talk with you about it. Why did you turn him down?"

"Aunt Elaine I didn't turn him down. I merely explained that I wanted to feel comfortable first. Besides there are too many people who still see me as a diva as you say. They won't want me to minister to them. I want to sing for the right reason not because Brother Jonas wants to impress the choirs visiting from the other churches these next couple of weeks."

Aunt Elaine nodded. "Okay, but can you do me a favor? The mother's board is leading the Wednesday night service and I am presiding. If I ask you to sing that song you just sang would you do it?"

Nina leaned toward her aunt to kiss her soft cheek. "Yes Auntie I would be happy to, but you have to do me a favor too. Don't tell anyone that I'll be singing that night."

"But I have to put you on the program," she protested.

"I won't do it if everyone knows. Brother Jonas will feel really bad if you do," Nina pointed out.

"How will the musicians know to play the song for you if it's not in the program?" she asked.

"Auntie I can play the song well enough by myself. Don't worry I won't embarrass you." Nina said with a smile and stood up.

Her aunt looked up at her expectantly. Nina told her that she was going out to her hair appointment and left.

Nina drove twenty-five minutes to the only hair salon she could find that did her hair right. It had been a nightmare these past few months finding anyone who could do it properly.

The salon was on the busiest part of Linden Boulevard. Nestled between a Farmer's market and a Real Estate office was Sophie's Hair Salon. She paid extra to go after hours because the first time she went there, it had been a fiasco.

Sophie herself insisted that she would stay open to do her hair if only she would come after hours. As a matter of course, Nina went every other Wednesday to have her hair done.

Nina had waist length locked hair. She wore her hair in that fashion since she was a young girl. Her dad told her that he had gotten tired of doing it and being a man who was rather busy with a career, he thought it was for the best. It wasn't easy trying to keep a young girl's hair looking neat, especially a bi-racial girl with red curly hair. He lucked out because Nina liked it.

As a teen, she tried different styles long and short and many colors in between before she realized that it was more becoming simple. The waist length became her unique signature style copied all over Hollywood and beyond. Today however, wearing locks was very fashionable and not the curiosity it had once been.

At the church, a few young girls approached her about starting locks and she told them that it was just a matter of taste and commitment. Her hair was long and evenly locked. It was hot in the summer and in the mild winters in California; she hadn't needed a hat as she did in New York.

There weren't many men in Los Angeles who liked the style either. They preferred the sleek style of processed hair. Since moving to New York, she found that it was very appealing to the men here. They called out to her on the street and if they happened to recognize her, she had to get away quickly. She stopped going for walks by herself for safety concerns.

As she sat under the dryer, Nina thought more about the church choir. There were a few new members in the church since she arrived and they were publicly welcomed into the fold. What Brother Jonas did was underhanded. She knew that he hadn't meant any harm, but in his enthusiasm in trying to get her to join the choir, he would have overstepped his bounds in not allowing the pastor to have the church welcome *her* as a member. It was something she wanted badly.

Being a celebrity was bad enough without having to seem to get special treatment. She knew that half the congregation felt that she wasn't a true Christian. Her perceived Hollywood past hindered them from seeing the real person that she was which bothered her a great deal. It was something she wanted to speak with the pastor about sometime, but he was busy man.

Pastor Darius Fairchild was a man she admired greatly. He had accompanied her aunt to California for her father's funeral services. Even though he was there to lend support to her aunt, he was respectful of her father's pastor and when asked to say a few words, was gracious and brief. He was a great source of comfort to her aunt then and Nina appreciated that of him.

She also found him to be intelligent and quite a powerful personality. She tried not to wonder too much about him fearing that it was some type of sin somewhere.

She felt sorry to learn that his wife died a few years ago. Once she had been attending services at Christ Tabernacle for a few weeks, she amused herself trying to spot the single women in the congregation who felt that they could be a great comfort to him. They sat up front, wore seductive clothing and always had to greet him after service.

It wasn't that she didn't find the young pastor attractive as well, she did but she also felt that her background and all the Hollywood hype stuck to her and no matter how hard she tried, she knew that it was going to take a very long time for her to shake it. Besides, the pastor barely gave her the time of day.

When Nina returned home, she found Elaine sitting in the living room reading the bible. Nina sat next to her listening. Her aunt read the Scriptures with confidence and ease that Nina vowed to follow her example to read the bible nightly for herself. She didn't read it on a regular basis because the wording confused her. Her aunt suggested that she buy a more modern version. Nina took her advice and now most nights she fell asleep reading. When Elaine finished reading, she patted Nina's hand and motioned for her to get on her knees for prayer.

Aunt Elaine's prayer was simple and to the point. Nina felt the tears burn behind her closed eyelids. Her dad used to pray in the same fashion. She realized that although her father left New York as a very young man searching for his place in the world, he carried what his parents taught him and his sister with him.

Her dad instilled strong moral values in her too and she never strayed from them. One of her dad's famous sayings was 'Do as I say and not as I do'. Hollywood changed him a bit especially after her mother died. He started drinking and smoking. He wasn't a very heavy drinker, but he smoked a great deal. Even after the diagnosis of lung cancer that claimed his life, he continued to smoke until the end.

After the prayer, her aunt told her that she was going to bed and headed up. Nina went to the award room to sit at the piano. She wanted to play but didn't want to disturb her aunt. Instead, she pulled out the photo albums she had of her past life in Hollywood from the piano bench.

There were many pictures of her parents at work in the album and of her as well on various stages singing. During those awful last days of her father's life, she sat beside him in his hospital bed looking through them. They talked and reminisced about all that they had done together. On his very last day, her dad told her that he would be very happy if she continued to sing. He said that was where her true talent lay.

He also told her to find a cause and to sing for it, not to let those bozos push her into anything she didn't want to do. That's what he called the producers, bozos. She sang Jazz with her dad because that's what his passion was, but what was hers?

She had one of those versatile voices that pulled off most any genre. Her dad helped hone her talents with piano and voice lessons. She wondered if she had any gospel in her. It was something that started to appeal to her and which she wanted to explore.

CHAPTER THREE

Since the revival began, the crowds packed in every night. Wednesday night service was no different. It was a challenge to get a seat if you didn't get there on time. Nina and her aunt always arrived early and always sat up front in the third row. She agreed with her aunt that the best seat in the church was up front. That way one didn't get distracted or miss anything.

Nina was feeling things she had never felt before and struggled to understand them. Most nights she cried and others she couldn't stop smiling. She felt a joy she couldn't describe and the beginnings of inner peace. Last evening she went up to the altar and the visiting preacher prayed with her.

When Elaine got up to start the service, Nina didn't feel nervous. She almost jumped up when her aunt told the congregation that Nina was going to sing. The musicians looked to one another in confusion but Nina smiled confidently at them and headed for the grand piano at the front of the church. She sat, closed her eyes and ran her fingers over the keys.

Following the example of other soloists on previous nights, she asked the congregation to pray for her and hoped that the song she was going to sing would encourage and bless them. With her eyes closed, she sang. She sang from her heart for the words of the song were her testimony. She felt that God had spoken to her and led her to a place of safety. He performed many miracles in her life and she had found peace.

The musicians joined in but didn't overshadow her piano playing. She sang true and when the she sang the last chorus, she heard the thunderous clapping, the shouting and the hearty Amen. When Nina got up from the piano, she wasn't surprised to feel the tears on her face and wasn't ashamed when an usher brought her a couple of tissues.

The highlight of the service for Nina was the sermon. Their pastor hadn't preached in three nights and tonight he was the speaker. After he read the Scripture, which he took from James, he prayed. Pastor Fairchild spoke of endurance and of faith. He encouraged the saints that gathered that evening to continue to hold on and to resist the temptations of the world.

He went on to point out what some of those temptations were and gave pointers on how to resist them. He spoke of lust, pride and boastfulness. "All is not lost my brothers and sisters. The fervent prayer of a righteous man availeth much. If you submit to the Lord and resist the devil, he will flee from you," said Pastor Fairchild at the end of his sermon.

Nina couldn't resist going up to the altar for prayer. When the pastor placed his hand on her head, Nina felt the presence of God, The Comforter and spoke in the heavenly language. It was amazing how good she felt afterwards.

When she returned to her seat, Elaine smiled at her from the pulpit. Nina returned her smile and wiped at the tears that spilled onto her cheeks.

The following services were just as comforting. Nina enjoyed the fellowship of the visiting choirs and other preachers who also spoke with power. With the last service came the invitation to those who wanted baptism. Nina didn't feel the need to do it again as she and her dad had done it in Los Angeles.

The church picnic was on the last Saturday of the month at Valley Stream State Park. Aunt Elaine along with a few other women from the church did most of the cooking and Nina was in charge of packing the food up for travel. Nina didn't think it was wise to wear pants, as it was a church affair, so she decided to dress for the weather and to dress simple.

She wore sandals with her white eyelet, just below the calf, peasant skirt. She complimented it with a sleeveless white cotton tee shirt. During the summer, Nina acquired a tan and she looked great in white. Her aunt advised her to use bug repellent and she sprayed her arms and legs liberally.

Aunt Elaine also chose to wear a skirt and blouse set and they were both comfortable and fashionable. Nina drove carefully as she was mindful of the food in the trunk of her SUV.

They arrived at the park early and Nina and her aunt delivered the food to the tables picked out for their group. By the time everyone who signed up to attend the picnic arrived, there were close to one hundred and fifty people present.

The pastor made his rounds and stopped to greet everyone who came. When it was time to eat, he blessed the food. Quite a few people from the visiting churches came to the picnic and most of them were young men. It was obvious that they were interested in some of the young women from Christ Tabernacle, and some were curious about her as well. Nina was enjoying herself until one young man approached her.

Nina was friendly and polite. The young man was nice looking but she really wasn't interested. When he walked away, Nina was grateful. "Now why did you turn that nice young man down?" her aunt asked. She remembered him from a visiting church. He was the lead singer in the choir.

Nina rolled her eyes. "He wasn't my type, and besides I didn't expect to be picked up at a church picnic."

"You know that is something I was wondering about. You've been home for almost six months now and you haven't gone out once. How are you planning on giving me those great-nieces and nephews if you aren't dating?" asked Aunt Elaine.

Elaine was loud enough so that several of the women sitting at their table overheard. They watched and waited for her response. Nina felt mortified. She didn't know what to say so she shrugged.

Suddenly, the pastor was at her elbow and she looked up at him. "Hello Pastor Fairchild, would you like to try some of my aunt's apple pie?"

He nodded and Nina cut him a piece. "Sister Elaine you know a picnic isn't complete without a piece of your apple pie, thank you," he said graciously then sat beside Nina. "So Miss Nina, how are you enjoying your stay in New York?" he asked making conversation.

Nina wanted to avoid eye contact with him but turned to face him turning red in the face in the process. "To be perfectly honest with you, I love it. California is great but I don't regret leaving." Nina answered honestly.

"So you are staying on then? I was under the impression that you were just taking a break, so the papers say." By now, everyone within earshot was very interested in her responses.

"No, I thought I made it very clear that I had quit? Hollywood and all of its trappings are in my past. I am a New Yorker now," Nina stated proudly with a smile.

"What will you do here?" he asked immediately regretting having started the conversation for Nina had that deer caught in the headlight look on her face.

"I was thinking of doing something for the community like my father did in Los Angeles. He bought a vacant lot to build a recreation center for the kids and added a wing to a nursing home across the street from it. I've been driving around the neighborhood surrounding the church and I don't see anything that would keep our young people occupied or out of trouble." Nina replied simply.

Her aunt squeezed her shoulder and the pastor nodded approvingly at her.

"That is very commendable of you Sister Nina. The young people in our community are a subject close to my heart. If you are serious about this endeavor; I would be very interested in hearing about your plans." Pastor Fairchild stated.

Nina nodded. "I do have very concrete thoughts about it. If you have time, I would like to discuss them with you Pastor. We can meet whenever you like just call the house and my aunt will give me the message." Nina agreed.

With everyone watching and listening to the conversation, she felt that it was the safest course of action. She would like nothing more than to spend time getting to know the man especially since he seemed curious enough about her to read about her in the papers.

Pastor Fairchild pulled out a palm pilot and scrolled through it shaking his head as he did so. "It looks like I am a very busy man these next couple of weeks. We can probably talk sometime in late September. Is that okay?"

"That would be fine Pastor." Nina replied then stood up to clear the table. She needed to do something, as she suddenly got very nervous. The women sitting at the table wore all manner of disapproving expressions on their faces that made Nina feel even more uncomfortable.

When the pastor got up to leave, he waved and smiled at the women, but Nina pretended to be too busy clearing the table to wave back. Aunt Elaine clucked like a mother hen and galvanized the women to help with the clearing up.

When she and Nina had a moment alone, she spoke. "I have a feeling that our young pastor is interested in you. What are you going to do about it?"

"Auntie, wherever did you get that idea? Let's not talk nonsense, look around you. The sun is shining, there's a cool breeze and I am full. Come for a walk with me," Nina suggested not at all sure, she wanted to talk about the very handsome pastor.

"I'm too old for those long walks you like to take," her aunt replied.

Nina laughed and pulled her aunt along. "You are not that old and you are healthy as a horse. Come on, the walk will do you good and it'll help you digest all that home cooking." Nina teased her, patting her stomach.

As they walked, she elaborated on the plans she laid out to the pastor. Her aunt expressed how proud she was of her and tried to steer the conversation back to the man who showed interest in her plans, but Nina wouldn't let her. Nina was afraid of that particular subject. The very idea of anything more than a working relationship between the pastor and herself was more inconceivable than her going back to California.

When they returned from their walk, it seemed that she and the pastor was the subject of much speculation. They overheard Sister

Dorothea Jackson saying that she didn't think that it was proper for Nina to be involved in any projects with their pastor. She was talking with Sister Rachel Winston who agreed wholeheartedly and who insisted that Nina's wild reputation would tarnish anything she did for the church.

Nina felt hurt, but her aunt squeezed her arm and pulled her along talking loudly. "I told you I was too old to go for walks with you. You've got me so winded I can hardly catch my breath."

Nina was instantly alarmed until she caught the wink her aunt gave her.

"I'm sorry Auntie. I really thought the walk would do you some good. Would you like me to get you something to drink?" she asked getting into the spirit of the ruse.

"No Baby just let me sit down for a few minutes and I'll be all right." Aunt Elaine told her. Nina led her to a bench then sat next to her. The women gathered all around her and then scolded Nina for tiring her aunt out. Nina didn't know what to say to them so she got up and walked away.

She found herself walking a path that led to a small playground. She stood there watching the children laughing and playing not realizing that she had tears streaming down her cheeks.

"Sister Nina, are you all right?" Pastor Fairchild asked suddenly appearing beside her.

Nina quickly wiped at her face and smiled weakly at the pastor as she accepted the tissues he handed her. "I'm fine thanks."

"Would you rather I leave you alone?" he asked making to leave.

Nina shook her head. "It's because of you I'm crying in the first place."

"Did I do something to offend you?" he asked with a puzzled expression on his face.

"I thought it was a good idea I had but some of the ladies from the church don't think I'm the right person for the job. My aunt and I just overheard them saying that anything I did for the church would tarnished it because of my Hollywood reputation and all." Nina put up her hand. "I'm sorry I'm gossiping but sometimes what people say about me hurts," she explained.

There was a kind smile on Pastor Fairchild's face. "I'm sorry your feelings got hurt. Maybe you have to let people know how you feel. I feel embarrassed to tell you this myself, but I thought of your past as well. I don't know anything about you so I cannot judge. All we know is what we read about you in the papers. Maybe it is time the people here know the real you," as he spoke he placed a hand reassuringly on her shoulder patting it gently.

Nina pulled her hair to hang to one side so she could lean on the tree. Looking up at the pastor, she nodded.

"My agent used to say that if I ignored the tabloids the gossip would go away. My dad used to be a great comfort to me when they wrote something really awful about me. One of the things he would say was to let it roll off my back. It worked sometimes and other times nothing helped, I just hurt."

"Whether what is said about you is true or not, that's just the way it is. Being in the limelight is something you have to deal with Sister Nina, and if you are as strong as your aunt, you'll be just fine," the pastor said reassuringly.

Nina nodded again. "Can you be honest with me Pastor? Do you believe that if we worked on this project together that it would hurt the church or you?"

"Celebrities are perceived differently than us normal people. If you do something, it most always seems to be some sort of publicity stunt. Either way, the children would be benefiting which is the most important thing." He said honestly.

Nina stared up at him with a very sad expression on her pretty face. "My father and I supported many charities and donated thousands of dollars to many causes that were never acknowledged by the press. We weren't looking for recognition. We did it because it was the right thing to do. I've visited sick children in Africa and personally cared for a dying woman with Aids. Famous people are just like you Pastor, we can care too." Nina was so upset she walked away from him hoping he wouldn't follow.

CHAPTER FOUR

When Nina returned to her aunt, she found her still surrounded by the women. Their demeanor had changed suggesting that Aunt Elaine had set them straight. Nina wished she had stayed to tell those busybodies exactly where to go, but it wouldn't have been very nice.

She plastered a smile on her face and asked her aunt if she was ready to go. Aunt Elaine nodded and together they gathered their belongings to place them in the shopping cart she insisted was useful on these occasions. They left wishing everyone they passed a good afternoon. Neither of them wished to stay for the rest of the planned activities.

They didn't speak on the drive back either. Nina needed to concentrate on the road because it was very congested. She thought everyone and his or her grandmother was on the road and laughed aloud. Her aunt laughed too when she told her what she was thinking.

By evening, Nina felt much better about the way she was treated and was determined to do what she planned with or without the pastor's help. *How dare he insinuate that she was doing it for publicity?* Richard always arranged the publicity stuff, but she always insisted that a charity she really cared about was private.

The public things that she and her father did such as the grand openings, telethons, received much publicity. They did many good works that only the people on the receiving end knew about and that was more rewarding than anything public was. Her dad instilled that value in her a long time ago and she believed it still.

He also taught her that if she was going to do something important that she plans it carefully and that was exactly what Nina intended to do. She planned to hire experts to go scouting for locations. Then when everything was in order, she would go to the pastor with a fait accompli.

Throughout the fall season, Nina and the scout she had hired searched the South Queens area. Nina wanted the center she intended to build to be close enough to the church because it would be part of the church. One evening while driving home from yet another disappointing meeting with her scout, Nina passed a row of houses that looked like they had been condemned. She drove around the block to pass them one more time. This is what she had been looking for it was perfect she thought.

There were several businesses in the surrounding area. A restaurant, a Laundromat and a bakery were across the street from the row of homes and behind them was a vacant lot. Why didn't the scout show her this location? It was perfect.

The following morning, she called the scout to tell him what she found and asked him to meet her there. The location was a few blocks from the church, which was exactly what she envisioned. One of the things she admired about the pastor of Christ Tabernacle was that he was truly involved in his congregation's lives. He knew their names and their children's names. That impressed her greatly. Having the recreation center so close to the church would make it easier for him to have an impact there as well.

She then instructed the scout to find out all the particulars concerning those homes after which she would get her lawyer to take her on to the next phase, which would be purchasing the location.

As luck would have it, there was a bidding battle going on with the nearby businesses. Each wanted to buy the burnt out homes to expand their businesses. It seemed that all three had been campaigning to purchase them ever since it became clear that the owners would not be rebuilding. The owners were waiting on insurance compensation for the fire that destroyed their homes.

Nina decided that she had enough preliminary information to approach the pastor. With a proposal on the buildings written out including the possible outcome on insurance payments to the families involved, Nina called the church to make an appointment with the pastor.

The appointment was set for the following Wednesday evening after bible study and Nina felt nervous. She was confident about what she wanted to do, but a little unsure if the pastor still wanted to be involved. He had after all, suggested that she was doing it for publicity. That stung more than a little; she was naïve to think that the pastor would see her suggestion as genuine. Once again, the false reputation of being wild and unruly stood in her way.

Did she really think that being a celebrity would automatically open doors for her in the religious community? Why did she think they would accept her into the fold wholeheartedly? She had been living among them for nine months now and they still couldn't see the person that she was. It was so frustrating.

The night of the meeting, Nina dressed with care. She hurriedly drove her aunt back home after bible study insisting she didn't need her aunt's support. She wore a long black wool skirt, a white turtleneck sweater and boots. She took a deep breath and parked. There were several cars still parked in the lot and Nina surmised that the meeting was going to include others as well. It was foolish of her to think that it would be just the two of them.

Nina entered the sanctuary and walked to the front where she was ushered through a side door behind which a set of stairs led up to the pastor's office. It was surprisingly big and tastefully decorated.

A huge mahogany desk dominated one end of the office. The sofas and matching chairs made for comfortable gatherings. He even had a small coffee station and a man whom she recognized as a deacon offered her some. Nina declined and sat on the chair closest to the desk where the pastor sat. He stood up to come around to greet and shake her hand.

"Good evening Sister Nina how are you?" he asked.

"I'm fine thank you Pastor." She replied. There were three other men gathered for the meeting and she had the distinct feeling that they going to pat her on the head then send her on her merry way.

"Are we all gathered?" she asked deciding to set the tone for the meeting.

"Yes we are Sister. I was surprised to hear from you so soon as these things take time and planning," the pastor said confirming Nina's suspicions. It had been months since they spoke about the recreation center.

"I was taught that if one is thinking about doing something that it is already planned. I assure you that I am very serious about this project." She pulled out the proposal and handed it over to the pastor.

While he read it, she looked around her. She didn't know who decorated his office but it was very nice. The furniture was masculine but it seemed to her that a female's touch was very evident.

There was a single picture window and the deep burgundy drapes and beige scarf valance was elegant. The plush carpet was also the same color scheme as were the cushions on the soft beige leather sofa. There were artificial potted plants in different areas of the office lending a homey feel to it.

The pastor put the proposal down to look at her. It was two pages long so he was able to read it all. "Sister Nina I don't believe that you've been introduced to Deacon Fitzroy, Trustee Worthington and Beecham." Each man raised his hand as the pastor said their name and nodded at her.

"Good evening gentleman. So Pastor Fairchild what is your opinion concerning what I'm proposing?" Nina asked turning her attention back to the pastor.

"I must say that I am surprised, it is a very good idea. The location you mentioned is ideal, but one of the problems I foresee is that the owners might not want to sell to the church. The other thing I would like you to understand is that we are still paying a mortgage on the church building, so getting another loan will be a strain on our finances," the pastor said spreading his hands. He spoke with a steady and even tone. He went on to fill the men sitting with them on what the proposal entailed.

Nina eyed each man in turn and when her eyes reached the pastor's once more she asked them if they had any thoughts on how to make the recreation center less of a burden on the church's finances.

Each man thought about it and came up with suggestions from fundraisers to donations. Nina stood up to walk around the office trying to find a way to say what she needed to say without offending them.

"Pastor you asked me at the church picnic what I intended to do while I was here and I distinctly remember saying that *I* wanted to do something for the community. I also remember you saying that you would be interested in *hearing* about my plans, as the youth were a subject close to your heart. I only asked how the church intended on making this happen just out of curiosity. I have millions at my disposal I did not intend to burden the church financially. You can either work with me on this as a religious consultant purely for the satisfaction that this community would eventually have a safe haven for its young people, or not. Since I have not been welcomed into the church as a member yet, I didn't want to offend you by doing this without your approval," Nina stated with much indignation.

"If you intended on paying for it, why did you come to us at all?" Pastor Fairchild asked. From the expression on his face, he was not happy with her tone.

"I want this to be attached to this church as I dictated in the proposal. I wanted not only young people from the area benefitting but also specifically young people from this church. It is also why I chose the location because of its proximity to the church."

"Did you say that you have millions at your disposal?" Trustee Worthington asked with a sheepish smile on his face.

Nina looked at him with such disdain that he dropped his gaze. She picked up her coat. "I hope that you will look at the proposal again and contact me in light of the *new* financial developments. Good night gentlemen." Nina said and walked out of the office.

She was at the bottom step when the pastor called out to her. "Sister Nina I would like to speak with you privately. Would you be available tomorrow evening?"

"What time?" Nina asked feeling that he wanted to put her down gently.

"Will you have dinner with me?" He asked.

"Will you be picking me up or shall I meet you somewhere?" Nina countered as her heart thudded in her chest.

"I'll pick you up at seven," then he turned to go back into his office.

Nina continued on her way out of the church. It wasn't until she was sitting behind the wheel of her car that she realized that she had a date with the pastor. She drove home and let herself into the house absentmindedly. Her aunt who was standing at the foot of the stairs startled her.

She came to meet her and took her arm. "Well how did the meeting go? Are they all pleased with what you've come up with?" Aunt Elaine asked.

"I gave the pastor the proposal and he read it. Then he said that it was a good idea. He also said that he didn't think the church could afford to get a loan as they were still paying on the mortgage. I got mad and reminded him that I was the one who proposed the recreation center in the first place and that he had only expressed interest. I then told them smugly that I had millions at my disposal and didn't need their money."

"Oh baby you really should watch that temper of yours," Aunt Elaine scolded gently.

"Yeah I know but I felt like they didn't think I was serious. Auntie I really want this to be part of the church so that the young people in it could benefit as well. That's why I agreed for the pastor to be involved. I know what I said embarrassed him and now he wants to take me out to dinner to speak with me privately. I thought it was a date but thinking back on what went on tonight, I think it is going to be a brush off," Nina said gesturing with her hand.

"Don't come to any conclusions yet, see what the man has to say. Now why don't I make you a nice cup of tea to help you relax?"

"I could go for a gin and tonic if it's all the same to you," said Nina.

The look her aunt gave her made Nina laugh and she had to tell her aunt that she was joking. What she said was a line from a movie she had done. They sat facing each other sipping on the tea when her aunt asked her what she was going to do for her birthday on Friday.

Nina hadn't really thought about her birthday like that. She hadn't celebrated her last birthday because she was still mourning the loss of her father and she hadn't celebrated Christmas for the same reason. Nina just shrugged.

"You think about it and let me know, we only have two days."

Nina didn't want her aunt to make a big fuss and told her so. "It is just another day Aunt Elaine. I want it to be quiet."

"You mean you are not going to give me a chance to wish you a happy birthday? The last time I did that you were still in your diapers." Aunt Elaine reminded her.

It was true that her aunt hadn't been around for her birthdays but that was because they had lived so far away. Her dad invited her to California that time because he wanted his family to meet his wife's family. Her aunt and dad were very close especially after their parents both passed on.

Throughout the years family members lost, touch until they were completely lost. Aunt Elaine was the only family he had known and her dad insisted on having his sister join in on the celebration. Nina's grandparents had been there as well and Elaine remembered how strained the festivities was. She got the impression that Nina's grandparents weren't very happy with the union their daughter made. They also made it plain that their granddaughter was not to their liking as well, even though their bi-racial grandchild had fair skin and green eyes.

After her mother's death, Nina hadn't seen her grandparents again. Elaine felt sad for her brother and his daughter. She was a newlywed herself and couldn't take on the responsibility of helping her brother care for her niece. She had always kept an open invitation to both of them if they wanted to return home.

Her brother carried on fine without her help however. Still it must've been painful to know that you had grandparents who didn't want you because of the color of your skin. Although Nina was fair-skinned, her father had not allowed her to deny her heritage. She was part Black and part Italian. They had never spoken of it and now she wondered if it mattered still to her niece.

"Do you ever see your family?" Aunt Elaine asked her suddenly.

"My grandparents moved back to Italy after Mom's accident and for all I know, they could both be gone now. It was just my dad and me and now I have you." Nina said.

"Did you miss them growing up?"

Nina shrugged. "I wrote to them once and my letter came back unopened. I figured that I would forget about them as well. My parents loved me and that's all that mattered."

"Still it would be nice if we celebrated your birthday here, just the two of us." Aunt Elaine insisted.

Nina couldn't refuse her aunt anything and agreed to a special dinner for her birthday. Kissing her aunt gently on the cheek, Nina went up to bed.

As the time neared for the pastor to pick her up on Thursday evening, Nina began to feel nervous. In California she hadn't dated much because her standards were a little higher than what was available. She didn't go for the sleek-must-look-like-a-million-dollars type that was everywhere either. She wanted someone who was genuinely interested in her, someone who wouldn't talk shop the entire night. She dated a person once who started out great but blew it later.

He was in show business as well and seemed to like her. It wasn't until she saw the tabloid a couple of weeks later that she understood that he was using her to boost *his* appeal. It is very hard to find a genuine soul in Tinsel Town. Afterwards, she gave up finding someone special and started going out with her friends in groups.

Nina was ready by six-thirty, dressed in a light green cashmere sweater and skirt set. She adorned her ears with small, round diamond studs with the matching chain hanging around her neck. Because the pastor hinted at her background Nina toned down everything she wore. Although her clothes and jewelry were expensive, they weren't overly pretentious.

She sprayed on her favorite perfume and stepped back to look at herself in the mirror. Nina nodded and grabbed her handbag and went downstairs to join her aunt.

Aunt Elaine smiled her approval and told her that once the pastor saw her he would forget about brushing her off and accept the recreation center as her gift to the church. Nina doubted it but mentally crossed her fingers.

When the doorbell sounded, Nina went to open the door. She stepped back to let the pastor enter. She couldn't tell what he wearing but admired his black wool coat. The pastor walked into the living room to greet her aunt. They made small talk while Nina went to get her coat. She signaled that she was ready and the pastor wished her aunt a good night.

The cold wind bit at Nina's face, as the pastor took her arm, and they hurried to his car. Nina didn't know what she was expecting but she was pleasantly surprised that he drove a black Dodge Charger. She had been curious about them and was pleased that she was getting a chance to ride in one.

It was the muscle car of choice driven in L.A. Of course, in L.A, the car had spinning rims and spoilers. The pastor's version was sleek and elegant. She decided that she liked it.

Pastor Fairchild drove them to the Bistro Grill Restaurant in Great Neck. Again, Nina was impressed. She began to wonder exactly what was on his mind. If this was a brush off, then it was an expensive one. If it wasn't then it was a good way of getting her attention.

She didn't expect to see this side of the man, he was a man who pulled her seat out for her and asked her if she wanted to wait before they ordered. She told him that she wanted some tea to warm up first and he expertly caught the waiter's attention and ordered two teas.

While they waited, he made small talk before getting into what he really wanted to discuss with her about. Nina decided that he was charming.

"Sister Nina, I wanted to speak with you tonight for two reasons. Firstly, I wanted to commend you for what you want to accomplish and secondly, I wanted to apologize for the other night. I realized that we offended you and gave you the impression that we were humoring you. For that, I truly am sorry. I didn't really think you were serious, but when you handed me that proposal I realized my mistake. Will you accept my apology?" he asked with a convincing smile.

Nina hung her head because she wanted to be angry. He's gone and apologized and stole her thunder, she thought. Nina looked up at him and smiled sweetly.

"I accept your apology," she told him putting him instantly at ease.

"Thank you. I was wondering if you would allow the church to do some of the work. It is obvious that we cannot afford to put up the building, but perhaps once the building is up, we can furnish it. Would that be all right?"

"Yes. I was angry when I left the meeting. I thought that I had made it clear that this was something *I* wanted to contribute to this community. Although I am well capable of footing the bills, I understand the need for the church to be involved. So yes, the church can do anything it wants once the building is up." Nina said.

Their tea finally came and when the waiter asked if they were ready to order, they both said yes. The pastor allowed her to order for herself and then followed suit. The place was famous for its steaks so Nina ordered a steak well done, a baked potato, mixed vegetables and a salad. The pastor ordered a steak as well but he wanted mashed potatoes, the mixed vegetables and soup.

While they waited, the waiter brought the soup, salad and bread. By the time their food arrived, Pastor Fairchild insisted that Nina address him as Darius. Nina told him that it was okay for him to call her by her given name, which was Catalina.

Darius questioned her on why no one knew her real name and she told him that her mother shared the same name. Her mother was Catalina and she was Nina. She only used her full name for legal matters.

Darius took the opportunity to satisfy his curiosity by asking her question after question. He also wanted to know why she decided to quit and Nina told him that she would tell him one day.

Nina asked him if he received any answer from her church in L.A. and he answered that he hadn't. Nina thought that it was strange, but after looking at her watch decided that it wasn't too late for her to call her old pastor to ask if they received the request for her transfer.

Pastor Fairchild was not offended or thought that she didn't believe him just impressed that she had the pastor's phone number and felt comfortable enough to call him at any time.

It turned out that they did receive the request. He said that his secretary would mail the permission to transfer shortly. Nina accepted the apology for the delay and told the pastor that she would be looking for the transfer's arrival in the next couple of days.

When she hung up, she smiled triumphantly at Darius who was staring at her in awe.

"It must be your celebrity status that got you through to the man, because I had been trying and was put on hold and transferred to the assistant pastor and so on and so forth." Most probably, it was because she was a celebrity and the need to protect her privacy that he received the runaround, he thought.

Nina turned suddenly when someone tapped her on the shoulder. "Nina Bennett?" a young woman asked uncertainly.

"Yes?" Nina confirmed but immediately regretted it.

"I don't mean to interrupt your dinner, but would you mind signing my napkin?" and she shoved the napkin at Nina.

Nina nodded and signed it with a gracious smile. Somehow, a line had formed and Nina was signing her autograph in earnest. Nina's smile began to slip after the tenth signature. The pastor came to her rescue then. He stood up to ask that they continue with their dinner without further interruption. There were a few grumbles but the crowd dissipated and Nina nodded her thanks to him.

"Thank you. I was never able to do that effectively. My agent usually allowed it when I made appearances and stopped it when I signaled him."

"So this sort of thing happens to you a lot?" he asked her, looking beyond her to see people pointing and whispering.

"Yes. When I was younger, it was fun but now it's not. I'm always afraid that I am hurting someone's feelings if I don't sign my autograph. But you know I just realized that I quit, I don't have to be treated like a celebrity anymore," Nina explained with a grin.

"That's not going to sink in for a long time. As long as your movies are still being shown and your records are still being played, you are going to be Miss Fabulous." Darius Fairchild teased.

CHAPTER FIVE

Their waiter approached them to insist that dessert was on the house. Nina accepted graciously. A few minutes later, the owner of the restaurant came to greet them. He wanted to know if Nina would consent to having her picture taken with him before she leaves.

Nina consented and she dug into her cheesecake with relish. Darius had pound cake with vanilla ice cream. Nina excused herself to go to the restroom and when she returned, she signaled for the waiter. She told him that she was ready for the picture.

Darius stood back patiently to watch as the owner had one of his staff take several pictures of him and Nina. After Nina buckled in, Darius turned to her shaking his head.

"I would like to see you again, but I don't know what we are going to do with your entourage," he stated.

It took Nina a few minutes to realize what he said. "Did you say that you would like to date me?" Nina asked him finally.

"I did," he nodded. "I would like to clarify that I was going to ask you regardless of the meeting yesterday. I just didn't know how to ask you. When I realized that you were offended last night, I took it as my opportunity." Darius stated.

"I'm not saying no, but I would like a couple of days to think about it. Is that okay with you?" Nina asked breathlessly.

"Take all the time you want," agreed Darius as he started the car.

The drive back to Queens was a relaxed and friendly affair. Nina wanted to know how long he had been a minister. He answered that he became senior pastor after the previous pastor passed away.

He was a youth pastor fresh out of theology school and eager to minister to God's people as he put it. The higher ups in the organization noticed him to give him many opportunities to preach. They recognized his talent and promoted him to assistant pastor until he was now the senior pastor.

Nina didn't pretend to understand the hierarchy of the church officers but she did agree with him, he really did have a great talent for preaching. By the time they parked in front of her aunt's house, Nina was laughing. Darius Fairchild had a wonderful sense of humor. She decided that she liked that as well.

He declined her offer to come in but instead took her hand gently in his to lift it up to his lips. "Catalina it was a pleasure to meet the real you. I'll be waiting for your answer," he said after he kissed her knuckles.

"Well good night Darius. I had a really great time and it was a pleasure to meet you as well." Nina declared then turned to insert her key into the lock.

The pastor waited until she was inside before he turned to head toward his car. Elaine waited until she was in her room before she pounced. There was a big smile on her face as she sat at the foot of Nina's bed.

"So was it a brush off or a date?" she asked expectantly.

"It was a date Auntie. He took me to a nice restaurant and we talked and he apologized for making me angry at the meeting and he wants to see me again." Nina told her aunt.

"That's what I'm talking about, a real nice man." Her aunt said standing up to do a little dance.

"Don't plan any weddings yet Auntie, I told him that I wanted to think about it first. He was nice about it and told me that he would wait to hear from me. This is not just any man. He is a *pastor*. I don't want to make any mistakes."

Her aunt's smile turned into a frown. "What makes you think you'd be making a mistake Baby?"

Nina went about undressing while she thought about what she was feeling. She didn't think she could adequately explain it to her aunt and told her so. It was just so sudden and she just wanted to think about whether she wanted to commit herself to being the pastor's girlfriend. Her aunt nodded and wished her a good night.

Nina tossed and turned most of the night because she was indeed troubled. Darius was on her mind. He wasn't just a man. What he represented concerned her. He was a man of God, highly respected in his community and as such, he had a tremendous responsibility. Just like her own celebrity status, Darius had his as well.

How would his congregation react if they dated? Would they accept or shun her because of her background? Although she was a potential member of the church, would anyone see her as a usurper if she and the pastor dated?

What if after a few dates, they both decided that it wouldn't work, how would the congregation take that? Would they blame her for hurting their pastor and possibly his ability to minister to them? Nina was very afraid of being the cause of any disruption in the church. She liked the church very much even though some people still kept their distance from her.

She didn't know what to do to make people relax around her and see her for the person that she truly was. How could she take on the responsibility for such potential discord? She just couldn't.

Apart from all that she imagined that could happen, Nina still wanted to satisfy her curiosity about the man finally. The man she saw in the evening was charming and courteous. Darius Fairchild was intelligent and he had integrity. From the pulpit, he oozed confidence and power. He gave one the sense that God was with him. That alone drew her to him from the very first sermon she heard him preach.

December 10th Friday morning, Elaine woke her up with a breakfast tray. It was Nina's birthday. Elaine decided to start the festivities early by giving Nina breakfast in bed. Her aunt wouldn't even let her wash the dishes afterward. Her aunt took the day off from her part-time job just so she could spend the day with her niece.

She told Nina to relax for the rest of the morning. Nina spent the better part of the morning in the award room playing the piano. She wanted to be happy and to feel happy but she wasn't. She awoke with her dad on her mind. She played all the songs he had written for her and listened to every CD they recorded together. They made her feel sad.

Elaine came looking for her around noon to find her crying. She heard the piano playing and the CDs too but she didn't know Nina was feeling blue.

She did her best to cheer her up and Nina made an effort to push the blues away for her aunt's sake. She apologized for putting a damper on the festivities and promised that the rest of the day would be better.

By early afternoon, Nina told her aunt that she was going for a drive and wanted to know what time their special dinner was so that she could come back in time for it. "A drive is an excellent idea. Go clear your head, but be back by seven." Elaine warned her.

Nina drove to the mall. She bought a couple of items she thought that her aunt would like. Giving them to her tonight was the best way to boost her mood. So with her purchases in hand, Nina returned home.

When she entered the house, Elaine called out to her. She was in the dining room. Nina shrugged off her coat and went to find her. Pastor Fairchild and quite a few other members of the church were seated at the table all wearing smiles.

"Surprise!" everyone shouted.

"Goodness, I really wasn't expecting this. Thank you." Nina expressed with a tremor in her voice. She went over to her aunt to give her a hug, and then greeted everybody else with a handshake. She greeted the pastor last and wasn't even surprised that her aunt arranged for them to sit beside each other.

Nina tried not to make a big deal of it to enjoy her birthday party. Once they finished eating, everyone took a moment to say something to Nina as they presented her with a gift.

Sister Dorothea stated that she enjoyed Nina's solo at the summer revival. She gave her a book of hymns. Sister Rachel wanted to make a toast and asked that everyone raise his or her glasses.

"You are probably used to the real stuff so I hope you don't mind the soda. I pray that God gives you joy and peace that only our Lord Jesus can give you."

Nina's smile started to slip after that. Being the experienced actor that she was, she kept her hurt hidden. The rest of the birthday wishes followed Sister Rachel's theme with the other guests saying things that hinted at her supposedly tainted past and hopes that she had reformed.

By the time the party broke up, Nina wanted to scream. Not being able to hold it in any longer, she let the tears fill her eyes. Apart from Darius and her aunt, everyone else thought that her tears were tears of happiness. She smiled her goodbyes at the door as they left.

It was only ten o'clock, but all she wanted to do was to go to her room to cry. Darius squeezed her hand and whispered that he drove everyone over and had to drive them home. He asked if she would see him afterward and she agreed. Nina closed the door and leaned on it. She was miserable but she couldn't blame her aunt for it.

She found Elaine in the kitchen sitting at the small table wearing a long face. Nina approached her smiling brightly and gave her a hug. She was finally able to give Elaine her gifts. Nina got her a hat she admired the last time they went to the mall. She also got her a scarf and some perfume.

"Aunt Elaine I want to thank you for a wonderful day. I wasn't expecting a party and I am grateful that you love me so much that you went to all this trouble. This morning I woke up thinking about my dad and how much I missed him, but tonight I want to thank God that I have you."

Elaine had tears in her own eyes as well and hugged her niece.

"Oh Baby, I didn't know those fools were going to say those things to you. I want to apologize for them." She said sadly.

"Those things they said hurt, but I forgive them because they don't know any better. What is important to me is that you know the real me and that you love me," Nina said in an effort to comfort her aunt.

A half hour later, the doorbell rang and Nina motioned for her aunt to stay put while she went to answer the door, she knew that it was the pastor. Nina led him to the kitchen where he sat across from Nina's aunt.

"Sister Elaine, I wanted to come back to talk with both of you if I may. I suspect that you've guessed my intentions concerning your niece and I wanted to show my respect to formally ask your permission to see her." Darius Fairchild said.

"I appreciate your respect Pastor," Sister Elaine said with a smile, "but my niece is 26 years old now and perfectly capable of making her own decision about such matters." Having voiced her opinion, she got up to leave them alone.

Darius turned his attention to Nina who sat beside him. "I know that I have jumped the gun by saying anything," he began, "because you asked me to await your decision, but tonight I saw something ugly. I also saw how hurt you were even though you tried to hide it. I wanted to do something to make you feel better."

"It's okay Darius. I had a chance to think and I feel that you and I need to talk. It is late and I have to respect my aunt's house. Could we meet tomorrow afternoon?" Nina asked him.

"I have most of the day free tomorrow. We could have lunch if you'd like?"

"Great," Nina said and stood up. She led the way to the door and waited for him to walk through it.

"Good night Nina and happy birthday." Darius Fairchild leaned down to place a chaste kiss on Nina's forehead before he walked out into the cold December night.

Nina went about calmly turning off lights and checking the front and back doors before climbing the stairs to her room. Only when she had gotten under the covers of her bed did Nina let go of her control and cry. She cried quietly because she didn't want to disturb her aunt's rest, but she couldn't hold the pain in any longer. For some reason what those ignorant people said to her face hurt more than anything that had been written about her. She couldn't understand why after all this time; these people still couldn't see her for who she was. This was something she was going to have to let the Lord handle for her. After a tearful prayer, Nina was finally able to fall into a deep and peaceful sleep.

Darius came for her exactly at noon as he promised. They drove around for half an hour before Darius could find a place they could talk without being disturbed. They found a small diner across the street from the hospital downtown where everyone was too busy to care who was eating there. They ordered burgers, fries and lemonade.

Nina waited until they finished eating before she spoke what's been weighing heavily on her mind.

"Last night you heard for yourself what some people think of me. I thought that if things didn't go well between us that the congregation would blame me for hurting you and that they would accuse me of being responsible for tearing the man of God down. The words that come out of people's mouths can do so much damage that I am really concerned about seeing you." She pointed out what the tabloids had done to her own reputation. People really believed that she was a boozer, a druggie and sexually free.

"I get the feeling that they believe that I am not Christian-like enough for them and therefore not acceptable enough for their pastor. Those busybodies at the church picnic insinuated that association with me would tarnish the church and its pastor." Nina continued.

She also told him that she thought that there were people watching his every move. Nina bet that since his wife died, that people were watching him to see if he would take a lover, chase the women in the church or go creeping in the dead of night when no one was looking.

She was afraid of what the repercussions could do to Darius' career, not to mention his future as the pastor of Christ Tabernacle. She hadn't really talked about the kind of life she led in California and she knew that he was curious, as was everyone in the church. Apart from her movies, and the albums she put out, no one knew the real Nina. She hadn't done many interviews in the past.

She told him that she decided she needed to speak with him and come clean about how she lived out there before the church knew that they were dating. She wanted to date him and wanted him to know who she was.

"So ask me anything you're curious about; nothing is too personal and I will try not to feel offended. If we are to see each other, then it is very important that you know everything you need to know about me," Nina told him.

"Before we talk about you, I want to backtrack to some of the things you said. It is true that I am the pastor and the congregation is my responsibility. I have to set an example for them. I am a man of God and my faith is strong in the Lord, otherwise I wouldn't be able to lead God's people.

Rest assured that no powers on this Earth could tear down what God has built up. I am a man who happens to be a pastor. You've given the awful gossip written about you much power over your own judgment I fear. I'm pretty sure that you aren't planning my demise so why are you so worried about what people *think* you are going to do?" Darius asked reasoning with her.

"But what if we date for a few months and then decide that it isn't going to work and break up, don't you think that the church folk aren't going to gossip about it and maybe blame me for hurting you?" asked Nina.

"Wow the gossip mill has done a number on you hasn't it? Nina, first I need you to understand something about me. When I step down from the pulpit, I am a man just like any other man. Being a man of *God* makes me conscious of my actions. I have to live a life that is holy and acceptable to God, but I am still a man. I do not need the church's approval to be one. In fact, if I had any doubts about seeing you, I wouldn't have asked you out.

The congregation had no say in who I married and they have no say about who I see now. If it doesn't pertain to the church building, the congregation, or anything spiritual then it is my business and only I can make decisions about it," stated Darius.

"Are you so confident about this that you are willing to take this chance? Can we still be friends if it doesn't work out?" Nina asked.

"Absolutely," Darius said nodding at her.

"Okay if that's how you feel about it, then I would be honored to go out with you." Nina told him with a smile.

"Good. Now tell me all about the fabulous Miss Nina." Darius said.

Over refills of soda, Nina told her new friend all about her life in California and Hollywood. She told him about her childhood, about her parents and her mother's death. She even explained away all he had heard or read about her. The damaging ones were a bit harder to explain especially since there were pictures but she was completely forthcoming.

Nina explained that her agent convinced her that the only way for her to maintain her popularity was to be with the 'in crowd'. She partied with them and networked. She told him that she didn't drink and if she had one, she'd nurse it an entire evening, or drink Ginger Ale instead.

Darius asked about her love life and reminded her that she had given him permission to ask her anything. Nina nodded and declared that it was none existent. She rarely dated and hadn't had a steady boyfriend in years.

"I recall hearing somewhere that you had married. That can't be a lie can it?" he asked confused.

"So you were willing to date a woman who may or may not have a husband waiting in the wings? Darius I thought you were smarter than that. I have never been married, engaged, gay or bi-sexual. I don't smoke cigarettes, drink or do drugs of any kind. My father smoked and drank occasionally, but he never allowed me to follow his example.

He advised me constantly about one thing he said was the most precious gift I'll have to offer the man I marry. He said that no matter how much talent I have the gift of my personal self will be by far the most treasured by my husband. I'm not trying to be crude but I feel that you need to know that I am untouched and will remain so until I marry. I promised my dad." Nina told him proudly.

"Your father was a very wise man Nina. In the kind of world we live in today, it is very hard to find many young women willing to save themselves for marriage. Even in the church, it is rare. That is why I try so hard to reach our young men and women in the church. There is so much pressure on them to give up their innocence that I hurt for them." Darius told her solemnly.

Nina reached over to touch his hand shyly then quickly withdrew.

"I would like to help the youth in our community too if only the church would stop seeing me as the enemy."

"That will come in time. I think once the recreation center is built, you should use it to re-create your image and I would be very happy to work on that with you," Darius insisted.

"That's just the thing Darius, people see what they want to see. I have always been me even while I was at parties and such. In Los Angeles, I have a reputation of being a party-pooper. Do you really think I can change these people's minds about me?" Nina asked skeptically.

Darius smiled reassuringly at her. "Yes Catalina, I do."

He reached over, took her hand in his to squeeze it. The look in his eyes told her that they had reached a level of trust in their relationship. Nina was glad that she talked with him and relieved that her fears about them seeing each other was all in her mind.

Still the enormity of it all made her feel just a little scared. She was excited that someone like him was attracted to her. If their relationship progressed further, Nina felt that she would be up to the challenge. Because Darius was a pastor, she understood the responsibility he had on his shoulders and because she understood, she could never stand in his way of doing his duty.

There would be times she knew that they would have to cut a date short because someone would need him for something only the pastor can handle. She knew that he had assistants but ultimately, most of the responsibility would rest on his capable shoulders. Nina could only hope that she was worthy of the man.

"What are you thinking about?" Darius asked when she had not said anything for a long time.

"I was thinking about how challenging our relationship is going to be," Nina answered.

"And what challenges do you foresee?"

"Well it wouldn't be a stretch to expect emergencies that would cancel a date or cut one short," she elaborated for him.

"So what would your reaction be if that happened?"

"Well it depends on what we had planned. I suppose I couldn't throw a fit if someone had a death in the family and needed spiritual comfort. Nor would I be overly upset if someone suddenly took a turn for the worse in the hospital either. But I think I would be just a tiny bit upset if we were interrupted by something trivial like say someone calling to ask about service schedules or something like that." Nina said.

Darius laughed and shook his head. Nina was glad that she could make him laugh. "Nina, I think you are very accommodating of my job as pastor. I promise you that short of something like what you brought up, when we go out, we won't be disturbed." Then his face grew grave. "Since you have been so honest with me about yourself, it would only make sense that I be honest with you as well. I admit that I am just a bit scared and excited about us. After my wife died, I didn't think I'd ever feel anything again.

I threw myself into my work and crammed so many activities into a day that at day's end I was too tired to feel lonely. Now I find myself tossing and turning because I am thinking about you. Last night I was really upset and I wanted to say something to Sister Rachel and the others about what they said to you, but I let it go because I wanted to talk it over with you first."

"Would you really have said something to them? At the church picnic, I almost did but then if I had, your opinion of me would have suffered greatly. I was so upset that the only thing I could do was to leave. Aunt Elaine was upset as well." Nina replied.

"If I have your permission, I think I can say something that will make everyone think twice about what they say to you in the future. I will not have that sort of behavior in my church. Everyone has the right to be in the Lord's house and as supposedly *experienced* saints I expect them to extend warmth and understanding to everyone." Darius said seriously.

Nina worked her features into a female in distress expression and exclaimed, "My hero!" and then because she couldn't help it she laughed.

Darius laughed too. Once they were able to control themselves, he suggested that he take her home. At the door, he asked if he could take her out to dinner Wednesday evening. Nina nodded her consent and he left.

CHAPTER SIX

On Monday and Tuesday, Nina was busy with her lawyer who pitched her bid for the recreation center. The lawyers for the owners had finally allowed her to talk with their clients for Nina to make her own appeal. She had done her homework and obtained background information. Mothers, fathers and children had once lived in those homes, so Nina was able to appeal to their sensibilities concerning the welfare of their children and the children still living in the neighborhood. She even sweetened the deal by offering to put up a plaque in their honor.

They told Nina that they would get back to her soon. Wednesday afternoon Nina's lawyer called to inform her that the owners decided to sell to her. Nina thanked him profusely and hung up. She was so happy that she began to run around her room screaming. Elaine who had just returned from work thought that something awful had happened rushed upstairs to Nina's bedroom to see.

"Nina child what on Earth is wrong?" she asked looking around the room searching for some kind of menace.

Nina screamed all the louder and ran to her.

"Auntie, they said yes! They are going to sell to me. The church is going to have its recreation center!" Nina exclaimed.

"That's great baby. How soon can you start building?" She asked disengaging herself from Nina's tight grip.

"I think it is going to take a few weeks before all the papers are signed, but I would like to start in the spring. I can't wait to tell Darius about this," then Nina's expression turned to one of horror. "Oh Goodness, I have to get ready, we have a date tonight."

Elaine advised her to calm down and that she would stall him while Nina got ready. It was almost six and Nina didn't much time. She didn't have the vaguest idea what she was going to wear. Tonight she wanted to celebrate. She wanted to wear something festive.

She went out into the hall to go through the closet out there. She had so many clothes that she commandeered the hall closet where she found an outfit that would be perfect for the evening. She bought it on a whim when she had been out shopping with her aunt.

Nina bought it because her aunt liked it so much. It was a red form fitting sleeveless dress with a square neckline. It had a matching bolero jacket with black trimming. Nina chose a pair of black pumps that would go perfect with the outfit. She decided that she would put her hair up. She twisted her long locks tight in order to pin it up with the jumbo pins she had.

When she stepped back to look at herself in the mirror, she was surprised to see her mother staring back at her. She never thought that she resembled her mother much but with her hair up and her face flushed with excitement, she looked exactly like Catalina D'orio Bennett.

While she was dressing, Darius came for her. Elaine sat in the living room entertaining him. She found them sitting across from each other talking quietly.

Darius stood as she entered smiling. "Good evening Darius," Nina said shyly.

"Good evening Nina. Are you ready to go?" Darius asked politely. From the look in his eyes, Nina could tell that he liked her outfit. She was impressed with his suit as well. She always thought that he was a well-dressed man.

"Before we go, I have some very exciting news to tell you. Today I got confirmation that the recreation center will soon be a reality. I feel like celebrating." Nina said barely able to conceal her excitement.

"You should have seen her earlier," her aunt butted in, "she was jumping up and down and screaming. I thought she got some bad news, until she told me."

"That is fantastic news indeed. We *should* go somewhere to celebrate. Sister Elaine would you like to join us?" Pastor Fairchild asked.

"Oh no, I couldn't. I've only just come home from work, but thank you for asking. You two go on and have a good time." Aunt Elaine said and she ushered them to the front hall.

Nina got her coat from the closet by the front door while Darius pulled his on. Nina couldn't stop smiling as they got in the car. She thought it was nice of Darius to invite her aunt out with them and told him so.

"She was bursting with pride and sounded so proud of you that I thought she would like to celebrate with you also. How far have you gotten with the building plans?" Darius asked turning to look at her quickly.

"I really hadn't gone that far yet because I wasn't sure I'd get the spot. My lawyer will be handling all that shortly. As soon as money changes hands, I guess I can go on to the next phase. Do you have any experience in putting up buildings Darius?" Nina asked him.

"I have dealt with contractors when we did some renovations on the church building. I know that it isn't on the scale of putting up a whole building, but it can't be that different." Darius said.

"No I don't think it is that different either. So if you have some free time will you accompany me when I go meet with the contractors?" asked Nina.

"I would be happy to. Now where shall we go to celebrate?" he asked.

"If you don't mind driving into the city we could go to the Four Seasons. I think we can have a festive dinner and not be disturbed by anyone. I hear that the place is usually crawling with celebrities." Nina suggested.

"The Four Seasons it is then." Darius agreed.

Since it was mid-week, the restaurant wasn't overcrowded and even though they hadn't a reservation, they were able to get in. Darius suspected that the host knew who Nina was. Their dining experience was enjoyable and Nina was right about not being disturbed. The staff respected their privacy. They dined on fine cuisine, laughed, and generally enjoyed each other's company. They also talked about the plans for the recreation center.

Over coffee, Nina recognized the tiny worried look on Darius' features when the waiter placed the check beside his elbow. When he looked at it, his facial expression turned to nonchalance. Nina felt horrible.

"Darius, would you be embarrassed if I paid the bill tonight? It was my choice to come here and I know that you agreed because you wanted to please me."

"I am not embarrassed Nina, I just wasn't prepared. I could leave the tip if that's okay with you?" Darius had a pleasant smile on his handsome face.

"I knew there was a reason I liked you," Nina answered as she pulled out her wallet for her credit card. She placed it in the little pocket in the booklet and Darius signaled the waiter.

When the waiter returned he handed the receipt to Nina to sign and Darius placed the appropriate tip amount in the booklet. The waiter nodded at them graciously and Darius escorted Nina out.

The wind had gotten bitter and Darius placed his arm around Nina as they walked the block and a half to his car. As she sat in the front seat beside him, Nina rubbed her legs. "I should've worn boots my legs are so cold I can't feel them."

Darius reached over to turn the heater on full blast as soon as the car had warmed up, then he adjusted the controls to blow on the floor. Nina nodded her thanks and leaned back to enjoy the warmth that thawed her legs.

"Do you mind if we don't do that again?" Darius asked suddenly.

Nina didn't have to pretend she didn't know to what he referred. She nodded and apologized softly. Darius reached over to kiss her. It was unexpected and Nina felt shaken. She decided that he was a great kisser. If she had been out with anyone other than Darius, she would have kissed him back.

How does one enjoy a simple kiss with one's boyfriend when said boyfriend is a pastor? Nina thought in a panic. She was terrified of doing anything considered sinful.

"Was I going too fast for you?" Darius asked taking in her downcast head and her folded hands.

"No, I really like the kiss but I'm not sure if it is okay to kiss you back. Is there a rule book on dating clergy I should read?" she asked.

Darius reached over to turn her to him as much as the seat belt allowed. "You are the strangest young woman I have ever met. We can kiss, hold hands, hug and be romantic. I would never let anything get out of hand between us and I know that you wouldn't either." He leaned over, held her face in his palms, to kiss her again.

This time, Nina kissed him back and timidly put her hands on his. When he pulled away, she opened awestruck eyes to him. "I wondered when and if we'd be doing this, and I'm glad I'm sitting down. Wow!"

"Don't tell me that you haven't been kissed before, I've seen you kiss in the movies." Darius said steering the car into traffic.

"That's stage kissing and it is very different. It isn't intimate and besides on the movie set there are anywhere from ten to fifteen people watching you, not to mention the ten or more doing their jobs on the set. And you have to practice and do so many retakes that by the time that everything is right, it doesn't even feel like a kiss anymore," explained Nina. She liked the idea that he's seen her movies.

"What about your old boyfriends, they've kissed you haven't they?"

"I had only one real boyfriend and we were both eighteen. We dated for five months and I think that I was his first real girlfriend as well. My dad put the fear of God in him the first time they'd met and even if he had wanted to try anything, the little speech my dad gave him kept him a complete gentleman." Nina recounted.

"You didn't answer my question Catalina." Darius stressed.

"I have never been kissed like that before if that's what you're asking."

"I wanted to do that on your birthday, to erase the hurt." Darius said stealing a look at Nina and reaching for her hand.

Nina didn't say anything. She squeezed his hand and dared not look at him. She didn't want him to see the hurt on her face. Darius was a sweet, kind man and now, Nina felt extremely lucky.

After he parked in front of her house, Darius got out quickly helping Nina out of the car. It had started to snow and it looked like this time it would be a major storm. Nina hurried to the door then turned to face Darius.

"Wow, it looks like it is coming down sideways. I hope your drive home isn't too long. Call me when you get in so I can stop worrying, okay?" Nina looked up at him nervously.

"Catalina I'm going to kiss you again," Darius warned her. He sensed her nervousness and murmured to her to put her at ease.

"You are becoming very special to me Nina and I am awed by how much." This time he pulled her gently into his arms. They pulled apart when a particularly strong gust of wind blew snow into their faces.

"Good night Catalina," Darius said and waited for her to unlock the door. When she was safely in and waving at him, he turned and rushed to his car.

"You know I wondered when that man was going to sound happy again." Elaine said behind Nina.

Nina jumped and turned to face her aunt. "You scared me," she declared. Nina pushed away from the door to take off her coat. After placing it in the closet, she faced her aunt once more.

"You weren't spying on us were you?" she asked.

"No. I happened to be looking out the window to see how bad the storm had gotten when you two came up the steps. I couldn't put the shade down because he would have seen me. That was a very nice kiss he planted on you there." Elaine said with a smile.

Nina smiled back shyly. "I thought so too." She brushed past her aunt to run up the stairs. She felt embarrassed that her aunt saw her kiss the pastor. She wasn't upset just feeling shy. This was still so new and she wanted to savor it privately.

Nina slid between the sheets and smiled to herself. Before she could daydream about Darius and any possible future they might have, she reached over to the nightstand to clasp her bible. She has been trying to read a few chapters every night and she was now at the Song of Solomon. There were only eight chapters to the book and what she read left her very confused.

She couldn't make up her mind whether it was about a man in love or a woman in love. The gender seemed to change from chapter to chapter and the emotions were intense. Because what she read left her feeling confused, Nina followed it with a couple of Psalms. Then she said a prayer to ask the Lord's protection for Darius as he traveled in the storm.

Nina was almost asleep when she realized that she hadn't heard from Darius. It had been more than an hour since he dropped her off, he should've been home by now, she thought further. Worried that something might have happened, she quickly unplugged her cell phone from its charger and speed dialed his phone. Darius answered his phone on the second ring.

"Hello?" Darius' voice sounded relaxed.

"Darius, are you okay?"

"Yes Nina I'm fine. I was wondering if you were ever going to call."

"You were expecting me to call?" Nina asked puzzled.

"I was," Darius replied simply.

"Why?"

"We haven't spoken on the phone yet. I figured that if you got worried enough you'd call," reasoned Darius.

"I see. So you're really okay?"

"Yes Nina I'm fine. Were you getting ready for bed?"

"I was almost asleep when I realized that you hadn't called." Nina explained.

"I wanted to hear your voice before I went to sleep. You have a great phone voice when you're worried," said Darius.

"Your voice sounds nice too. So you won't mind if I call you whenever I need to hear your voice?" Nina asked him.

"You can call me anytime as long as it is not for something nonsensical like asking for the church schedule." Darius teased.

Nina frowned a little. She realized that she was acting silly. Darius and she were going out and she had every right to call him when she wanted to speak with him.

"I'm sorry if I'm overly cautious. I am really paranoid about making mistakes with you," Nina admitted.

"I thought we cleared that up Nina. When I'm with you, it's all about us. I don't understand why it is still an issue with you. Are you having second thoughts about us?"

"Please don't think that Darius. I feel good about us. I just want things to be perfect. I forgot to ask you about my transfer, did you get it yet?"

"As a matter of fact I received it today. I made a stop on my way home to pick up the mail at the church. Be ready for me to announce you as a new member on Sunday, okay?"

"Great. Brother Jonas will be glad to hear that I'm a member now. He wants me to join the choir badly. What do you think, should I join?"

"That's entirely up to you," Darius answered.

"I was dragging my feet because I feel that he wants me to sing lead. Sister Jennifer has a great and powerful voice and I don't want to be the cause of resentment in the choir ranks."

"This isn't Hollywood Nina. At Christ Tabernacle, we are one big happy family. There can be more than one lead singer," he explained.

"Then I'll let him know that I am ready to join."

"I believe that it is a step in the right direction and people will start to see you in a different light," he pointed out.

"I hope so. Darius are you happy that we are seeing each other. I mean am I what you expected?" Nina asked him.

"I thought you might be shorter up close, but you're just the right height."

"Very funny, what do you really think?" Nina asked seriously.

"I didn't know what to expect. You are this superstar living among us mere mortals and I felt in awe. I realized that there was more to you when you sang during the revival. I couldn't hold back any longer. You are a very beautiful woman and I thought that even if you had shot me down like you did that young man at the picnic that at least I had tried." Darius answered.

"Wow what does a girl say to that? I'm used to Hollywood handsome but you are better than that. You aren't phony and your appearance isn't what is always on your mind. I'm glad that you are in my life Darius." Nina told him truthfully.

"I'm glad that you are in mine also. I'm going to say goodnight now even though I don't want to. I have to be up early in the morning. I'll call you sometime during the day, okay?"

"Yes. Goodnight Darius." Nina murmured.

"Goodnight Catalina."

Sunday morning Nina awoke early. She was excited and wanted to start celebrating early. Aunt Elaine agreed wholeheartedly and allowed Nina to take over the kitchen to prepare a big breakfast. She shooed her aunt away insisting that she would call her when everything was ready.

Nina served waffles with strawberries and whipped cream, a side of bacon and toast. She made a pot of coffee for herself and some herbal tea for her aunt. Elaine ate everything Nina served with relish.

Nina decided that she didn't care what anyone thought and dressed like the Hollywood star that she was. She chose a mint green, calf-length sequined dress that shimmered when she moved. Because of the color, her eyes stood out more and she put her hair up and wore makeup. She never liked big bulky jewelry so she felt comfortable wearing her emerald stud earrings and matching necklace. Since it snowed, Nina pulled out her white leather quarter boots and its matching purse. When she stepped back to see her image in the mirror she smiled knowing that she looked good.

Her aunt announced how difficult it was going to be for the pastor to focus on his sermon with her looking so pretty. Nina was alarmed for a minute until she realized that Elaine was teasing her.

When they arrived at the church, Nina parked as close to the side doors as she could. Elaine was a basket case with her driving even though Nina assured her that her SUV had four-wheel drive, which meant that she wouldn't lose control readily. They had gotten five inches of snow. They held hands as they approached the door and stomped their feet on the mat to shake off the snow.

Sunday school was just starting and Nina was still shy and sat in the back while her aunt sat up front. Trustee Worthington taught the adult class and his lesson was on the miracle of Christ's birth. Nina realized that Christmas was literally around the corner. She and her aunt would have to start decorating the house soon, she thought.

After Sunday school, Nina got up to go sit with Elaine. Sisters Dorothea and Rachel turned to watch her as she approached the pew. Nina gave them a big smile.

"Praise the Lord, good to see you." Nina greeted them.

"Praise the Lord sister Nina." Sister Dorothea answered in returned.

Sister Rachel waved as she was on the far end of their pew. Nina smiled and waved back. She noted how phony her smile still was and decided that she didn't care. Today she was going to be welcomed as a member of the church and nothing was going to change that.

When the praise team got up on the pulpit to lead the congregation in song, Nina was happy to sing, clap and praise. She didn't know if it was just her but she felt something in the air. The air was full of excitement and as the service progressed, she felt it more and more. It became apparent that she wasn't the only one who felt it. The air was thick with the Holy Ghost.

The songs the praise team chose to sing were powerful and moving. By the time the pastor got up to deliver his sermon, the Lord had seen fit to direct his every word. When he ended his sermon, he opened up the doors of the church to receive new believers, five people had come to the altar for prayer and two asked for baptism.

Finally, seven others stood as new members of the Christ Tabernacle Church with Nina. As was the custom, the assistant ministers, Deacons and Deaconesses, all the other church officers lined up to welcome them. Darius Fairchild brought up the rear and had a few words to say to each of them. When he got to her, he lingered to give her a hug. Nina flushed with pleasure and smiled at him and then at the congregation.

Darius made a little speech on how he expected the saints to treat their new members. Nina knew he did it because of the way she was treated.

After service, Brother Jonas rushed to her side to ask her if she had given any thoughts to joining the choir and Nina asked him for a schedule of the rehearsals. He wasted no time as he sifted through the folder in his hands to find a schedule. Nina took it and promised that she would be at the next rehearsal.

CHAPTER SEVEN

Nina felt good and wanted to go out to eat but Elaine insisted that the weather was too cold and the roads too icy for them to be out in it. Besides, she had already cooked Sunday brunch. Instead, Nina drove home a little subdued and she rushed up to her room to pout.

When Elaine called her down to eat, Nina almost didn't want to go down. She wanted to celebrate because she finally belonged to an organization that would not ever desert or use her. When she eventually went down to join Elaine, she found Darius sitting at the dining table as well.

"For a minute there we thought that you weren't hungry." Elaine told her with a sly smile.

"I didn't know you were coming to eat with us, Darius," Nina said ignoring her aunt's comment.

"Most Sundays I am invited to different families' homes so I decided that today I would break bread with you fine ladies." Darius answered.

"Great," replied Nina. She felt embarrassed for having thrown a tantrum earlier even though no one knew that she had.

Nina helped Elaine serve the food and soon they were eating and laughing. Darius told them that he planned to schedule a meeting about the recreation center. He wanted Nina there to answer questions and she agreed. Darius spent the rest of the day with the Bennett women. Elaine discreetly left them alone and Nina was grateful. She and Darius spoke more of the plans for the recreation center. Nina was full of ideas and ways the church and the surrounding community could use to keep the center functioning.

"I was thinking that we could have an opening ceremony when it is complete with something like a concert or a maybe a battle of choirs," she suggested.

"Sweetheart, you are really excited about this center aren't you?" Darius asked suddenly.

"Yes I am, aren't you? I mean you mentioned that you wanted to help the young people in this community and this is one way of doing that," Nina pointed out.

Darius' features turned serious and he stared at her.

"What's wrong?" asked Nina.

"Nina you didn't do this because of what I said did you?" he asked.

"I wanted to do something for the youth and I thought of what my father did in L.A. He made a difference in the lives of a good number of young men and women who would have otherwise hung out on the street corner.

I wanted to do something similar. Since you expressed your interest, I didn't think that it was wrong to pool both our concerns for the youth into the same project. As you said before in the end the kids are going to benefit." Nina explained.

The expression on Darius' face made her afraid that she had said something wrong until he leaned over and caught her lips in a kiss.

"You are the most selfless person I have ever met. You just keep amazing me more and more. What am I going to do with you?" he asked.

"You could kiss me again." Nina suggested as she leaned into his embrace.

They kissed and held each other close. Nina closed her eyes tightly as she breathed in his scent and thought that it was the most wonderful in the world.

"What are you going to do once the recreation center is up and in use? Have you given any thoughts to whom might run the place?" He asked suddenly.

"Do you have anyone in mind?" countered Nina. She's decided that sitting next to him and having his arm around her holding her close was the second best part of the day thus far.

"Why don't you run it? This could be the vehicle you need to gain everyone's trust." Darius pointed out.

"Darius I don't have the credentials to do that. I'd have to go to school all over again and I really don't want to do that." Nina insisted.

"Did you or didn't you get a degree in psychology?" Darius asked suddenly.

"How did you know that?" Nina asked wide-eyed.

"Honey I have been studying you since I laid eyes on you. You can do this if you want to. And if you need more schooling you can take correspondence courses to get up to speed."

"So you've given this a lot of thought haven't you? Just because I'm putting, the center up doesn't mean that I have to be at its helm too. Perhaps I could coordinate with whoever is running it when there is an event. How does that sound?" Nina asked leaning away from him so that she could see his face.

"I take it back you are not amazing, you are a coward." Darius accused Nina.

Nina's eyes widened. "I am not! The idea was to get more people in the community involved. I don't want to be in the spotlight Darius because it would seem like I want to control everything."

"Trust me, this perfect for you. Take a couple of business courses and run the center." Darius insisted.

"What about you; how much time are you going to contribute to the center?" Nina wanted to know.

"I will be around here and there," he replied vaguely.

"You have some nerve calling me a coward Pastor Fairchild. Your yellow streak probably glows in the dark!" Nina accused him.

"I just get a kick out of watching you get riled up, you are so cute!" Darius told her. He caught her lips in a quick kiss.

"Seriously Babe, don't you want to be involved in the center?" Nina asked while she tried to compose herself. Darius was a very affection man and he was always showing it. She liked it very much. It was just that she wasn't ready to go public with their relationship yet. In her opinion, it was still too new.

"In the event that I'm needed for anything spiritual, I'll step in. I also have a degree in psychology and can help counsel some of our youth. You do understand that I have a job outside the church too. I can only do so much." Darius explained, spreading his arms wide.

"You have a job? I thought the church paid you a salary for you to minister to the congregation and the community." Nina's expression was one of disbelief.

Darius smiled at her indulgently. "The church you went to in L.A. was probably capable of supporting their pastors but there are a few churches that cannot support their pastor so he takes an outside job to support himself and his family."

"But this isn't a storefront church. Christ Tabernacle belongs to a bigger organization so why aren't they paying you enough?" Nina asked agitatedly.

"Sweetheart, that's just the way it is. You are right I do get a salary but it isn't enough. I like nice things so I work to get them. Although we have a healthy membership, the money coming in isn't enough to keep everything running smoothly, so I work to supplement what the church pays me."

Nina stood up then to look down at him. "You called me amazing but you are many times more that than me. Maybe I am being a little prejudiced about this, but you do more for these people than they realize. You never refuse them whenever they call on you. When Sister Richardson read the card that family sent to the church for the monetary help they received for their rent this past week, I got the feeling that it was all you because I was watching the faces of some of the people sitting near me and they looked puzzled. It was evident that they didn't know to what she was referring. Last week alone, you've visited several members in the hospital, and officiated at one funeral." Nina said counting on her fingers.

"It's true that I do a lot, but it's not just because I'm a pastor and it's my job, I do those things because I want to and also because I feel that whatever I do in the capacity of a clergyman, I am influencing someone to come to the Lord." Darius explained. He stood up too because he was getting excited as well.

"You must have gone back for seconds when God was handing out goodness," Nina said smiling up at him.

"You give me too much credit Nina. Let's get back to the subject at hand; I promise you that I will be there on a regular basis if you agree to run the place." Darius said and put out his hand.

"That's blackmail Darius," Nina grumbled but she put her hand in his and they shook on it.

Darius left shortly thereafter and Nina went into the kitchen to make sure that her aunt hadn't gone in to clear up. She promised that she would do it herself.

Nina had a lot on her mind as she washed the dishes. She's committed herself to running the center once it was up. It wasn't something she wanted to do, but she supposed that she would have to do something to keep occupied. She didn't need to work for wages because she had plenty of money, so maybe running the center wasn't such a bad idea after all.

When she was done with the downstairs, she went upstairs to check on Elaine before going on to her room. Nina found her sitting up in bed reading her bible as usual. She looked up from whatever passage she was reading to smile at Nina.

"Is Darius gone?" she asked using his given name, but she still addressed him as Pastor in his presence.

"Yes, he left a while ago. I was getting the kitchen straighten out," Nina answered. She walked further into her aunt's room and sat on the edge of the bed.

When Nina first moved in, Elaine's house although was well kept, it was rundown. The renovations it had undergone transformed the house into a showplace. Her aunt's bedroom was elegant, done to suit her personality. Elaine was very fond of Earth tones and Nina was happy to oblige her. Now Elaine's bedroom was all browns and beige and burnt orange.

"Auntie may I ask you something?" she asked as she got more comfortable on the bed.

Elaine put the bible down to nod at her. "What's on your mind child?"

"Darius is insisting that I run the recreation center once it is up. I don't know if I am up to it. I mean I could probably do it but I don't want Christ Tabernacle getting the wrong impression of me. I don't want to seem too controlling. What do you think?"

"Well I don't see why you shouldn't. Our community leaders make all these promises for better conditions within the community and nothing happens. I think that if you can come out of pocket for something for this community then, you should be able to have a say so in how it runs. It wasn't like what your dad did when he put the center up in L.A. He wasn't required to run it because he did it as a charity.

You are doing this because you care about the community into which you've moved. If anyone has a problem with it, they will have to prove why it isn't a good idea," her aunt expressed.

"I'm pretty sure that the community in general will see it as a good deed, but I was more concerned about the church community. I'm still getting dirty looks from some of the members and I haven't done anything to them. I can't understand why they resent me," said Nina.

Her aunt shrugged. "If you ask me I think they are just plain green with envy. I'm sure that once they get to know you, they'll change their tune." Elaine advised her.

Nina nodded then went to her room. She hoped that Elaine was right and that one day the people she wanted to accept her will come around. Sister Rachel Winston came to mind; she just couldn't see what it was that made the woman dislike her so.

Nina prayed about her coerced deal with Darius to run the center and hoped that people would start to see her in a different light after the meeting

Darius planned to set up.

The following morning, Nina received a call from her lawyer. He called to give her an update. The families wanted reassurance that she really was going to erect a recreation center and that she was going to place a commemorative plaque in their honor in it. They also wanted to know if they could participate in putting up the structure, as one of the men was a licensed carpenter and the other a plumber, both out of work.

Nina closed her eyes and took a deep breath. Nothing was ever simple, she thought. She didn't know how it would work since she'd planned to hire a contracting firm. She told her lawyer that somehow she would work it out. Maybe after the building was up, she could have the church hire them to help with what they planned on doing. She asked for their contact information, jotted them down, and then she hung up.

The next day, she met with the bank and the families. Each family was getting the market value of their respective homes. Her lawyer explained that mortgage balances were issues the owners had to deal with, that Nina offer was fair.

Nina thought back to when her dad had done this and didn't recall him having to go through any of what she was going through. It brought to mind what Elaine said the other night. What he did was charity and good works. He merely threw money at the project, he wasn't directly involved as she was.

However, she hoped that she was up to the task. This was all new to her and she was glad that she had her lawyer beside her. As far as contractors go, her lawyer was instrumental in connecting her with several companies that would be perfect for her project. Richard advised her to keep her lawyer because he knew her and been with her for years and more importantly, he wouldn't cheat her. Richard was right. Mr. Ethan Dullard of Dullard, Dullard and Edison was very patient. She liked to think that after fifteen years they were also friends. She was in capable hands in that sector.

By the end of the week, Nina felt frazzled. Each family insisted on having separate and private meetings with her and their lawyers. She repeated the simple act of writing a check three times when she could have done it in one meeting. Her lawyer insisted that he handle any extra negotiating if it came up. As it was, each family tried to ask for more money, which was why they wanted separate meetings. Mr. Dullard was firm, insisting that market value for their properties was fair. He went on to inform them further that any reneging on their part would result in dissolution of the contract between them and his client.

Nina was looking forward to Saturday. She planned to stay in bed for most of it. Naturally, early in the morning her aunt came knocking on her bedroom door. Nina had a headache and felt miserable.

"Nina, are you awake?" Elaine asked through the door.

"No." she answered piteously.

"You have a visitor," Elaine elaborated.

"Who is it?" Nina asked dreading to hear that her lawyer had yet another document for her to sign.

"It's Darius honey," Elaine replied.

"Tell him to go away I don't want to see anyone," Nina replied.

"I'm sorry child but you will have to tell him yourself. Are you decent?"

"Why?" Nina asked alarmed.

Elaine opened the door and there stood Darius. She pushed him into the room and closed the door behind him.

Nina squealed and scrambled to cover her head. She didn't want him to see her morning face or her hair tied up in a scarf. What was her aunt thinking shoving the man into her room like that?

"Why do you want me to go away, Nina?" he asked calmly as if being in her bedroom first thing in the morning was normal.

"What are you doing here?" was her muffled query.

"Answer my question first and then I'll answer yours," said Darius.

"I'm tired. I've had meetings all week and I have the grandfather of all headaches. Now why are *you* here?" asked Nina.

"I thought I'd have breakfast with you this morning to ask for your help in decorating my house for Christmas. I like what you and your aunt have done with yours. Every Christmas Eve, I host a dinner after service at my house. I usually have the women's auxiliary help me, but this year I wanted you to co-host it as my girlfriend." Darius explained serenely.

Nina pulled the blanket off her head to stare at him. She did a quick calculation in her head and came up with a few weeks since they started dating.

"Don't you think that's a little soon?" she asked sitting up to settle her blankets chastely up to her chest.

"It's too late for you to back out now. I've been calling all of last night to ask but your phone wasn't on. So in my panic I came over as soon as I thought it was appropriate to see if you were okay." Darius explained further as he looked around.

For a mega-star, Nina was ordinary. He was expecting her to be in silks and satins but she slept in what appeared to be a big cotton nightshirt and she tied up her hair just like any other black woman he's ever known.

He liked what she'd done to the bedroom too. Her color scheme was the palest lavender. He figured that it was her whimsy side. Her furniture was sturdy mahogany and he thought that it was her practical side. Whatever clichéd ideas he had about Nina were all wrong. She surprised him all the time and he loved it. He learned something about her every time they were together. Watching her trying to hide from him brought home how deeply he felt for her. It was amazing how quickly his feelings for her had escalated.

Nina slowly got out of bed on the other side tugging her knee length nightshirt to its limit and walked over to the dresser where she pulled the top draw open. She reached in and came out with her phone, which she proceeded to plug in. Turning to smile at him, she yanked the hair scarf off and threw it on the bed.

"Two of the owners of the burnt out homes are an out of work carpenter and plumber. They've been blowing up my phone about work on the center. They just won't stop calling, so I put the phone in the draw so that I wouldn't hear it anymore." Nina explained weakly.

Darius nodded. "So what about my house and Christmas Eve dinner, why don't you think it is a good idea?" Darius asked, "And why do you think it's too soon?"

"We've only been dating a short time and I really don't think it will go over very well. There are still too many people who see me as an intruder and a Christian wannabe," Nina answered sneaking a look at him.

"You are the most insecure person when it comes to these people. Why is them liking you so important to you?" Darius asked.

"I can't think right now, I need to brush my teeth and wash my face," Nina murmured and brushed past him to go to the connecting bathroom she shared with her aunt.

As she past him, Darius caught her hand to pull her close. "I know you have morning breath, but I just need to hold you," he said with a smile.

69

Nina allowed him to pull her closer until she felt his warmth envelope her and she threw her arms around him as well. They held each other and without words communicated how they felt. When Darius let go of her, Nina practically ran into the bathroom.

She had emotions swirling around in her heart she had never felt before and although she understood what sexual attraction was, she knew that it was much more than that. When Darius held her, she felt loved and safe. Could she be falling in love with him?

Nina hurried to brush her teeth and to look presentable. Even though she still had a headache, Nina felt that she could suffer through it to have breakfast with Darius. She showered quickly and peeked out to see if Darius was still in the room; he wasn't.

It was getting colder by the day out so Nina dressed warmly. She wore a pair of tan corduroy pants and a brown sweater. In case they went out, soft brown leather boots completed the outfit and then she went downstairs to join Darius and her aunt.

She found them in the kitchen. Darius was sitting at the table with a cup of coffee while Elaine stood at the counter with a cup of tea. They were talking and laughing. They sobered up when she entered, but Nina knew that they were talking about her.

"What's so funny?" she asked them suspiciously.

"Pastor was just telling me that I scared you when I pushed him into your room. He said you hid under the covers, is that true?"

"You have no couth Auntie, none at all." Nina expressed and ignoring them both went over to the coffee pot to pour a cup. Then she reached up into the cabinet and took out a small vial of Tylenol. She tossed two to the back of her throat and swallowed them with a cautious sip of the hot coffee.

"Do you think you'll feel better by the time we get to my house?" Darius asked her.

"What about breakfast? I distinctly remember hearing you say that you wanted to have breakfast with me." Nina reminded him, she was hungry.

"I meant at my house. My housekeeper is there now preparing it for us. Didn't I mention that?" he Darius.

"No you didn't. Is your housekeeper someone from church?" Nina asked feeling curious about the person who kept his house.

Darius flashed a quick and nervous smile. "As a matter of fact it is. Sister Rachel Winston has been my housekeeper for three years now."

Nina's mouth dropped open. She didn't know what to say. She let it sink in for a few more minutes before she looked over at her aunt. "And why didn't you tell me, she's supposed to be your best friend isn't she?"

"Why should what she does for a living be of any interest to you?" Elaine asked. She too wore a nervous expression.

Nina looked from her aunt to Darius. *Were they being deliberately obtuse? They both knew that Sister Rachel didn't like her. As Darius' housekeeper, she would be privy to everything that went on in his house. It wouldn't even be a stretch to imagine them sitting at his table just talking. Nina decided to grasp this opportunity to win the woman over and perhaps find out why the woman disliked her so much.*

Nina shook her head and suggested that they go before she changed her mind. As Darius was in a very good mood, she tried to be cheerful as well. She decided to keep an open mind and deal with Rachel as the situation dictated.

Darius didn't live far from the church, he could walk if he wanted to, which he probably did in good weather. He held her hand as they entered his house. Wonderful aromas greeted them as they made their way further into the house. He took her into the kitchen to greet Sister Rachel. She looked up from what she was doing to smile at them.

Nina saw the surprised look on her face and realized that Darius hadn't told her who was coming. Nina waved and tightened the grip she had on Darius' hand.

"Good morning Sister Rachel." Nina said hoping her voice sounded steady.

"Good morning Pastor, Sister Nina," the stunned woman replied.

"Good morning Rachel." Darius said. Then he tugged Nina along telling her that he was going to give her a tour of his house.

"She didn't know that I was coming did she?" Nina asked him when they were away from the kitchen.

"No. I called her while I was on my way to get you. I told her that I needed her to have breakfast ready for me and a guest," he explained.

"I see. Does she know that I am your girlfriend?" asked Nina.

"No she doesn't and it isn't any of her business who I see."

Darius took her to the living room and explained that the house had three bedrooms and then he took her into his office, which was off the living room.

Darius had great taste. His house was a beautiful brick cape. For a man who was on his own like he was, Nina expected the walls to be papered in no nonsense generic colors like green, blue or stripes of some kind. Instead, he painted the walls in a very nice shade of blue with white trimmings. The furniture was light blue with royal blue pillows.

She expected wood paneling in his office, but it too was painted and decorated in mellowing browns and tan. On the walls, he hung his framed credentials and several commendation plaques from various organizations.

Nina sat down on a comfortably stuffed chair in front of the desk. He pulled a thick album out from one of the desk draws to show her. He told her that it contained pictures of past Christmases and dinners.

Nina looked through the album to see quite a few people she recognized and from the expression on their faces; they were having a good time.

She even saw her aunt, Sisters Rachel and Dorothea in the album as well. The album went back quite a few years but one picture caught her attention. It was one of Darius and a woman whom she thought couldn't be anyone but his deceased wife.

"Darius, is this a picture of your wife?" she asked looking up at him.

He walked over to where she sat to look over her shoulder.

"Yes," he said in a tight voice. "That was my wife Rebecca. She died six months after that picture was taken."

Nina closed the album, got up to give him a hug. "I'm sorry if I've called up painful memories. She was a very beautiful woman. Was she sick?" Nina realized that they never talked about her.

"No. She died of asphyxiation. We didn't know that she was allergic to aspirin. She had a headache, and we had run out of the Tylenol she usually takes. The only thing that was on hand was aspirin left over from when my dad used to take them for his heart. By the time we got to the hospital, they couldn't revive her. She's been gone five years now."

"Oh Darius, I'm so sorry." Nina said. She hugged him tighter.

There was a discreet knock on the door and Sister Rachel opened the door. Nina tried to pull away but Darius held her tightly to his side.

"Pastor I came to let you know that breakfast is ready." Sister Rachel told him but her eyes never wavered from Nina.

"Thank you, Rachel. Nina and I will be right out."

Sister Rachel left and shut the door behind her. Darius let Nina go and she turned to face him. "Did you see the look she gave me? What have I done to her?"

"I don't think it's as serious as you think. She needs to get to know you better." Darius said encouragingly.

"Does she see me as a threat of some kind? Was she related to your late wife?" Nina asked with a searing dread in her heart.

"No, she wasn't related to Rebecca, and I don't think she thinks you're a threat either, Nina. Why don't we go eat before the food gets cold?" Darius suggested.

He led the way back to the kitchen but Sister Rachel insisted that they eat in the dining room. He steered Nina to it and seated her, and then sat opposite her.

The dining room was huge. Apart from the enormous china cabinet, it held a table that sat twelve. Nina realized it was why he was able to host a dinner at his home. He had enough room for a big dinner party. After Sister Rachel served them, the pastor asked her to join them. Sister Rachel hesitated but he insisted and she went to get a plate for herself. Once she joined them, Darius blessed the food and they began to eat.

"I've invited Sister Nina over to help me decorate the house this year. Have you seen what she and her aunt have done to their house? I think it is very nice. I would like her to co-host Christmas dinner as well." He told Sister Rachel.

"Sister Elaine mentioned how Sister Nina had gone all out. And I guess with her background in entertainment, she would do a great job hosting the dinner." She turned to Nina. "Can you cook Sister Nina?"

"Please call me Nina and yes, I've been cooking since I was thirteen years old. My Dad insisted that I learn to cook, clean and keep house. I even took a culinary course in college." Nina replied hoping to impress the woman.

"That's nice, but can you cook for black folk?" she asked with her I'm-better-than-you expression on her face.

Nina took a deep breath and nodded. "Sister Rachel, I don't know what misconceptions you have of me but I'd like to take this opportunity to set you straight. My father was a black man who married a white woman. My mom died when I was only eight years old, but my dad raised me to embrace my heritage. Although I don't look it, I am as black as you." Nina spoke with as much attitude as could muster.

"Oh I didn't mean to upset you child, I just thought that since you've lived in California all your life and your lifestyle was so different from ours, that you weren't exposed to our culture."

"Well now that we've gotten some clarity, I'd like to get started with the decorations. Sister Rachel, while we are clearing the air, I would like to inform you that Sister Nina and I are seeing each other." Darius said simply. His tone was assertive and didn't invite any comment.

Sister Rachel smiled and nodded but it was a strained smile; the expression on her face was of one disappointment.

They finished breakfast quickly and Sister Rachel went about clearing up. Nina and Darius went back to his office to discuss his decorating plans.

For the next hour, Nina and Darius made shopping lists. Nina was finally able to get into the spirit of decorating Darius' house. She went back to the album to get ideas and realized that she wanted to do something different. As nice as the previous years had been, Nina wanted what she was about to do to stand out. She found that she didn't want any comparison to Darius' deceased wife. She surmised that Rebecca had had a hand in the festivities up to her sudden death.

After Rachel's comment on her Hollywood background, she wanted to be different but not showy. Once the lists were completed, she insisted that they go shopping. Rachel popped in to say her goodbyes and left. Nina felt less shy about walking around the house with her gone. Darius wanted only the main floor and the basement decorated as no one would be going upstairs where the bedrooms were.

The first thing on Nina's list was a Christmas tree. She asked him if he wanted to get a real or an artificial tree. Darius was very enthusiastic about a real one and Nina agreed so he stored the big white fake tree from last year in his garage. They also inspected the rest of his decorations. She put aside what she could use and Darius stored the rest.

Since Nina didn't know where to go for the tree, or if they'd find one so late in the season, she insisted that they go early before the choice trees were gone. Afterwards they would visit the party goods store for the rest of the decorations.

Thanks to Nina's celebrity status, they arranged to have the tree delivered to the house later. Darius had a very small budget to work with and it presented a very delicate situation.

"Darius, would you feel uncomfortable if I paid for some of the purchases? I mean what I want to do is going to be a little costly and since you've given me free reign, I want to do it right."

"Honey, I already knew it would come to that. Just as long as my house isn't turned into a circus you can do pretty much anything your little heart wants." Darius had a big grin on his face. Nina felt such a rush of affection for him that she couldn't stop herself. She threw her arms around him to hug him tight.

"I love you Darius," she said quietly in his ear.

Darius went still for a moment and Nina pulled back horrified at what she said. Her face was red from embarrassment. Darius realized that she hadn't meant to say those words to him. It was a complete surprise to her as well. Being out in public, they couldn't pursue the subject until they were alone.

"Well now, what do you want to get next?" he asked quietly trying to put her at ease.

"Garland." Nina answered even more quietly.

He took her hand and together walked toward the shelves containing garland of every length and description. By the time they purchased everything Nina felt she needed, it was mid-afternoon.

Nina decided that she would return to the house after Sunday's service to put everything together. Darius agreed but warned her that he had commitments he couldn't get out of, that she would be alone. Nina insisted that she did her best work alone.

They had a late lunch before Darius dropped Nina off at home. They were both aware that their relationship had changed but Nina was too afraid to talk about it. Darius wanted to but he didn't have the time. He had a meeting and a couples' counseling class to conduct.

After Darius left, Nina changed quickly and went in search of her aunt. She found her in the basement doing laundry. Nina routinely helped with the laundry and started folding clothes that her aunt pulled out of the dryer.

"Aunt Elaine we need to talk and I would like you to be honest with me. Darius and I had breakfast with Sister Rachel and it was the most disturbing meal I have ever had. She was deliberately condescending and I would like to know why. I got the feeling that she didn't resent me; rather it felt like she resented my presence. What do you know?" Nina stopped folding the towel she had in her arms to stare at her aunt.

"Well the only thing I could think of is that maybe her hope of her daughter and the pastor marrying is shot. They dated for a short time and she often said that she would be proud to have him as a son-in-law. But the relationship didn't progress past a few dates." Elaine wore a guilty expression on her face.

Nina watched the towel fall to the floor. She stared at it for a moment before she had the presence of mind to realize that she dropped it. She bent down slowly to pick it up then shook it before folding it once more.

"Who is her daughter?" Nina asked quietly.

Elaine looked up at Nina quickly, this time her expression one of surprise.

"Nina you know who she is. We see her every Sunday and if you weren't so busy with the center, you'd be singing with Jennifer in the choir, which reminds me. Brother Jonas called to remind you of practice tonight."

"Jennifer is *Rachel's* daughter? The woman can hardly bring herself to say hello to me, she certainly wouldn't introduce her daughter to me. Does Jennifer resent me too?"

"I couldn't tell you."

"Auntie you knew this all along and you didn't warn me, why?"

"I really didn't think about it. Rachel never let on that she was upset that Jennifer and the pastor stopped seeing each other. We're friends but this was something she never discussed. In fact she used to say that she didn't want to intrude in any way shape or form."

"Now I know why she resents me and after today, I'm pretty sure Jennifer is going to know that I'm seeing Darius. She may change her tune about me as well. We discussed singing duets together and now it may never happen." Nina said shaking her head sadly.

"Jennifer isn't like her mother Nina. For all you know, Rachel may be the only one who is upset about the relationship not working out," encouraged Elaine.

Later, while Nina got ready for choir practice, she thought about what her reaction would be if Jennifer turned hostile. She wasn't the type that liked conflict and usually shied away from those sorts of situations. For that reason alone, what the tabloids printed about her hurt. Jennifer didn't look the type either but one never knows. Nina decided that she would improvise and go on from there.

When she got to practice, she felt so self-conscious that she couldn't look anyone in the eye for the first half-hour. By the time they got around to their second song, Nina loosened up enough to look Jennifer's way. She was surprised that nothing happened. In fact, Jennifer was the same courteous young woman that she's always been.

Nina relaxed to sing, laugh and enjoy herself. When practice was over, she greeted everyone as she gathered her song folder. As she neared her car, she heard her name. It was Jennifer. Nina waited nervously for her to catch up to her.

"Nina can you give me a ride home?" she asked.

"Sure," said Nina. They continued to the car and Nina unlocked the doors.

Nina started the car then blew on her fingers. "It sure is cold out. This is my first real winter up here and I totally get why people love the tropics." Nina said conversationally.

"Yeah I know what you mean. My parents are originally from Barbados and we used to vacation there every other year," replied Jennifer.

When they stopped at a red light, Jennifer turned to Nina. She touched her shoulder lightly. "My mother told me that you and the pastor are dating. She was very upset about it." Jennifer stated. Her face was expressionless.

"My Aunt told me earlier today that you and he dated a while back; are you upset too?" Nina asked darting little nervous glances at her.

"No. I wanted you to know that my mom told me. He and I didn't work out because we didn't have anything in common. Mom was the one who pushed us to see each other. Besides, there is someone else." Jennifer said with a small smile.

Nina stopped the car to hug Jennifer. Their friendship had solidified by the time they reached their destination.

CHAPTER EIGHT

Sunday morning Nina jumped out of bed. She hurried to shower before going downstairs to start breakfast. Elaine was just waking up by the time she finished setting the table. When she came down, Nina was on her second cup of coffee.

"Good morning Auntie. I have breakfast ready so we can eat as soon as you'd like."

"Good morning Nina. We can eat right now. I've had to use all kinds of willpower to finish my morning prayer, since you've got the whole house smelling so good. What did you make?" She asked with a smile.

"I made pancakes, sausages and toast. Would you like me to make you a cup of tea?" Nina asked getting up.

"Oh goodness child, you need to lay off that coffee. You're so jittery you could jump right out of your skin. I can make my tea." Elaine went to the stove to reach up into the cupboard to pull out the box of teabags she preferred.

As they ate, Elaine regarded her curiously. She was fidgety and couldn't sit still. Her restlessness reminded Elaine of a child with a secret she couldn't hold.

"Goodness Nina, say what you are dying to say before you burst. I gather something good happened to put you in this mood so out with it." Aunt Elaine said finally.

"Jennifer asked me for a ride home last night. We had a nice little chat. Her mother told her how upset she was about my dating Darius. She also said that her mother pushed them together. The relationship didn't work because they didn't have anything in common," Nina gushed.

"Good. Now you can stop worrying about what other people think. You spend more time worrying about others than you do about yourself. See if you could muster some more of that energy and help me with my hair. I fell asleep before I could put rollers in it." Elaine replied as she got up from the table to place her plate and cup in the sink.

Nina hurriedly washed the dishes then followed Elaine upstairs to her room; they had plenty of time before they had to leave for church. Nina realized that her aunt was right about Rachel's daughter. Jennifer wasn't upset that her relationship didn't work out with their pastor. Perhaps this mysterious someone else had a lot to do with it.

Fretting over hair and outfits caused Nina to lose her coffee buzz. They got to church in time for Sunday school regardless. As an official member, Nina took her rightful place up front with her aunt.

This morning the choir sang a most edifying song. Jennifer sang the solo and Sister Rachel beamed at everyone on her pew. When Nina returned to her seat, she smiled and nodded sweetly at Sister Rachel. Sister Rachel returned her nod but didn't smile. Still Nina didn't allow the woman's coldness to bother her because she now knew what was bothering the woman. She merely had to get over it, after all Jennifer did.

After service, Nina went home first and planned to go decorate Darius' house after brunch with Elaine. The doorbell rang as she was finishing the dishes. She was completely surprised to find Darius standing there with a smile on his handsome face.

"What are you doing here?" asked Nina.

"Why good afternoon Sister and yes it is a fine afternoon. What do you mean what am I doing here? Aren't you going to decorate my house this after- noon?"

"Come in you're letting the cold in," Nina said pulling him in. "I'm still going but didn't think I'd see you until much later. You said that you'd be busy and that I'd be on my own. You gave me a key remember?"

Nina reminded him and fished in her pocket for the key, he had given her to show him.

Darius did the only thing left to a man when his woman talked too much. He kissed her quiet then he held her close.

"I came to pick you up so that we'd have some time together, but I have to go back to the church for a meeting and then I'm invited to Bethel after that. I figured that if I drove you home afterward we'd have some more time together. Now I ask you Sister Nina, do you have a problem with that?" Darius asked pulling away from him to see her face.

"I really liked that kiss." Nina said and for the first time in their relationship, she took the initiative to pull his head down to hers. It didn't take Darius long to take over and if it weren't for a discreet cough somewhere behind them, it could've gone on much longer.

"Sister Elaine, we didn't hear you there." Darius said weakly, acutely embarrassed.

"I suppose I should try to get used to catching you guys this way," Elaine said with a smile.

"Darius came to pick me up so I won't have to drive. He has a service at Bethel Temple so I probably won't be in till late since he will be driving me back." Nina replied neatly evading the issue.

"Good evening then Pastor, and Nina I'll see you in the morning." Aunt Elaine said. The couple watched her climb up the stairs.

Darius shook his head then turned to Nina. "Catalina you are going to get me in so much trouble with your aunt."

"I'm sure I don't know what you mean Pastor, I was just saying hello."

"If that was hello, I can't wait for your goodbye." Darius stated. Nina took a step toward him as if to show him, but he held up his hands and shook his head.

"I'm sure I can wait for your demonstration Babe. I have people waiting on me and I would hate to have to explain why I'm late."

Nina smiled and grabbed her coat. "Oh to be a fly on that wall," she said playfully as she walked past him out the door. Darius shook his head once more and followed her out of the house.

Once in the car, they got quiet again. Darius could feel the slight tension in the air and he knew that their relationship had quickly reached another plateau. He didn't know what he could say to make things less strained between them. Men and women have been grappling with these feelings ever since time began and for all that time it hadn't gotten any easier. No one it seemed had come up with anything that made it less awkward.

"We need to talk Nina and I'd like you to do some thinking this evening while you are at my house. Our relationship is changing and I think it would be prudent for you to think seriously on what is happening between us." Darius said. When Nina hadn't said anything, he reached over to squeeze her hand.

"Nina?"

"Yes Darius. Will you be thinking about us too?"

"I've already done so. I know what I want but I want you to know your own mind."

They drove the rest of the way in silence. After he helped her into his house, he kissed her gently on the cheek then left her standing in his office.

Nina shrugged off her coat to gather her hair into a bun then set to work. It took her a half hour to unwrap their purchases and while she did so, she mentally placed each item.

After half an hour of hanging garland, Nina felt thirsty and went to the kitchen to get some water. When she entered the kitchen, she found a bottle of iced tea on the counter next to the refrigerator with a note saying For Nina, in it. She smiled and opened the freezer for some ice. Darius was so nice and thoughtful she thought, and it brought to mind what he asked her to do.

It wasn't hard to recall what she felt the day before. It started with Darius' morning visit. He wasn't uncomfortable with people knowing that he was seeing her, which was why he felt that she could stand beside him and co-host the Christmas dinner. Moreover, he was very comfortable with their relationship; *she* was the one who wanted to hide it. Did she feel unworthy of him, was that why she wanted to keep it private still?

When they were together, she felt comfortable, unpressured, safe and loved. Why did she feel self-conscious, shy and unsure of herself when they were in public? Nina couldn't seem to shake the feeling that people would see her as a heathen and unworthy of the man of God. Didn't men of god fall in love, marry, and have children just like everybody else? Because her background was a little different from the average person, did that make her not as good as the average woman interested in a man of god?

As she grappled with her thoughts, Nina put the decorations up in the living room, basement, and dining room and then turned her attention to the Christmas tree. Darius made her promise that they would decorate it together when he got back later. She unraveled the strings of multi-colored lights and placed them in a coil on the floor by the tree, then she inspected the manger she couldn't resist buying. It was an African-American version and she arranged it carefully on the hutch in the dining room.

Nina's finished product was just what she wanted. The living room came alive with wreaths and hung garland. She placed scented pinecones in strategic areas so that the scent was continuously evident throughout the house. The mistletoe she placed in the entryway of the living room was sure to be a hit with married couples.

Although Darius warned her about the upstairs not being included, Nina strung leaf garland up the balustrade as far as the eye could see. In the dining room, Nina also hung wreaths with flowers. She bought two potted poinsettia plants, which she placed on either end of the table atop of the Christmas themed runner she bought. Along the runner, she placed pinecones and red candles.

As she stepped back, she bumped into Darius who had returned.

"Oh you scared me!" she cried as she turned to face him.

"I called out but you didn't hear me." Darius said clasping her hand. Looking around he smiled and nodded. "The place looks great."

Nina smiled and flushed with pleasure. "Thanks. How did everything go?"

"Very well, one of my assistant ministers preached tonight. He was good. That young man has a wonderful gift." Pastor Fairchild said.

Nina nodded her agreement. "I guess having assistants sort of gives you a break every now and then. It must be nice to sit and listen and be ministered to once in a while," said Nina.

"It is. Come show me what else you've done. I can see your personality coming through and it's kind of nice." He commented.

Nina dragged him along eager to show him what she did in the living room and his office. When Darius walked into his office, he looked around and nodded. "It is very nice. Not showy but portraying Christmas as it was meant to be. Although our Savior had a humble beginning, he had dignity and that's what I see here." Darius said. He pulled her close to kiss her forehead. Then he led her back into the living room.

She did the most in the room. She hung three different colored garlands. The Christmas wreaths between them kept the theme going along the walls. She then placed poinsettia plants beside the couch and the loveseat. In the windows, she installed single solar powered candles that came on at night when charged during the day. She bought enough so that he could put some on the windowsills upstairs. When they came to the tree, he squeezed her hand and told her that he needed to go change so that they could decorate it together.

Nina watched his retreating and felt a small pang of sadness at his leaving. She shook her head and tried to focus her attention on the tree. She was opening boxes of ornaments when Darius joined her again. Quietly they worked and it took them a little over an hour of steady work to get it done. Darius asked her to sit while he went to plug the lights in.

The tree came alive with the multicolored lights and ornaments. Darius had ordered a special ornament and picked it up after he left her the previous day. He pulled it out of his pocket to show her. It was small enough to fit in his hand. Nina stared at the porcelain miniature of her father and herself. They promoted it as a collector's item when she and her dad recorded a Christmas album one year. She was in her late teens then and looking down at the ornament, she recalled how special it made her feel when the people from Columbia House presented them with it.

"Oh Darius where did you get this, I didn't think they made them anymore." Nina asked looking up at him.

Darius pulled her up to her feet, smiling as he did so. "It wasn't easy but I wouldn't take no for an answer. Why don't you hang it?" he suggested.

When she had done so, he pulled her into his embrace once again for a kiss. This was a different kiss. Nina felt shaken by the kiss and its meaning wasn't lost on her. Darius was asking for forever. How she knew this, she couldn't put it in words, but she knew.

The last place he inspected was the basement. He instructed her to limit what she did in it, as it was where the bulk of the invited guests would gather. He had six long tables arranged. Nina bought red vinyl tablecloths for them and placed white candles on top. She hung wreaths on the walls and thought that it was festive if meager.

"Now before we talk Nina would you like something to eat or drink?" he asked as he led her back upstairs to the living room.

Nina shook her head. She looked at him and felt her heart flutter in her chest. She was so nervous her hands shook.

"You asked me to think about our relationship and I have. I think you are a wonderful man Darius. You are kind and sweet, giving and you have integrity, and something my father said was very important, you make me feel loved.

Because you are a minister, I feel that I have to be a certain way and I am still unsure if I fit the bill." Nina raised her hand to stop Darius who opened his mouth to speak. "I know that we've talked about it before and I am really trying to believe that I don't have to change, but I guess I'm not as confident as I thought I was."

"We can work on that Nina but that isn't that I wanted you to think about. Yesterday you blurted out something you didn't know you felt. Your whole demeanor changed afterward. You said that you loved me. Have you thought about that?"

"Yes I have and I really feel what I said." Nina replied. *There she said it and now there was no going back.* She lifted shy eyes to him and waited.

"Do you really? This isn't a movie set and there won't be anyone to call out 'Cut' and you get to start over. You said you loved me and it changes things between us. I know how I feel, but because I felt that it was too soon to feel that much for you I didn't tell you. I do love you and the feeling gets stronger every time we're together. We are not the typical couple because for one, my life is hectic with a job and being a clergyman and the whole world knows who you are. As daunting as it sounds I know we can find a happy medium where we can have quality time together, like now."

Darius clasped her close and his head swooped down to capture her lips in a sweet kiss. This time Nina didn't wonder at the intensity because she also allowed her heart to lead and kissed him back with the love she felt for him.

"Darius," she said when they came apart. "I'm not afraid of what people think about us. I love you and although I feel that the congregation should give us their blessings, this is ours and ours alone. I won't let them matter anymore."

"Good."

He watched the glow of the Christmas lights play across her features and thought that there wasn't a lovelier sight. Nina was the sweetest and most humble person he had ever known. *He first suspected how he felt about her when he caught sight of her at the park. He stayed back to watch her at the picnic because he felt unsure how she would receive him.*

She had only been coming to the church for a short time and he was captivated. He thought that she was beautiful and he felt that she was sincere in her praise too, evident particularly when she sang her solo. He also tried to keep in mind that she was an actor skilled in the art, that it might have been an act. Yet there was a yearning in her voice he thought was very sincere about the love she felt for the Lord.

He'd been alone these past five years but he hadn't felt lonely until Nina. Even when he dated Jennifer, he hadn't felt the need to take things further. He felt guilty about taking her out when he didn't really want to but he also felt that maybe the Lord had plans for him that he hadn't understood.

After the fourth date however, he knew Jennifer wasn't the woman for him. She confessed then that she had feelings for their choirmaster. Darius remembered feeling relieved then and told her that he hoped that things worked out for them. He also knew that the feeling was mutual between the two. Sister Rachel was quiet afterward but came around later. They never discussed it but he thought she discussed it with her daughter.

Nina was special and he could see a future for them. That day at the park, he had shamelessly followed her around and when she stopped at the playground to watch the children, he felt confident enough to speak with her alone. He was surprised to see tears streaming down her face. He wanted to comfort her. He learned quite a few things about her that day.

He learned that she was sensitive and had standards most people her age with her advantages didn't. She was sweet and honest. He had to admit that the things she said to him stunned him. He went home thinking that she wasn't what the magazines said she was.

When the opportunity came for him to see her, he grabbed it with both hands. He found that she was a remarkable sight when she was angry and often tried to get her riled up because her eyes flashed so brilliantly at him. At the meeting she'd attended to discuss the center Trustee Worthington commented about her money; Darius worried that Nina was going to explode at him, but she just stared him down with those eyes embarrassing him. He remembered following her out the door to catch her at the foot of the stairs from his office. He asked her to dinner to apologize and to soothe her. He felt that she was earnest and he came to understand that she would do the project without any input from the church. What impressed him was that she came to him at all.

He chastised the men after she left. Both trustees suggested that he ask her for financial support for the church. Trustee Worthington suggested that since she had those millions just sitting there and she wanted to do something for the church, that she should pay the mortgage off. He felt embarrassed for him and glad that Nina wasn't privy to *that* conversation.

He was afraid that Nina might see his attentions as a sort of prelude for monetary gain as well so he made it a point to avoid talking about church business of any sort instead he just wanted to enjoy her. The center was a great idea and the community would benefit from it and so would the youth from the church.

Now looking down at her smiling face, Darius felt at ease. He was confident that they were going to be fine. Regardless of how anyone felt about their relationship, Nina and he were going to be fine.

"Nina it's getting late and I have to work in the morning. I wanted to take you out for a late night snack but I can tell that you are tired from the work you've done here, so why don't we make a date for tomorrow. I want to thank you for making my home extra special this year."

"You've got yourself a date." Nina agreed. She was relieved that he was taking her home. She had the most unchristian thoughts running through her mind and she was fighting the urge to act them out. She realized that being with Darius was getting more and more difficult because she didn't want their time together to end. Going out somewhere public was just the thing she needed.

Darius dropped her off with a chaste kiss on the cheek and took off only when she was safely inside her aunt's house. Once inside, Nina took the stairs two at a time and hurried to get into bed. She was tired but she was excited as well. She and Darius Fairchild were in love. Surely, God was smiling down on them.

Nina went to sleep and dreamt about the Christmas dinner. When she awoke in the morning, she found that she couldn't remember much of the dream except that Darius was smiling and that made her feel good. She got up and spent most of the day pouring over Christmas menus.

When she lived in California, her dad and she hardly enjoyed the formal Christmas fare. Because it was just the two of them most of the time, they often prepared a roasted chicken instead of turkey. Her father was a cornbread freak so they always made that and she definitely remembered dessert. It was their personal tradition to have apple pie with whipped cream and a scoop of vanilla ice cream. For as long as she could remember they spent Christmas day by themselves and after dessert, they'd opened their gifts.

Elaine suggested that she wait on the women's auxiliary meeting because regardless of who hosted the dinner, they always did most of the cooking. She went further to say that if she attended the meeting; they would be partners. Nina nodded but pulled several recipe cards from her own collection of recipes and put them aside. She planned to take them with her to the meeting.

When Darius came for her, Nina was impatient and ready. New York during the holiday season was a sight to see. She'd been to Colorado to ski with friends so it really wasn't about the snow and besides, it hadn't snowed much. It was the special feeling New Yorkers exuded. The people were friendlier and smiled more at each other. As they drove, she caught sight of lighted trees in gaily-decorated homes. Just like the movies, there were roasted chestnut vendors on the corners as well as the Salvation Army Santa.

Darius took Nina to Rockefeller Center to see the tree. They ate at a restaurant nearby and Nina insisted that they walk around for a while. She was like a little kid at her first circus. She dragged him from one storefront to the next just to see the displays on Fifth Avenue. She marveled at how each store tried to out-do each other. To her, they were all ingenious and fun to watch.

At the door, they kissed deeply before Darius walked down the two steps from the porch to his car. He waved to her once more and watched her go into the house before he drove off.

Elaine was in bed as usual reading her bible when Nina poked her head in to say goodnight. She waved her in and Nina sat at the foot of the bed. "Did you have a good time?" she asked.

"Yes we did. He took me to see the sights in Manhattan. I know that you are probably sick of hearing me say it but New York is the most wonderful city in the world. It just comes alive during the holidays." Nina told her aunt excitedly.

"It is nice this time of year. Rachel called me with some wonderful news of her own. It seems that Jennifer and Brother Jonas are getting serious and he has formally asked for her hand in marriage. I thought you should know so that you can stop fretting over whether Rachel likes you or not. She sounded very happy."

"That is good news and when I go to rehearsal this week, I will pretend that I don't know. Until she is wearing his ring I won't say anything." Nina got up from the foot of her aunt's bed, reached down to kiss her aunt goodnight, and went to her room.

Just as she was settling into her bed, her cell rang. She answered it quickly. She knew that it was Darius calling to say goodnight.

"I just wanted to hear your voice before I go to sleep. It makes being alone just a little easier." He said.

"In that case, you should get a teddy bear so you won't feel so alone. You've seen mine. Sometimes when I think of you I hug it close and I don't feel so alone anymore. We should take a trip to Build-a-Bear and pick you out a real nice one. You build it and dress it to your liking." Nina suggested seriously.

"Woman you've got to be kidding. I'm much too macho for a bear in my bed. I have it down to a system now. I call you and hear your wonderful voice and then I fall asleep. That is better than having Sister Rachel see a bear in my bed."

"Suit yourself. I am secure in my womanhood to have a bear in my bed and not feel like a baby. Just like now, I am talking with you, he is right here close enough for a hug." Nina teased.

Darius made a strange sound in his throat and bade her goodnight. Nina smiled and hugged her bear tight. She fell asleep soon afterwards.

The next couple of days, Nina and Elaine met with the women's auxiliary to discuss the menu for the pastor's dinner. In turned out that Elaine was right about the women's auxiliary doing all of the cooking, they wouldn't hear of her doing any more than her assigned share.

Christmas Eve dawned cloudy as expected. Nina spent most of the previous evening listening to the weather report. New York City and the surrounding boroughs were going to get their first major snowstorm. They'd get five inches to begin with and more if the storm system hadn't moved on. She also spent the time wrapping gifts. Although she knew that she didn't have to be secretive about wrapping her aunt's gifts, it was just more fun to wait until she was asleep to sneak them under the tree in the living room.

Just as she had done at Darius' house, she did a fine job of decorating her aunt's house as well. She went all out to compensate for the fake tree her aunt insisted on putting up. She used the pine-scented pinecones to give the house the Christmassy aroma. Gay Christmas lights blinked on and off, to cast hues of wonder throughout the living room.

Knowing that she'd be seeing Darius later on, she kept his gifts in her room. She also had a huge bag in which to pack and carry the gifts for various members of the church. This year Nina was able to participate in the secret Santa and she giggled in anticipation at the prospect of her gift exchange, which was to take place at the dinner later.

The night before, she and her aunt started cooking. Because they were a team, their task was to make desserts and cranberry sauce for the turkeys.

Elaine was like a general in the kitchen. She worked Nina to the point of exhaustion. All morning and most of the night before they baked sugar cookies and cakes. They made several apple, pecan, and peach pies. Nina decided that she would never eat another sugar cookie or any of the pies they baked again. She was sick to her stomach with their aroma.

Before going to the church, they needed to deliver the food to the pastor's house so Nina rushed her aunt. Neither wanted to miss any of the service as Nina and Jennifer were singing, Ave Maria. They'd been practicing for two whole weeks with Jen sometimes coming over to practice with Nina at her house where she accompanied them on the piano.

They agreed to wear the traditional Christmas velvet clothing. With Nina's complexion, they thought that she would look best in black or red. Jen wanted to wear red so Nina went shopping and bought a black velvet gown. It had a simple square neckline and an empire waist. The rest of it hung snug but not tight her to curvy body. Nina asked her aunt what she thought of it and Elaine merely smiled. She took that to mean that it was nice for Christmas and chaste enough for Darius. Nina had her doubts. She wore her emerald studs and its matching necklace and then they set out.

Both women carried their shoes separately because they couldn't wear them in the snow. Once they delivered the food, several women caught a ride with them. At the church, Nina changed out of her boots and into her shoes in one of the classrooms downstairs.

She joined the choir mere minutes before the service started. The mass choir and the children's choir did most of the singing. When the time came for the choirs to merge to sing with Jennifer and Nina, Nina strove to get rid of the butterflies in her stomach. The song went off without a hitch and the congregation gave them a standing ovation.

Pastor Fairchild got up on the pulpit to comment on how wonderful his church family looked. That brought many smiles across everyone's face. Then he got serious.

"The Bible tells us that Jesus was born away from prying eyes. It tells us that our Lord had only the animals in that stable to witness his coming. Oh what a blessed thing his coming was saints. As powerful as He is, he chose the humblest beginning he could find to come into this world much like the lamb that he represents.

That also tells us how comfortable He was in his power; he didn't have to make a big deal out of it. Mary named him Jesus but the Bible tells us that he is Emmanuel, the Prince of Peace, the Way and the Light. Tonight we gather to pay him homage much as the three wise men that followed his star in the heavens did. We don't have frankincense, gold or myrrh to present to him tonight.

We have what pleases him the most saints. The least of us can give it to him freely because it is affordable. We don't have to shop at Macy's or Bloomingdale's to get it. We have it in abundance. He came into this world of sin and sadness to bring life, joy and happiness. All we have to do is pledge our allegiance to him. We give him our hearts and he becomes our God, our way-maker, our salvation and our hope. He came so that finally, forgiveness was ours to have and *all* of our hopes and dreams may come to fruition. With Jesus we get to live in peace and we get to have all of our needs supplied and all because a child was born in a manger. Can we stand up all over this sanctuary and give our Lord some praise! Can we shout Hallelujah?" Darius urged.

All of the saints that could stand stood up to give praise to God and when the praising ended, the choir sang their rendition of *Joy to the World*. After the benediction, Pastor Fairchild announced the dinner. Then he urged the congregation to be quiet as he had more to say.

"Sister Nina will you come join me?" he asked holding his hand out to her. Nina stood up and wanted to faint, but she walked up to stand beside him.

"Brothers and sisters as you know that it had been some time now since my wife Rebecca passed and I know that many of you worried for me. The Lord has seen fit to send me a woman whom I may love. Sister Nina and I have been seeing each other and tonight she will be hosting our annual Christmas dinner with me." Pastor Fairchild then did something Nina had not been expecting. He clasped her hand in his and together they stepped down from the pulpit. There were a few catcalls but mostly they heard hardy amen and clapping.

The business of getting their coats and boots took a few minutes. Quite a few people stopped Nina and the pastor to comment on his announcement. They received many heartfelt well wishes that put a lump in Nina's throat. No one gave them the impression that they were upset and finally, Nina felt silly that she had worried at all.

A program led everyone through the order of things at the pastor's house. As everyone sat, the deacons and ushers passed out the gifts. Only when everyone received their gifts did they find out who their secret Santa was. Nina received a jewelry box with a twirling ballerina atop it. When she opened it, the ballerina danced to a Christmas tune. The gift was from one of the older women in the church and Nina got up to thank her with a kiss on the cheek.

Nina's gift was to Sister Rachel of all people. Nina hadn't told no matter how much her aunt badgered her. She agonized over the gift she would get the woman. Although her demeanor had changed the last few days, Nina felt that the woman just didn't like her. It brought to mind how Jesus taught about turning the other cheek. She didn't allow how Rachel felt about her to cloud her judgment in getting her gift. Nina got her a gift certificate to Bed, Bath and beyond. The rules were that one couldn't spend more than fifty dollars and Nina went to the max.

Sister Rachel was gracious and Nina could tell that she wasn't feeling very comfortable. She accepted the gift with a stiff smile because she had no choice as everyone was watching.

It took over an hour to serve the food. Nina's feet and back hurt because as host, she felt obliged to make sure that she served everyone. By the time she went to sit beside Darius, she didn't feel like eating. It was close to midnight and she and Darius meant to exchange their gifts on Christmas.

"You look beat Honey, eat something and then go home." Darius said to the tired woman sitting beside him.

"It would be rude to leave now and I'm not very hungry. Have you eaten?" Nina asked turning to face him.

"Yes. You served me first if you recall," answered Darius.

"That was ages ago, and I don't remember. I think I'll have just a salad." Nina said to Darius' worried expression.

"Good, just sit tight and I'll get it for you."

"Thanks," Nina said gratefully. Once she sat down, she just couldn't get back up. She watched his progress to the kitchen and smiled. The house was full of happy people. She got rave reviews for the décor and that made Nina's night.

"You've got a good man in our pastor. I'm glad that he's finally happy." Rachel said as she sat down in the seat the pastor vacated.

"Thank you." Nina replied shyly.

"I know you feel that I've been unfair to you, but that's because I am very protective of him and I don't want to see him hurt again. He's been through a lot and after his wife passed, I feared for him. Rebecca died just a few weeks after his own father had and it was too much for him. He looks and sounds happy now and I appreciate that." Sister Rachel said. She got up to leave just as quietly as she approached her.

"I'd like to talk with you again sometime if that's all right. I sense things that he won't talk about and it would help if I knew how to help him." Nina said before Rachel got further away.

"He leaves for work by eight and doesn't return until after six, so feel free to stop by and we'll talk." Rachel told Nina and left.

"What was all that about?" Darius asked as he placed a large salad in front of Nina.

"Sister Rachel was telling me that she's glad that you are finally happy." Nina said searching his features. Darius nodded and smiled. He reached over to squeeze her hand and urged her to eat.

Nina ate her salad. She smiled at those who caught her eyes and tried to look confident. From now on, she knew that people would be watching. Not that she felt any hostility but she felt that she had just been elevated to potential first lady.

She smiled to herself. It was a wonderful thought but she didn't feel ready for that yet. She thought back to how the pastor's wife from her old church in L.A presented herself and knew that she wasn't a good example. The woman wore designer clothes and shoes. She seemed to breathe rarified air. The pastor and his wife weren't your typical couple. They were high powered and their assistants had assistants.

This church needed a humble woman who served not only her congregation but her community as well. Nina turned to watch Darius as he made his rounds. There was a smile on his face and although Nina knew that he was tired, if any of those people gathered in his home this evening needed him he would be ready and steady. He needed a woman who would serve as he served.

At midnight, someone put Nina's Christmas duet with her father on and it startled her. Suddenly Darius was standing in front of her with a small rectangular box wrapped in shiny silver paper in his hand. You could've heard a pin drop as the few people remaining quieted down to watch. Darius handed her the box and Nina took it from him with numb hands. She was very nervous.

Because people watched her, Nina made a big production of tearing the wrapping paper. She opened the box to reveal two pairs of hair clips specially made for her. Nina stood up to show everyone who clapped with approval. Nina reached under the table they had been sitting at to pull out a big box, which she picked up to place in his arms. Everyone quieted down once more to watch them.

Darius stood up to balance the box on a chair as he opened his gift. He kept darting puzzled looks at her as he did so. It wasn't until he pulled out the big fluffy clergy bear that he understood the gift. He lifted the bear high for all to see. People clapped and cheered, until someone pointed out that the bear was wearing a watch. Nina got him a Rolex. She had the band especially made with a cross and a bible verse along the length of it. It read, "Ye are blessed of the Lord, which made heaven and earth". (Psalms 115: 15 KJV).

Darius bent down to place a kiss on her forehead. "We will talk about the bear later," he said gamely.

Nina smiled sweetly at him and reached over to pull the watch off the bear. She hammed it up for the crowd watching them as she fastened the watch onto his wrist. The crowd clapped and cheered. Nina thought this was a great night. Shortly afterwards, Darius said a prayer dismissing everyone to go home. The women's auxiliary shooed Nina to the living room to sit and relax with the pastor while they made short work of cleaning up. Nina was grateful and leaned her head onto Darius shoulder, as they got cozy on the sofa.

"I really like the clips Darius, I can create better ways to wear my hair," she told him.

"It was really hard to shop for you. You have everything already. Then I realized that the best gift for you would have to be something practical. I thought of your hair and it got easier. I'm glad you like them," Darius explained.

Nina sat up to see his face. "Why don't you like the bear?"

"Baby men don't do the bear thing. Now the watch I can deal with and it was very nice of you to get it for me." Darius said seriously, as he admired it sparkling in the light.

Nina jumped up to her feet to glare down at him. "I am not returning the bear Darius. I built it especially for you," Nina said with her hands on her hips.

Darius stood up as well. As much as he tried, he couldn't hold his composure a minute more. He smiled and took in the beauty that was

Nina. Her eyes flashed and her cheeks were turning a shade of red he hadn't seen before. She was breathtaking!

"I will never tire of seeing you excited. Do you know that your eyes turn a shade darker? Your cheeks turn so red I am expecting smoke to come out of your ears. You are the cutest thing."

"I'm going home." Nina said calmly and made to walk away from him.

Darius clasped her arm before she got away and pulled her to him. "I'm sorry baby I didn't mean to tease you. I love the bear and I promise I'll put him in bed with me tonight. Okay?"

"Man you are so easy." Nina said smiling brilliantly at him. "I knew you were teasing me all along."

"You had better thank the Lord that we are not alone otherwise I'd make you very sorry," warned Darius.

"Oh yeah, the big and bad pastor can dish it out but he can't take it?" teased Nina.

"No the big and bad pastor would have kissed you clear down to your toes but since I know how shy you are about showing affection in public, I will restrain myself." Darius said suddenly serious again.

"Oh well in that case, I think I should go home and I also think you should take Holy Bear upstairs and get acquainted."

"Is that his name?" Darius asked looking at the bear seated on the chair opposite them.

"That's the name I gave him but you can change it. You can call him pookie or boo-boo or whatever." Nina lifted the bear up into her arms and gave it a little squeeze. The bear was soft and cuddly. "He resembles you a little, don't you think so?" Nina turned the bear to face him.

"Catalina I'm going to kiss you," Darius said and before Nina could react, he lips were on hers.

As they were in public, Darius didn't linger too long. Nina was devastated. She felt eyes on them and when she felt comfortable to look around, she blushed even more. Sister Rachel had just come into the living room and she was rooted to the spot. Her expression was serene.

Someone coughed and shattered the moment. "I think we'd better take the mistletoe down," someone said playfully. The tension immediately dissipated as the few people who were still in the living room laughed.

"I'm sorry but you are so irresistible. Say you forgive me," Darius pleaded softly for her ears alone.

"It's fine really, I just have to get over— excuse me," Nina brushed past him to go to the bathroom down the hall.

Nina locked the door, closed her eyes and leaned against it. She hoped that no one realized that she had fled. Opening her eyes, she inspected her features in the mirror. Darius was right about her eyes, they did get a shade darker but this time they weren't flashing. Her eyes sparkled.

There was a discreet knock on the door and Nina knew it was Darius on the other side. Her heart beat faster and she feared that it would beat itself right out of her chest.

"I'll be right out," she called out. She flushed the toilet and washed her hands. She unlocked the door and turned the knob. Darius pushed the door open and Nina smiled up him.

"Are you okay?" he asked uncertainly. Nina had never seen him this way before. She decided that he was cute when he was worried.

"Yes I'm fine. Are there still a lot of people out there?" she asked him.

"No everyone is gone except for your aunt and two others. Why?"

"Could you come in here for a minute?" asked Nina sweetly.

Darius walked into the bathroom and closed the door quietly behind him. Nina pushed him against it and closed the space between them. "I am trying very hard to contain what I feel for you sweetheart but you make it so hard. I love you more and more each day and tonight I think I'll burst if I don't do this." Nina said and quickly pulled his head down to hers.

Her kiss told him how deeply she felt for him and the feelings she evoked in him bordered on the dangerous as she pressed her body a little too close. He thought he could hold her just a little longer, but Nina moaned deep in her throat and he pushed away quickly.

She blushed crimson and covered her face with her hands. "Oh God Darius I'm sorry, I'm so sorry," she said miserably through her hands.

"Hey, no need to be sorry Baby. We just have to get out of here and get some air." Darius opened the door and together they walked back to the living room.

"Oh there you are. I was wondering if you'd gone and left me," Aunt Elaine said. She was sitting on a chair with Darius' bear on her lap.

"Has everybody gone?" Pastor Fairchild asked quietly.

"Yes, Brother Jonas drove the church van; he came back for Jennifer and Rachel. They just left."

"I see that you are getting acquainted with my bear," he said finally.

"Nina was so secretive about it. I just couldn't figure out what she had in that big box. He is cute," Elaine admitted and then looked past the pastor to her niece standing behind him. "Are you ready Nina, I am dead on my feet."

"Yes Auntie I am, I'll just go get our coats," Nina said and left to go retrieve them from Darius' office.

"I am happy that my niece has found love and I'm grateful that God is giving you a second chance, mighty grateful." Sister Elaine said quickly.

"I thank Him every day for her too," replied her pastor.

Nina returned with the coats and seemed to have regained her composure. She was able to look at Darius without blushing. She smiled confidently at him.

"I'll call you when I get home," she said as she helped her aunt with her coat.

"I will be waiting. Be careful Honey, Merry Christmas Sister Elaine." Darius called out as he helped them into Nina's SUV.

"Merry Christmas Pastor Fairchild," Sister Elaine rejoined.

"Merry Christmas bye," Nina called out.

The drive home was quick and uneventful. The streets were clear and it wasn't cold enough to freeze so there weren't any icy patches. Nina parked the car in the drive and hurried to help Elaine out of the car. Holding hands, they walked up the front porch steps and into the house. Nina insisted that they leave the Christmas lights on as the house was cheerful looking.

Elaine complained about being too tired to open presents and suggested that they get some sleep. Nina agreed.

Nina undressed and got into bed before she picked up her phone to call Darius. She had been trying to collect her thoughts while she drove home. She didn't know what to say to him. What she did was reckless. Even now, thinking about it, she couldn't keep from blushing.

She spoke quickly when he answered. "Hi. We got home just fine and I was just getting ready for bed."

"I love you Nina and I know that you are not fine. Talk to me."

"I feel so ashamed and I don't know what to say." Nina said tearfully.

"Nina you didn't do anything wrong. We weren't in any danger of anything happening between us. Tonight was very emotional for you and you were expressing how you felt. I feel it too baby and it is very hard to walk away from you sometimes. It is cool knowing that you feel so deeply for me because I've felt like that about you for weeks now. It's good to know that I am not feeling like this alone. However, we have to be careful from now on. Before, I thought that it was just me but knowing that we are both in the same boat will make things more difficult. We can pray for strength and use common sense. Can you do that?"

"I love you so much Darius. Please pray with me before I hang up."

"Yes love I will." Darius said a prayer of thanksgiving, for holiness and for strength. Then he hung up.

Nina had a little trouble falling asleep but once she had fallen asleep, it was peaceful.

CHAPTER NINE

The following morning the sun shone brightly but the air had gotten colder. The snow on the ground was beginning to turn to ice and Nina worried for her aunt. She got up early trying to spread the ice melt evenly on the front steps and walk. Being conscious about their neighbors walking past the house, Nina made sure to shovel the sidewalk and she threw ice melt on it to keep it ice-free as well.

When she entered the house, she found her aunt up and making brunch. It was almost lunchtime. They slept in since it was past two in the morning Christmas day when they got home.

Nina told her aunt that she was going to shower and change before they opened their presents. Her aunt shooed her away urging her to hurry up because she was excited and hungry.

She smiled as she hurried to shower. This was the first holiday since her dad passed that she's celebrated. She felt happy and blessed that she had her aunt.

Nina dressed in a long flowing black lounger she bought just for Christmas morning. She got one for her aunt as well and was pleased that she was wearing hers too.

"I hope you aren't going to a lot of trouble Auntie I don't think I could eat that much," Nina began. She stopped to stare at Darius sitting at the table with her aunt.

"Darius you're here, good morn—, afternoon." Nina stammered, and blushed uncomfortably.

"Good afternoon Catalina."

"Don't call me that," Nina said annoyed.

Darius smiled then, "You look like the star that you are and so does your aunt. I called her Ms. Bennett-Hughes." He continued to smile.

"Well if we can all agree, I think we should eat. Maybe some people can stop being so grouchy," Elaine said pointedly at her niece.

"I'm sorry Auntie." Nina murmured.

Elaine served them and they ate. While they were in the living room opening gifts, the doorbell chimed. Nina got up to answer it and her aunt and the pastor could hear her raised voice as she spoke.

Nina returned with a tall, Caucasian man who looked at her with fondness. Nina turned to her family and smiled as she made the introductions.

Darius stood up to shake the man's hand. "Merry Christmas and pleased to meet you," he said.

"Hello, Merry Christmas." Aunt Elaine said.

"Darius, Aunt Elaine this is Richard. He was my agent and manager practically my entire life in California." Then she turned to the man questioningly. "What are you doing here? And why didn't you call to warn me that you were coming?" Nina ushered him to a seat and then sat down next to Darius. She took his hand and held it tightly.

"I missed you Nina and I wanted to see you. Also something came up that I hope you won't pass up." Richard said carefully.

Nina's grip got tighter on Darius' hand. "You could've called and what came up?" She asked him.

Richard spread his hands. "Can we talk freely?"

"You can say anything with my family here." Nina said defensively.

"Wow family eh? That's great sweetheart. A few weeks ago, a script came across my desk from an independent filmmaker. She wants to do a biographical film on your father. After looking it over, I called her and she came to see me. What she had to say was very flattering. She was a great fan. She heard about you retiring and thought that I might be able to approach you with it," Richard explained. He opened the worn leather attaché he always carried to pull out a large thick manila envelope.

"Dad's career was very public. If she wants footage, she can go to any film library to get them. She doesn't need my permission for that, but I will give it to her if she needs it," Nina offered.

"No darling that's not what she wants from you. She wants you to do a cameo of your mother. You have to know that you are the spitting image of her." Richard said as he handed her another envelope.

Nina took it and pulled out pictures of her mother at her age. It was true. She was the very image of Catalina Bennett. Her mother had red hair and the same green eyes. Nina's eyes filled with tears as she passed the pictures to her aunt and Darius.

"If it weren't for your locks, no one would be able to tell the difference, Nina." Her aunt pointed out.

"My mother has footage at the library also; she could use those couldn't she?" Nina suggested to Richard.

Since she was getting agitated, Nina got up to unplug the tree. The gay lights were getting on her nerves. She wasn't feeling the Christmas spirit at all now and she had Richard to thank for it. His visit called up painful memories for her. Looking at her mother's pictures, she realized that she hardly remembered her mother anymore. She only had vague memories of hugs and very little memories of the three of them together.

"What if I say no? I quit the business if you recall and besides this is too personal."

"Word around town is that you've embarked on a big project that's going to take a big chunk of money. I know that you've invested wisely darling and you won't run out of money anytime soon, but why use your savings when revenue from this project could pay for all of it?" Richard asked coyly.

"How did you find out?" Nina's gaze turned suspicious.

"When are you going to realize that it will be about eighty years before you are forgotten? Everything you do is news. Oh and Dullard should be approaching you soon about royalties for one of your songs. A fresh young face is trying to break in and wants to use your song to do it. It is like you never left." Richard countered.

"Richard what is this film maker's name?" Nina asked.

"All the information you need is in the packet you have in the envelope including how to contact her. Why don't I give you a few days to look it over and then we can talk again. You can contact either her or me with your answer. I have some gifts in my car, so let me go get them and leave you to enjoy the rest of your day." Richard said and he stood up.

Darius offered to escort him to the door and when they were alone her aunt asked Nina, what she was going to do.

"Auntie I can't think right now. Thinking about my mother is very hard for me and then there's dad too." Nina raised shiny eyes to her aunt.

Richard came back with a shopping bag with gifts for Nina as well as her aunt. He told her that he would be in town for a few more days and then he'd be flying back to L.A. When he left, Nina was a nervous wreck.

Nina tried to pretend that it was a normal everyday thing to unwrap a five hundred dollar gift. She felt Darius' eyes on her and even her aunt was a little surprised when she opened her gift. Richard got her a very expensive handbag. Nina could feel the tension in the air, so much so that she couldn't finish opening her gift. She put it down.

"All right we will talk about it now," Nina announced suddenly.

"I don't think I have a right to say anything in this matter Nina. This is something you will have to figure out on your own." Darius said.

Nina turned to him quickly, "Yes you do. You are a part of me now and I really don't want to feel alone right now." Nina told him.

"Baby this is a matter you have to decide for yourself. Do you want to portray your mother in this movie or not? It is that simple. You may have reasons why you do and why you don't, but ultimately the choice will have to be yours," insisted Darius.

"If you want my opinion, I think you should look this script over and see what it is all about. You might be able to make a decision once you've seen how this woman wants to present your parents to the world," Aunt Elaine suggested.

Nina couldn't keep still and stood up to pace. Her mind flashed images of her parents and she felt the remembered pain from her father's death. Regardless of how her parents appear in the movie, the fact that they were both missing is that she would have to go away. Since this was an independent filmmaker, she probably is searching for someone to produce the project. That being the case, money will be tight and there will be delays. It won't be a quick thing at all. Nina felt torn because it would be a great way to honor her family but at the same time, it would be an emotional drain on her not to mention that as a Christian woman involved with a clergyman, she would have to be careful of what she did on screen.

"Don't you guys get it? I'll have to go away for a while to do this. Richard was hoping something like this would come up. He didn't want me to leave in the first place. He will be behind the scenes orchestrating ways to keep me there."

"He's not your agent anymore so why are you so afraid that he'll be involved?" Darius asked.

"Richard was the one who accepted the packet from for her and if I agree to do this, he'll have to be around. Richard is waiting in the wings for me to go back to California to pick up where I left off." Nina explained.

"You are afraid of him," Darius stated plainly.

"I am not. I trusted this man with my life once. He decided almost every aspect of my life and I let him do it because he'd proved that he knew what he was doing. I'm all grown up now and no one need tell me when to come and go. Being away from that environment has shown me how sheltered I'd been. Richard ran my life." Nina realized that she was on the defensive and it rankled.

"Would you be able to get something in writing that would ensure that you do just this one project with this woman and then walk away?" Darius asked.

"It sounds like you've decided for me," Nina accused him.

"I haven't decided anything I'm just pointing out your options. They obviously need you in order for this to be authentic and they'd be fools if they didn't cater to you." Darius added.

"Look this is Christmas and I'm sure that there are other things we could be talking about. Richard gave you a few days to decide so put it aside for now." Aunt Elaine suggested.

"You're right Auntie I don't have to dwell on this right now," Nina agreed and went to sit beside Darius again. She took his hand and tried to pretend that a few minutes ago she wasn't trying to hold back tears after seeing pictures of her mother.

"So did you give the bear a name yet?" she asked changing the subject.

Darius shook head, "No he is going to have to go by Bear for now. Sister Elaine I want to take this opportunity to thank you for your part in last night's dinner. Everything was wonderful." Darius said changing the subject as well.

"It was my pleasure. This year was the best because I have Nina to celebrate with me," Aunt Elaine explained.

"Yes this year Nina's presence has made a big difference. I'm glad she's here too." Darius admitted. He placed a soft kiss on her hand.

"I'm doubly glad because after the loss of my dad, I avoided all the holidays, but this year I have both of you," Nina said just a little tearfully.

Then she jumped up to plug the Christmas tree lights on once more. She turned to her loved ones and smiled.

Nina had one final gift under the tree and she pulled it out. It was a large white envelope. She gave a little excited squeal and opened it.

"This gift is for all of us. These," she said as she took out several sheets of what appeared to be miniature blueprints. "These are the plans for the recreation center. I received them a week ago. It took a while to get them approved and I thought it would be a wonderful present."

Darius took the plans from her to examine as soon as she sat down again. Even her aunt squeezed in beside them to see what the recreation center would look like. After a few minutes of looking at the drawings and finding that she still couldn't understand what she was looking at, Aunt Elaine got up announcing that she was going to get some rest as she was still tired from the festivities from the night before. She took the expensive Louis Vuitton handbag Richard gave her and went upstairs murmuring to herself about what was she going to do with a bag that was more expensive than her entire wardrobe.

"I think she likes the bag," said Nina in a conspiratorial manner.

"It'll grow on her. What was your gift?" Darius asked suddenly interested in the box on the floor by the tree.

Nina reached over to pick it up. She pulled out two very nice looking cashmere sweaters in different shades of green. "Richard couldn't possibly have picked these out himself; his wife still dresses him in the morning. I'll have to call Trina to thank her." Nina said admiring the sweaters.

"Is Trina his wife?" Darius asked.

"No she's his secretary; his wife's name is Agatha.

"Those are very nice sweaters Nina and I'm hoping I can take you out somewhere nice so that you can wear them," said Darius.

Nina placed the sweaters back in the box and turned to face him. She was no longer smiling.

"About last night I want to apologize for my behavior. I should have more control since I was the one who expressed concern about behavior in dating a pastor. I promise to be more on guard from now on."

Darius looked at Nina and recognized the bewilderment across her features. He smiled at her reassuringly. "Baby what happened last night will happen again and sometimes it will be me who forgets self-control. What you have to understand is that we are human and we all fall short of God's perfection. God's wonderful gift to us is forgiveness and no matter how many times we fall we can get up knowing that He will always be there with grace and forgiveness."

"Is being in love always going to feel like this? I mean will being close to you always make me feel funny and lightheaded?" Nina asked.

"I can tell by your question that being in love is new to you. I don't know how it is for everyone but for me it is a constant need. Being with you is always on my mind. I think about you all the time and when we are together is the only time I am satisfied."

"Do you think about me when you are preaching too?" asked Nina. She had a serious expression on her face.

"Before I go up to preach I pray. I pray and ask the Lord to remove me and to replace me with the Holy Spirit. On the pulpit nothing and no one matters but the Word."

"I have noticed the change when you are up there. My very first time at the church, I felt as if it was the very first time hearing the Word as you preached. You are filled with the Holy Spirit and there is power in everything you say." Nina replied.

"I take preaching very seriously and I am glad that the Lord chose me to work through."

Nina frowned. "The night you asked me to see you, I went home and agonized about my decision all night. What I see when you are preaching is very special and powerful. I thought what right I had to tamper with something so vital. If something went wrong between us and it broke the connection you have with God, I would surely go to hell."

"Nina because you are so very careful about how you act when we are together shows how much you care not just about me but about God's work. I feel encouraged that you want to be careful."

"That's why I felt so ashamed last night and scared too. What you do is important and sacred. If our relationship were to progress into a marriage I have already made up my mind that I would never stand in your way of doing God's work. I would try to help you in any way I could although I can tell you right now that I am an actor not a preacher and would not care to preach. I could probably lead a service, read a passage in the Bible, but that would be the extent of my help."

Darius had a big smile on his face. "You thought about being my wife?"

"Seriously Darius, this is very important stuff. I care about your standing with God. I don't want to do anything to jeopardize it. Who am I that I would want to do such a thing?"

"Baby, relax you are going to make yourself sick with worry. I am not worried. I didn't come into this relationship lightly. I prayed and fasted. I wanted God's approval on this. There's not much that I do that I don't ask for God's counsel with. I prayed for a wonderful woman who is kind-hearted, cheerful and giving. I asked that she be a helpmeet in my ministry and I asked that she be gorgeous. He sent me you." Darius had a big grin on his handsome face.

Nina blushed and covered her face. Since all afternoon, what was upper most on both their minds was the kiss they've been denying themselves. Darius reached over and gently took Nina's hands from off her face and cupped it.

"You are exactly what I prayed for Catalina. I am happy and I love you very much," he said. Then he did what he had wanted to do since he'd come over her house. He kissed her.

Nina tried to keep her body as rigid as possible ever conscious of the previous evening, but Darius pulled her closer and wrapped his arms around her. It was all she needed. She relaxed and leaned in kissing him with all the love she felt for him.

"Darius, do you remember asking me why I decided to quit show business and come here?" Nina asked him when they parted.

"Yes I do. You said that one day you would tell me. Are you going to tell me now?"

Nina pulled away and nodded. "My father got sick and then all of the sudden he grew worse. The doctor diagnosed him with lung cancer and gave him a few months to live. I was angry because he knew he was sick for a long time and kept it hidden from me. Anyway, I was in the middle of putting an album together and finishing a movie. I was glad that it was local and didn't have to travel. I couldn't get out of either of those things so I worked long hours with Richard pushing me to do more.

At the end of every day, while he was in the hospital I would go and spend the night with him. I'd fall asleep holding his hand. Every morning I would leave fearful that, I wouldn't see him again. After a month, he was able to go home and I thought that we had gotten a reprieve and the cancer had gone into remission but after another month, he got sick again.

This time I knew that he wouldn't be going home and I hurried to finish both the movie and the album. The day he died, I sat with him and we talked for hours. Then we went through our photo albums. He'd tell me the story behind each picture, especially the ones of me as a baby and young girl. Then he asked me to get in the bed with him, he wanted me to hold him. I held him tight because he was slipping away.

"He died in my arms Darius and I felt so alone. He told me that after he was gone that I should do whatever made me happy. He also said that he'd be watching over me."

"You quit because your father told you to?" Darius asked with a confused expression on his face.

"No of course not, I made up my mind that after my mourning

period that I'd do some soul searching so when I ventured out into the world again, I went crazy. I did many things I hadn't done before. I ate foods I never ate before just trying to feel independent. I broke all the routines I had and I partied with friends. Then one night I broke down and allowed the depression I'd been keeping at bay to take over.

I cried for seven days straight. I didn't eat or sleep. I didn't talk with anyone and I didn't answer the door. On the eighth day, I got up, showered, and got dressed. My house was a mess so I cleaned it. I even got the courage to go into my dad's bedroom to clear it out. I put his belongings in boxes. By the following day, I had his room completely done. I gave away the clothes and shoes. I put his jewelry in a safe deposit box and I packed away all his awards and albums.

That night I went to bed and I dreamed. I dreamed of my wedding day. In the dream, my dad walked me down the aisle to the front of the church and when we got there, I turned to him and he smiled and kissed my cheek. Then he took my hand and placed it in yours." Nina told Darius.

"Your father placed your hand in mine?" Darius asked incredulously.

"Yes he did."

"You saw my face in your dreams? How could you see my face in your dreams, we hadn't even met?"

"We did meet briefly at my dad's funeral services. You came with Aunt Elaine. You said a few words and then we spoke at the luncheon at my church. I thanked you for coming with her."

"If I remember correctly you were in no shape to remember anyone. At one point, you fainted and that broke up the gathering. Your aunt worried about you and she decided to stay a few days with you and I flew home alone." Darius recalled.

"It took six months to acknowledge the dream. It confused me and I didn't even remember what you looked like so I couldn't even be sure it was you. Instinctively I knew that I had to come here. When I finally got my affairs in order and put the house up for sale, I called Aunt Elaine to ask her about coming here to live with her.

"She said that nothing would make her happier, so I came but I still didn't think about the dream until the picnic. It finally dawned on me that you were the man in my dream. I was scared and tried to rationalize it away with reasons why I dreamed in the first place."

"What reasons did you come up with?" Darius asked her. He was curious.

"Well I thought that most dads wanted their daughters protected and cared for and for some that means marriage."

"But how did you explain away him giving you to me?" Darius wanted to know.

"That was a little harder to explain but I tweaked it until I was satisfied with my reasoning. I figured that since I hadn't been able to find a decent man in L.A, that there would be a man for me in New York. Aunt Elaine introduced you to me at the funeral and I thought you were very kind in flying to L.A. to be with her."

"Boy you went out on a limb there didn't you. Did you never think that it was a divine sign?"

"You have to understand that even though I was a devout Christian in L.A, I didn't spend my days contemplating the mysterious ways that God works. I was a performer who had a busy schedule. When I had the dream I had been cramming so many activities in my day that when I got into bed, I fell into a dead sleep."

"Baby the reason I'm finding this so incredible is that I was praying for God to send me someone around the time your father died. I had been in a funk about losing both my father and then my wife so close together, but I was recovering by then. I felt that I was finally ready to share my life with someone again and after dating Jennifer didn't work out, I prayed in earnest."

"It is kind of eerie isn't?" Nina asked as she rubbed her arms to smooth away the goose bumps that appeared there suddenly.

"God does work in mysterious ways and I'm not saying that we should grab this dream of yours as proof positive that we were meant to be together, but it certainly isn't an impossibility that there had been a divine hand in us getting together."

"I think we should pray on this some more Darius. I am trembling inside because I prayed for you too." Nina said.

She'd been reading on spiritual gifts and wondered if she had any. That was the subject of the last bible study. She asked him about it.

"Some people have the gift of prophesy, but I think that your spiritual gift is the same talent you'd been born with. Your ministry lies in music. When you sing, you are ministering with your soul and you can encourage others to come to the Lord."

"I think I will pray about that some more too. Aunt Elaine was right about taking the time to look the script over. I guess that afterwards I'll be able to make a decision with more confidence." Nina said.

"Good. Now," Darius said pointing to the blueprints. "Have you decided when you want to start construction on the center?"

Nina picked up the blueprints and smiled at him. "I thought that it would be better to start in the spring because the weather will be nicer. I estimate that it will take several months to put up the structure. I was hoping that we could have a dedication ceremony by late summer to open it."

"That sounds like a plan. Once the building is up, I'd like to get the board together to discuss furnishing it." Darius told her. He took the blueprints from her and drew her close for a kiss.

He felt glad that she was doing this wonderful thing. It was his wish to do something for the community. He couldn't do it by himself and it was impossible for the church to take on any more burdens. Nina's coming was indeed beneficial to all concerned. Expanding his ministry to the surrounding neighborhood was something he dreamed about ever since he took over after the passing of the honorable Rev. Jacob Riverton. He had the same dreams too. He spoke about buying up the surrounding area and turning Christ Tabernacle into a real community leader.

However, it was a dream he put on hold. What he was doing was enough and until the flock grew a little more, he couldn't even entertain the thought of the church buying anything. What the board suggested made him squirm almost every time he was with Nina. They suggested that he talk her into financing the church's influence in the community besides the center. It was a thought that made him feel ashamed for them.

He supposed that executives were mercenary even in the church. Business was business to the Trustee board and they didn't care that Nina might feel offended or feel used. He already made up his mind about never broaching the subject with her and he dreaded the day when the board would go over his head to approach her themselves.

He prayed that by God's miraculous hand that his dreams would become a reality. Just the thought of reaching out to those in need in the surrounding area made him feel good. He doubted that Nina would be opposed to helping, but it just didn't feel right in using her money.

Darius hugged Nina tightly to him and sighed. "Baby it is getting late and I have a few more stops to make before I call it a night. One of the mothers is recovering from pneumonia. She got out of the hospital recently. I promised to meet a group of the mothers at the church to visit and pray with her."

"I understand. I'll say a prayer for her as well. What is her name?"

"Mother Winifred Easington. She is in her nineties and we thought that we might lose her quite a few times, but I guess the Lord isn't ready for her yet." Darius told her.

Darius finally was able to bring himself to pull away from Nina. It was surprising how hard not being with her had become. She walked him to the door and helped him with his coat. When she pulled the door open for him, the cold blast of air hit her square in the face.

"My goodness, it sure is cold out there. Darius be careful driving and call me when you finally get home," she said as she rubbed her arms.

"I promise. Shut the door before you get sick yourself," he scolded her gently.

Nina peeked through the blinds to watch his progress to his car. He was lucky to have gotten a spot in front of the house so he didn't have far to go. As he drove away, Nina felt a gut wrenching sadness. She hoped that one day they wouldn't have to part.

As it was still early, Nina went into the kitchen to fix herself a snack. She smiled, as did so. If she were living in California, she wouldn't have dreamed of eating between meals. In fact, she probably would have slurped down a low calorie drink and hit the gym.

Christmas in Tinsel Town was hardly the affair she's experienced these past couple of days. Had she not made this life-changing move, she would have house hopped through various parties, saying meaningless things to people she hardly cared for. Going home afterward to her Dad had been the only good thing about the holiday. They would have had their version of Christmas dinner and their ritual of gift opening. How she missed him. She felt comforted that her father was no longer in pain. He truly was in a better place.

Nina finished her sliced turkey sandwich and potato salad. She left the kitchen to go check on her aunt. She felt warmth spread through her as she climbed the stairs. Her aunt took her in and shared her home with her not because she was family but because that was the kind of person, she was.

Nina knocked on the bedroom door then pushed it open. She spied her aunt sitting in the rocker beside her bed. She was asleep with the bible in her lap. Nina tiptoed to her aunt, pulled the afghan more snuggly around the sleeping woman, and left the room.

With nothing else to distract her, Nina had no choice but to look over the package Richard brought her. She entered her room and dropped it onto her bed.

"Dad I sure hope that this isn't a waste of time. Both you and mom deserve recognition for the work you'd done but I don't see why I have to be involved," Nina sad aloud.

She sat up in bed and pulled the contents out of the envelope. The first page was a letter from the filmmaker introducing herself. She listed her accomplishments and collaborations. Nina felt encouraged to read about the woman's accomplishments and about her awards.

The film chronicled her parents' earliest beginnings when they performed at parties, benefits and hole in the wall nightclubs. It went on to include the performances her parents did apart. The segment about her mother's last show in Chicago, which had been a qualified success, was almost clinical in its presentation. Nina didn't know what she was expecting but she felt so relieved that it was tasteful.

Seeing that the script was appealing, Nina took time to read it and found that it was good. She frowned at the excitement she felt. All that fuss she'd made earlier made her feel foolish now. Her parents' story deserved recognition even post humorously, and this woman's vision was going to do a very good job. The material was probably worthy of the several awards she felt.

The other thing that worried her was that consenting to do the project, would mean that she'd have to travel and be away for an indefinite period. She didn't know if she wanted to go away now.

There was the construction work to oversee and she didn't want to leave her aunt. More importantly, she didn't want to leave Darius for any length of time. She didn't know how long it would take to do the project, but she knew that she would miss him terribly if she decided that she was going to do it.

Nina decided that she would simply think about it and then maybe contact the filmmaker to talk. By speaking with the filmmaker, she would learn how long it would take and whether she would have to travel farther than California to shoot the film.

Nina felt better about it. Thinking about just talking with the filmmaker made her stop worrying. She's learned these past few months that God was at work in her life and that she shouldn't question the direction He took her.

It was incredible how much her faith had grown. Almost a year ago, she was a mediocre Christian. She went through the motions but didn't live them. Reading the scriptures was scant at best and only done when she and her dad were at services. She couldn't vouch for her father, but she never would have thought to get in bed and read the bible until she fell asleep. Even though she and her dad did some charity work, it wasn't out of any sense of doing the Christian thing. Instinctively, Nina knew that she was a good person but it didn't mean that she was Christian person. She was sure that the God in her hadn't shone through when she was doing good works.

Darius and her aunt have greatly influenced her in her walk with Christ. Her whole outlook on life has changed for the better because of them. She's had extensive discussions with Darius on passages in the bible that puzzled her. Her old pastor was great but he didn't really care about her soul like Darius did and it isn't because they were romantically involved. Darius truly cares about the people he is shepherding. He has great passion for Christ and he conveys it in everything he does which makes her strive more and more to be Christ-like as well.

Even when Darius was expressing his incredulity about the reason why she came to New York, he told her that regardless of whether it was fated to be or not, he consulted the Lord first. She felt that if she approached him to insist that she was his soul mate he wouldn't have believed her. She could even envision him asking her why would the lord say something to her and not to him as well. She wanted to be the kind of Christian who consulted the Lord for everything. She's learning to put God first in everything she does. With that comforting thought, Nina closed her eyes in prayer asking God to lead her in the way she should go with this project.

CHAPTER TEN

The next couple of days were quiet and the weather turned colder. New Year's was approaching and Darius became a hard man to pin down. He traveled to other churches to preach and there were happy things and sad things. A couple had been trying for a long time to have a baby and suffered through three miscarriages, but the Lord blessed them with an uneventful pregnancy and a nine pound baby girl. Nina recalled the couple coming up for prayer. The woman was at term and they were afraid that something would go wrong. Darius prayed for them insisting that God was in control.

Nina called and spoke with both Richard and the filmmaker. She told them that she was interested and wanted to wait until after the New Year to talk more in depth about doing the project. The woman eagerly agreed and Richard sounded happy that Nina was even considering it.

New Year's Eve was full of activity. Nina and Darius hadn't been out on a date in almost a week and they went out the night before. The church usually conducted service from 10:30 to midnight and Nina was eager to attend.

Darius invited a much-anointed man of God to preach. Evangelist Emmanuel David delivered an amazing sermon.

He spoke about endurance to finish the course. He said that the enemy was so devious in his ways that he excelled at camouflaging sin so that it didn't appear as such nor did it feel as such.

"A great many of our young folk are losing their way because they are fooled into sin never realizing that they have sinned. The Scriptures tell us that God destroyed a whole town for their immorality. He could have spared some of those folks for sin that society today tells us is not sinful, but he didn't. God doesn't categorize sin. One isn't less repugnant to him than another is. In God's eyes, sin is sin and distasteful to him.

God is awesome in his power to punish and to bless. The Bible teaches us about his chosen people. The more he loved them the more they disappointed him and turned their backs on him. So God punished them and when God punishes he does it big. The Israelites sinned and God came swooping down to punish them. He displaced them, allowed them to become slaves.

The Israelites of old fascinate me. They were a loved people and they were a stubborn people. No sooner would they find their way back to the God of Abraham, they would get distracted and be right back where they started.

I like to teach about the Israelites because their story teaches us and encourages us today. By grace, we became co-inheritors with Abraham's descendants. By way of adoption, we have the same privileges afforded them. No matter how many times we fall short, God will always come running when we call on him. Even when God hardened his heart against the Israelites, there was some prophet praying and begging forgiveness for them and God acquiesced and saved his people. The God of yesterday is the same God today folks; he never changes and always loves.

I would like to end with a short story I heard a few days ago from an evangelist friend of mine. He said that he had gotten together with two other friends. They got into a heated discussion about the crossing at the Red Sea. If you recall the story, the Israelites left Egypt and Pharaoh's whole army were in hot pursuit. They came to the Red Sea where they realized that they were between it and the army chasing them.

Moses stretched out his staff and the sea parted. Well these two fellows were arguing back and forth about it. My friend sat listening to them. One fellow was a scholar and said that it was impossible for the sea to part, that the Israelites didn't get away from Pharaoh by crossing the Red Sea. He listed all the reasons why it was impossible for such a huge body of water to part like that. Then he said that alongside the Red Sea was a marshy piece of land. He said that at a certain time of the year it got windy enough so that the two feet of water in it dried up. That was where the Israelites crossed he insisted.

The other fellow argued that the Bible clearly stated that the Israelites crossed the Red Sea. The Israelites crossed and when Pharaoh's army pursued, the sea came together again and drowned them. This went on for a length of time until my friend stopped them. He said that the Bible did state that the Israelites crossed the Red Sea and that Pharaoh's army pursued and drowned. Even if you are right about it not being the Red Sea that they crossed, how awesome is God to have these people cross that little marshy land and then drown an entire army in just two feet of water!"

The thunderous shout that filled the sanctuary was impressive to say the least. Nina was right there standing and clapping and praising God along with everybody else.

She wondered how an unsaved person could come to a service to hear a sermon like that and not crave salvation. Evangelist David made an altar call and Nina felt blown away at how few people went up for prayer. She was on line for prayer and wondered why so few people felt as she did. She wasn't going up there to ask for salvation, but rather to ask for the endurance the evangelist spoke about and then just to praise God for being so awesome.

Having introduced her as his girlfriend on Christmas Eve, Nina wasn't surprised that Darius introduced her to the evangelist and his wife. Nina smiled and accepted the hug from the man. She was further surprised that his wife wanted an autograph. She insisted that she was her biggest fan.

Nina signed her name on the back of the service program and smiled hesitantly at her. "I wouldn't have thought that you listened to my music." Nina said.

"Your music is romantic not offensive. I like that about you. Knowing that you are saved says a whole lot," she replied.

Nina didn't know what to say but her smile widened. Later on as she was getting ready for bed, the evangelists' wife came to mind and she realized that she had been worrying needlessly about her image. Thinking back on all the performances she's done in the course of her career, she had maintained a positive self-image and perhaps projected it across to her fans.

She always insisted on being fully clothed in videos and movies. After having done the wholesome Disney movies, she went and did other projects that were more grown up. The movies dealt with more mature subject matter and told stories that were current with what was going on in the world. Nina agonized over romantic scenes until she pulled the director aside to voice her concerns. He understood and allowed her to interpret a scene tastefully. She hadn't been ashamed to see the finished product afterwards.

In the film about her parents, there were a few scenes where she had to drink or hold a cigarette in her mouth. Her father was a smoker, a social drinker but he never did any drugs. Her mother as far as she knew was squeaky clean as Nina was. She made her living with her voice so she protected that religiously.

In the course of their career however, her parents encountered a lot of the drugs and alcohol and groupies. There was a difference between a fan and a groupie. A fan enjoyed an artists' work and praised it. A groupie enjoyed the work also but they wanted to be part of that artist's life. They followed the artist on tours and tried to find ways to be with them.

Nina toured with a rather popular artist who allowed a busload of groupies to follow them. This artist didn't mind them and had his manager pick one out each night after a show to sleep with. Nina felt disgusted by the offer of her choice of the people that played in the band. She politely declined and insisted that Richard move her to another hotel. That kind of life was not for her and never appealed to her.

She felt that she had a responsibility to be a role model to the public. She would rather people think of her as eccentric than be another sensational story in the news. In fact, there was a feeding frenzy in the media this very week. They were crucifying a very successful golfer for his indiscretions. He was young, successful and married. The couple has young children who may not understand what is going on and the media doesn't care about the fallout. All they were after were ways to sell more magazines and newspapers, even if they had to speculate which they did aplenty, Nina thought.

That was the pitfall of being in the lime light. One's entire life is under scrutiny and considered public domain. The poor man may have been wrong to do what he did but Nina felt that as long as it didn't affect his golf game that it was a private matter between his family and himself. The media attention was not helping the hurt he and his family were experiencing. The people involved were not caring either; they were out to get monetary gain or their fifteen minutes of fame.

In the end, this man's family would be damaged or worse. Nina felt that she was fortunate that her father brought her up with the right values. Even with the right upbringing, a popular performer must exercise discipline not to fall into the traps, which were the nature of the industry. It seemed that being rich and famous made for a whole set of rules that regular folk weren't privy to. All manner of illicit wares were readily available and sometimes free.

Most of Nina's peers were into one type of drug or another. Behavioral taboos were also the other things in which they indulged. She often wondered what the gain was by those obviously destructive behaviors and never really came across an answer that made sense. One friend explained that she was bored and another said that he had one life to live, that it was short and he was going to get as much as he could get out of it.

In Nina's opinion, it all boiled down to what she had been hearing a lot of in church recently. This world's morality is on a downward spiral and it was getting worse. Just watching the news on television made her cringe. Did one have to be a Christian to see it? Apart from the drugs, there was violence that a few short years ago were shocking. Today people are so desensitized to it that they are not appalled anymore. Children killing children is considered a mere tragedy and not the morally wrong thing that it is.

There are psychologists who are giving credence to this lack of morals by categorizing it as a new disease or syndrome. It made Nina sick and she knew that Darius was fighting a very hard battle. The following Wednesday Nina attended bible study and found that Darius was a little distracted because earlier he had to go bail a young man out of jail.

As a minister, he took his job very seriously. She knew how frustrating it was for him when he ministered to a victim of violence or drug abuse among the congregation. He hurt for them and he was always searching the word for ways to help his flock. He always said that the answers were in the word. He had many interpretations of the bible, which Nina had seen for herself in his church office and his home office. He was always trying to find new insight.

As much as he tried to comfort himself that the things that plagued people were slated to happen, he felt almost helpless. He would then pray for strength to hold on because the alternative was damning. The fight that he fights and all Christians fight is going to get harder.

Nina started paying more attention to the concerns of the church and she saw what Darius saw. Sometimes, the enemy attacked the children tearing families apart. The youth were the ones who were more vulnerable at this time because they were young and impressionable. Darius taught that although we live *in* the world that we needn't live *like* the world. For young people, their inexperience made it all the more difficult; everything was still exciting to them.

He also taught that even the saved have to be more watchful lest they fall into acquiescence. Today the train of thought was that it wasn't wrong so long as they were going to church. He gave a long speech after the bible study about how even certain churches were falling into complacency with what was going on in the world. There was a lot of controversy concerning gay rights that had him heated.

He said that there were things that the saints didn't have to swallow. We should be able to see it for what it is. "Didn't God destroy Sodom and Gomorrah for their lack of morality and for their sins? If He didn't stand for it then, why should he do so now?"

The many attending the bible study agreed, Nina along with them. Later after she got ready to leave, she insisted that he take her to his house so that they could talk. She sensed his unease and wanted to soothe him. She called her aunt to let her know that she would be late.

"Baby you have to calm down a little. I know how much you care but you also have to comfort yourself in knowing that you are in the battle and that you haven't given up. As the general of Christ Tabernacle, you are leading your troops. It is a hard battle and I do understand that it will get harder, but honey you have to calm down. I worry that you will get sick." Nina told him.

"I know Baby, I know. It just bothers me and I feel that it should bother others as well. I know that the Bible tells us that these things will happen but it hurts when it affects God's people. We have teenage parents and addicts and marriages falling apart right here in this church and I feel hard pressed to help them," Darius lamented.

"You always say that the answer is in the Word and you just admitted that it says that what you are seeing is supposed to happen. What you are also failing to see is that since it is supposed to happen, you cannot stop it. I know that you feel that it shouldn't affect the saints but it is. It is not your fault that some will fall by the way side while others go on to glory. It's just like the Scripture about sowing. Some seeds will fall on fertile ground and others will fall among thorns and not flourish; and just like you said, this is a war and there will be casualties. The saints have to pray harder and resist harder than they have ever before. Just remember that you are right here encouraging them."

"Truly the Lord is watching over me, he sent you to me. I'm sorry if I'm worrying you. I get so excited and frustrated that it gets to me, but you are right. I am in the perfect position to help God's people wage war on the enemy." Darius said pulling her close for a hug. "Do you still see yourself as a minister's wife? That little speech you just gave me is exactly what I'd expect for my wife to say."

Nina pulled back to see his face. "I see myself as your wife one day but I'm not ready yet. I'm still searching and growing, but I am glad that I was able to help you tonight. Now if you are feeling better, take me home so you can get some rest," said Nina.

"Catalina what am I going to do with you? It is getting to the point where I don't want to be without you. I love you very much." Darius said before he kissed her.

"That's why you have to take me home now. You have holy bear to keep you company, it's why I got him for you, so you won't feel so lonely," replied Nina softly after the kiss. She realized that Darius was feeling vulnerable now, not to mention the physical changes she could feel happening in him.

"Can you even understand that it is not just sexual? I just want you near all the time," he explained in a strained voice.

"And how long would it take being together for it to become sexual Darius? I love you too and sometimes it is hard to be away from you, but the reality is that we can't take the chance, there is too much at stake."

"Come on then let me take you home. One of these days I will put a ring on your finger and you won't have to go away from me," he grumbled.

"What a wonderful day that will be," sang Nina.

"Do not mock me woman!"

"I wouldn't dream of it," laughed Nina.

"Get in the car Catalina," Darius said gruffly. He opened the car door for her and handed her in.

Nina got in, clicked on the seatbelt and continued to smile. She found that humor was the best way to deal with her grumpy man when he was like this. It was happening more and more and she'd been trying to find ways to defuse it, she found that humor worked best.

"Did I tell you that I am thinking about going to the recording studio? I have been writing a lot lately and I think that I could have enough for a gospel CD. What do you think?"

"That would be wonderful Babe, and don't think that I am shooting you down. I just don't feel like talking right now. Okay?"

"No it is not okay. Stop being so hard on yourself Darius; the stuff with the young man will sort itself out. Even if it doesn't who's to say that God isn't using it to save this young man? Honey you need to realize that you can't help everybody. You are always saying that God is in control so let Him control it. Step back, pray and let God do."

Darius was in the process of clicking on his seatbelt when he stopped to face her. "Baby I am not even thinking about that young man. I already prayed and left it at the altar. I am frustrated about you wanting to wait for us to be together. If I had it my way, we'd be married by now. We are so right for each other. You know exactly what to say to make me feel better. If you recall when we first started I told you that although I am a minister that I was also a man." He looked at her with such intensity, that it made Nina angry.

"All right then we're going to settle this right now." She unbuckled her belt and unlocked the door. She stepped out of the car and hurried toward Darius' front door.

Darius was slow to follow and when he reached for her to take her back to the car, Nina pulled away angrily from him.

"Unlock the door Darius. We need to come to an understanding and tonight is the night."

Darius fished for his house keys to unlock the door. Nina rushed in, took off her coat, and hung it on the coat rack by the door. She turned to him with eyes flashing and cheeks flushed crimson.

"Where do you want me, here or upstairs in your bed?"

"Nina this isn't what I meant. Baby put your coat back on and let me take you home." Darius approached her slowly and reached for her hand.

"No, it is *exactly* what you meant," Nina said and turned from him. She rushed from the foyer and ran up the stairs. She hesitated at the top because she didn't know exactly which way his bedroom was. She found it on her second try. The first door she opened was one of the spare bedrooms.

She took a deep breath and walked in. She looked around quickly and spotted his bed. The bedroom wasn't very remarkable; everything was green and white right down to the comforter on the bed. She sat gingerly on the edge of it waiting for him.

Once again, Darius followed her slowly. He found her sitting on the side of his bed holding the bear. She looked up at him expectantly and his heart began to ache.

Nina watched his approach and realized that she had achieved what she sought. Darius appeared confused and his steps toward her were full of trepidation. She decided to press on.

"I guess this is where I leave off and you take over. I've never made love before so you will have to teach me what you want me to do."

Darius stopped in the middle of the room and dropped his gaze. He couldn't look at her anymore. She was offering herself to him and all of the sudden he just couldn't bring himself to get any nearer. They were in love and they had God's approval didn't they? Yet seeing her sitting there trying to look brave stopped him cold. She trusted him to do the right thing. It was something they promised each other they would do and yet look at them now.

Darius found the strength to get closer and when he was close enough, he knelt down beside her. "Forgive me. God knows how utterly ashamed I feel right now. I promise you that there is no pressure to rush anything between us. We've only known each other a short while and it would be prudent for us to grow together as a couple before we can be husband and wife. Please say you forgive me." Darius asked lifting tortured eyes to her.

"I love you Darius. I was confident all along that this wouldn't go any further. But don't ever make me do this again." She bent her head to kiss his lips.

Darius kissed her as if it was the last time he'd get to kiss her. When they came apart, he took her hand and together they left the room.

"So do you forgive me?" he asked when they were in the car once again.

"Yes Darius I forgive you. You do realize that I was acting and I would never have gone to bed with you tonight. I just thought that a dramatization would be better than trying to talk you through."

"You mean to tell me that you offered yourself to me and it was all an act?" Darius asked as he pulled out of the parking spot.

"Yes I would never have found the guts to offer myself to you for real. As many love scenes as I have played and have seen I wouldn't know how to act or what to say. When the time comes for us, it will be all on you." Nina said shyly.

Darius reached over to clasp her hand. "I can't believe how lucky I am and I want to thank you for being the voice of reason tonight. Even though I said that it wasn't sexual, I confess that I lied. It was a little bit. Please be comforted in knowing that I would never have pressured you to do anything."

"I know but if we have to go through this again, give me a few months okay. My knees were shaking so much I *had* to sit on the bed," Nina admitted finally looking at him.

"Really, so the high color on your cheeks and the death grip you had on the bear was because you were scared and not excited? I thought you looked cute."

"I was trying to look seductive not cute. Forget it. Let's talk about something else. I really think I can pull off a gospel CD," said Nina.

"I would have something else to be proud of you for. Do you need a PR man? I can go around and hype you up and such," he said. He was feeling better and he had Nina to thank for that.

He was glad that Nina hadn't tried to make him feel better further by placing blame on the enemy. This was a case of lust and he had been feeling it a lot lately. It was sin of the flesh and not induced by the devil. Sometimes it was so easy to blame the devil that the saints continued to sin thinking that once they prayed for forgiveness that it would be okay. He had to be on guard for his own flesh. He needed to rebuke it and know that the Lord would bring Nina and him together in his own time. Tonight Nina proved to be the strong one and had held firm. A woman like that was worth waiting for.

When they pulled up in front of her house, he got out eagerly to help Nina. Together they walked up the steps and once they were at the door, Nina turned to face him. "Even though you've already prayed for that young man, I know that tomorrow you are going to check on him. I'll say a prayer for him tonight too."

"How did you know I'd check on him?" Darius asked taking her in his arms.

"It is the kind of person you are. I love that about you." Nina said and drew his head down to hers.

Their kiss was warm and passionate, but because it was cold, they could not linger longer. "Good night, beautiful lady."

"Good night, Darius." Nina replied.

Darius waited for her to get inside before he hurried to his car. It was cold out and there was a storm brewing he thought. As he drove home, he thought again, about how fortunate he was in having Nina in his life. She was perfect for him.

When Darius got home, he went up to his bedroom to get ready for bed. He felt good and realized that Nina's scent still lingered in the room and it was on the bear as well. After saying a prayer of thanks and asking for strength, Darius climbed into bed with the bear. Because it held her scent, he held it close. If he could get Nina to douse the bear with her perfume every now and again, Darius thought he could probably tolerate it in his bed.

The following morning, he got up earlier than usual just so he could stop by that young man's house to see if he was going to go to school. Darius felt comforted by the fact that once he got to the young man's home, he was getting breakfast ready for his younger brother and sister. They were all getting ready for school.

Their mother was a single parent who worked two jobs to make ends meet. She needed her oldest child's help. She had already left for work and probably wouldn't return until much later in the evening.

Darius prayed with the children and left the home confident that they would be all right. The young man was surprised that his pastor had shown up at his house. He promised that being locked up even for those few hours was something he wouldn't forget for a long time, nor was it something he wanted to repeat.

Nina stretched luxuriously before getting out of bed. She had a full morning and wasn't even motivated to get to it. She promised Richard and the filmmaker, she would get in contact with them to set up a schedule of meetings to discuss her part in the venture after the New Year. This morning Nina planned to call her to tell her that she was ready to speak with her.

As Nina lay in bed trying to convince herself to get out of it, she could hear her aunt getting ready for work. Elaine was in her late sixties and recently hinted that she might retire soon. Nina insisted that she needn't work so hard anymore but her aunt was the independent type who didn't like to lean on anyone. Part of Nina's Christmas gift was paying the taxes on the house for the year.

The current economic state has played havoc with many work places and her aunt was grateful to have a job. Her hours were down to part-time and she was barely making ends meet. She no longer had a mortgage, but other expenses plagued her. Nina coming to stay with her had eased the burden. She worked now because it was something to do as Nina took over paying the monthly utility bills.

Nina finally got out of bed just as her aunt was leaving the house. She had a meeting with the builders to get a start date on the recreation center. It brought to mind how right Richard was about using the money she would make from doing the film to fund the center, and it made sense to do it that way.

Last Sunday she was privy to an announcement made in church at the end of the service. They were short a few hundred dollars to pay the mortgage and the trustees appealed to the congregation to donate as much as they could to fill the gap. The church came up with the difference but the fact that they had to ask left Nina feeling concerned.

She recalled the conversation she'd had with Darius about the church not being able to fund the recreation center because of its financial burdens.

She couldn't understand how any congregation would let their church go without. She came to realize that many churches had the same difficulties paying their mortgage too. Since she started attending this church, it was a common occurrence for the treasurer to announce that they were short. Darius never discussed the church's financial situation with her and she wondered if he felt embarrassed to do so; or perhaps fear that he was hinting that she might pay it off.

Trustee Worthington expressed interest in her millions she said she had at her disposal when she had first approached the church about the center. Perhaps she should have a talk with him to get a better picture of the church's financial situation. Would the congregation feel indebted to her if she paid a portion of the mortgage? Alternatively, would they resent her intrusion? She didn't know which way it would go and decided to speak with Darius about it.

After finally getting out of bed, Nina called long distance to speak over an hour with the filmmaker to get a better understanding of what she was hoping to accomplish. After Nina hung up, she knew that she was very interested in doing the project. According to Ms. Rubinowitz, the project would take about four to five months to complete. They wouldn't have to travel much and Nina would only be working six weeks at the most. With the amount of footage the film library had, they only needed her for the real-time speaking parts.

Nina agreed. Ms. Rubinowitz would send her a contract and start date. Richard called her later in the day to express how happy he was that she consented to do the work. Nina suspected that he thought that she was edging her way back and for now, she would let him think that. She intended to be on guard with him. She would read everything twice before she signed anything just so she wouldn't fall into any traps. It would be horrible if she mistakenly signed something that was long term.

Next was a face-to-face meeting with the constructing firm she and her lawyer had agreed to hire. As luck would have it and because of downsizing, the construction company had need of the two men from whom she bought the properties. They would be able to keep their jobs simply because the company had an upsurge of work. Her lawyer explained that because she was using the company, others sought to use them too.

When Nina returned home from her meeting with the builders, she found that Darius was waiting for her. She smiled and waved as she approached him. Darius leaned forward to unlock his car door so that she could get in.

"Well this is a wonderful surprise. Do you want to come inside and have dinner with us? My aunt should be home," Nina said leaning over to give him a kiss.

"No baby, I've been waiting for you because I got a call about your aunt. She had an accident and an ambulance rushed her to the hospital. I didn't want you to drive in a panic so I came for you," Darius told her as he started his car.

"Oh my God, why didn't anyone contact me? What kind of accident, is she all right?" Nina asked as her face got paler and paler.

"Relax baby, she's fine. She fell down trying to get off the bus and when she got to the hospital, they found that she fractured her hip." Darius relayed to her.

"What hospital is she at? Is it a good one?" She asked visibly relieved.

Visions of her father lying in the hospital crossed her mind and she got scared.

"She's at New York Hospital and it is excellent. She was resting comfortably when I left her and she wasn't even in pain. The doctor said that it wasn't a very bad fracture but it wouldn't hurt to observe her for a few days."

"Oh thank God," Nina expressed.

When they approached the hospital, there was a crowd of people there along with a mobile news truck. Nina had a sinking feeling that they were there because of her and she wasn't up to dealing with the media.

Darius watched as she tucked her hair inside her coat and then fish for her shades. "I wish I knew this hospital well enough to get you in the back way but I don't. There isn't that many people so we might be able to push our way through," Darius told her. He steered the car into the parking lot adjacent to the hospital's entrance and parked.

Crossing the street was uneventful until they had reached the other side. A reporter spotted her and pointed. That was what the crowd needed. They converged all around her and she saw no way to get past them.

Darius put a protective arm around her and they tried to push their way through. A television camera operator and a reporter were directly in their path and Nina had no course left to her. She stopped and waited for the reporter to finish his introduction. She smiled when he put the microphone in front of her.

"I haven't gotten any information yet about my aunt, so I would appreciate the chance to go see her. Thank you for your concern and I'm sure my aunt appreciates your concern as well," she announced graciously. They walked past him easily after that.

"There you have it, ladies and gentlemen. Miss Nina Bennett is entering the hospital to see to her ailing aunt. "This is Brad Crosby, up to the minute news," they heard him say as they entered the hospital.

Once inside the hospital an impeccably dressed man approached them. He introduced himself as the administrator. He insisted that he would be delighted to escort them to her aunt's room. While they were in the elevator, he informed them that he moved her aunt to a private room and that she was resting comfortably.

When they reached the room on the sixth floor, he stepped back to allow them to enter. The room was brightly lit and spacious. There was a nurse with her whose eyes lit up when she saw Nina but because the administrator was at the door, she dared not do anything more than smile.

Nina broke away from Darius and rushed to her aunt. "Auntie I came as soon as I heard. Are you all right?" she asked.

Aunt Elaine was smiling brightly. "Child I really don't know what the fuss is all about. I feel fine. I'm not in pain but they won't let me go home."

"I haven't spoken with the doctor yet but Darius tells me that you have a fractured hip. Are you sure you aren't in pain?" Nina asked smoothing her aunt's hair.

"No pain sweetheart."

"What happened to your cell phone? Didn't you have it on you?" Nina questioned her further.

"I did but as I was trying to tell the police, my purse was snatched and I was trying to rush after the young man who took it. He yanked it harder than I could hold on to it and I fell. I doubt I'll get it back so you are going to have to help me cancel cards and such. I didn't have much money in it, but I had all those pictures and now they are all lost," bemoaned Elaine.

Nina hugged her aunt close. "I'll take care of the cards Auntie, what matters most is that you are okay." Nina assured the suddenly old looking woman in the bed.

Darius approached the bed on the other side and he took her hand. "Sister Elaine don't you worry about your stuff, we just thank God that you are all right."

The doctor entered the room just then and the nurse handed him the chart. He scanned it and then looked up first at the patient lying in the bed and then at Nina. "Ms. Bennett, I'm Doctor Wilcox, it certainly is a pleasure to meet you. Your aunt has suffered a fractured left hip. It is what we call a hairline fracture, which means that it is very fine and not as serious. However, because of your aunt's age, we are going to be careful not to stress the bone. We intend to observe her for a few days to ensure that infection doesn't set in and that she is healing nicely. It might even be wise that after she leaves the hospital that she have some rehab as well." The doctor informed her.

"How long do you think her hospital stay will be?" Nina asked squeezing her aunt's hand.

"I'd say a week to ten days to see and then after we x-ray again we'll know better," Dr. Wilcox replied matter-of-factly. He left shortly after shaking Nina and Darius' hands.

"Ten days, I can't stay here ten days!" Aunt Elaine cried out after the doctor.

Nina turned her attention back to her aunt trying to soothe her. It was clear that she was agitated. She probably was worried about her job Nina thought.

"Auntie, try not to worry I'm sure that everything will be all right. "I'll call your job to explain what happened." You've worked for them too many years for them not to understand. Besides, I think they already know. You are a celebrity now, you're on TV."

"Whatever for?" she asked even more agitated. Nina could clearly see that her aunt was curious as she eyed the television set up on the wall opposite her bed. Darius reached for the remote on the bedside table and clicked the television on.

After going through several channels, they found a news channel. The news that Elaine Bennett-Hughes who is the aunt of the famous Nina Bennett, brought by ambulance to New York Hospital for injuries she sustained getting off the bus at the bus terminal in downtown Jamaica was extensive. They interviewed the police officer who was at the scene. He said that he was investigating the crime that was committed against Ms. Elaine Bennett-Hughes. He explained that the victim got hurt because of resisting a purse-snatcher. He went on to advise people not to struggle or resist in cases like these because it always resulted in someone getting hurt.

The picture they used was one of Nina's most recent publicity photos. She looked glamorous, not at all like the woman sitting at her aunt's bedside. They had a picture of her aunt as well and it looked they photographed her while she was being loaded onto the ambulance.

"That policeman is right Auntie. Resisting him wasn't a good idea. I know that you weren't thinking at the time, but it could have been worse. As much as I hate to think this way, but had this happened in a more secluded area you could've gotten seriously hurt," said Nina.

"I was only thinking about what I'd be losing if I let go. I realize now that it was foolish. Look at me now lying in a hospital bed with a broken hip. Won't he get a surprise when he realizes that he got very little out of it? Apart from my phone and store credit cards I only had about twenty dollars in my purse," Aunt Elaine explained.

Darius patted Sis. Elaine's hand and told her that in most cases, once the crook went through the purse, it most likely is thrown away, someone may find it and she may even get her pictures back. Nina agreed and that seemed to make her aunt feel better.

Nina looked over to him and smiled her thanks. She had never been privy to him ministering to anyone before and she realized that he was good at it. Her aunt looked to him for comfort and he gave it easily. How she loved him!

The nurse came back to let them know that visiting hours would be over soon, but that they could stay longer if they wished. The administrator left instructions that her aunt had VIP status.

Nina smiled at the nurse and insisted that she wasn't going to disrupt hospital routine and would be leaving shortly. She did ask that they call her if her aunt was in any distress. Nina gave her the house number and told the nurse that it wasn't a private number after she saw the excited expression on her face.

"Auntie I'll be back in the morning with your own night gown so that you can be comfortable. Is there anything else you'll need?" Nina asked.

"If you could bring some of my tea, I think I can bear being here," was her reply.

Nina acknowledged that her aunt was nervous about being in the hospital. She hurried back to her side and hugged her close. "Auntie I'm so glad you're okay. I wish I could stay with you tonight but I can't. Darius brought me and he's had a long day. I promise to stay the entire day with you tomorrow. What would you like for breakfast?" Nina asked her.

"You don't have to go to any trouble for me baby," she smiled slyly. "I think that I'll be fine. My niece is famous you know. People around here will be bending over backward to cater to me if they can get an autograph."

Nina shook head. "Don't get carried away Auntie. I don't mind signing a few autographs, but just don't promise them anything," warned Nina.

She straightened up and smoothed her aunt's brow. "I'll see you in the morning okay?"

Her aunt nodded and looked to her pastor. He approached the bed once more to take her hand in his. After saying a comforting prayer, he released her hand and escorted Nina out.

Outside the door, Nina waved once more and slid on her shades. As they walked toward the elevator bank, she tucked her hair into her coat and waited. Ever conscious of the media, they got off the elevator cautiously. The administrator was waiting for them in the lobby. He led them to a side door with instructions on how to get to the street.

Somehow, they were able to walk across the street and enter the parking lot without trouble. Darius led her to the car and they exited without the reporters outside the hospital seeing them. When they had come to a stop light, Darius reached over to clasp her hand.

"Are you going to be okay tonight?" he asked her.

Nina shrugged. "I haven't been alone at my aunt's house before, but I guess it wouldn't be any different than when my dad was in the hospital. I'll be okay." Nina squeezed his hand before he pulled away to steer the car.

The drive back to the house was quiet with Nina thinking about her aunt. When they reached her block, there were two news vans and several reporters camped outside the house. It never ceased to amaze Nina how resourceful these breed of people could be. It probably wasn't very hard to get her aunt's address, but someone had to have let him or her know that she left the hospital.

Darius brought the car to a stop and turned to face her. It was too late to try to get away. The reporters were approaching his car and they stood beside the car with microphones ready as soon as Darius parked.

"What do you want to do Babe?"

"Sometimes if I cooperate like earlier, we might just be able to get this over with," Nina said. She plastered a dazzling smile on her face and unbuckled her seat belt. Darius watched her transform before his very eyes.

Nina closed her eyes and reached deep inside her soul to pull out the Hollywood star she left behind. She slid her shades on and then unlocked the car door and stepped out before Darius could react.

He watched her take off her shades in a coquettish manner to smile alluringly at the reporters. She took a step forward and the reporters stepped back. She took another step and still they moved back. When Nina was on the front porch of her aunt's house, she stopped, turned and smiled luminously at the cameras.

"I will answer just a few questions and then I must go inside gentlemen, it has been a horrendous day." Nina said in a voice that dripped diva with a capital D. She nodded at one reporter.

"Miss Bennett, can you tell us more about the recreation center that you are building?"

Again sporting that million-dollar smile, Nina answered. "My father once told me that the young are truly the most treasured resource mankind has and that we must protect and nurture them. Building the center and having it serve the young in the community would certainly be a way of doing that. With the center I am doing my part in giving a young person who otherwise would have become endangered a safe haven."

"Who is that man with you?" Another reporter asked.

By this time, Darius came to stand behind her. Nina leaned back slightly to whisper to him. "What shall I tell them?"

"Tell them the truth." Darius whispered back.

Nina then reached behind her to clasp his hand then pulled him into the glare of the lights. "This is Pastor Darius Fairchild of Christ Tabernacle of Jamaica Queens. He is a wonderful spiritual leader who will be of service to the young in the community at the center. He is also the man in my life."

"Is it serious?" Another reporter called out.

"Yes. And if there aren't any more questions about the center or my ailing aunt, I would like to retire now." Nina announced politely.

"It is the hope of the up to the minute news family that your aunt makes a speedy recovery," the reporter said. He then turned to face his camera operator to make his final remarks.

Nina took that as a sign that the interviews were over. She handed Darius the house keys and they entered the house unhindered.

When Darius shut the door to the sea of people and the news crews that had gathered, Nina leaned on the door and closed her eyes.

Again, Darius watched her transform into the woman that he had grown accustomed.

"Do you know that you do that?" he asked her in awe.

Nina opened her less brilliant green eyes to stare at him. "Do what?" she asked him. She pushed away from the door to shrug out of her coat. That was when Darius saw what it had cost her to do what she had just done. Nina was shaking. She was trembling so hard she could hardly hang her coat in the closet.

She brushed past him and headed for the kitchen where she poured herself a glass of orange juice.

Darius stood back unsure of what to say or do as he watched her drink the juice. Then she did something he wasn't quite expecting her to do. She walked over to him and asked him to hold her. She had been in control all afternoon the minute she got the news about her aunt. Now she needed comfort that which he was willing to give to her wholeheartedly.

Nina held onto the man who instinctively understood what she needed. She clung to him now unable to stem the flow of tears that streamed down her face and knowing that he was there for her, Nina cried in earnest.

"Don't cry baby, I've got you." Darius cooed to her. When she cried herself out, he led her to the stairs and together they climbed up to her room. Nina opened the door and they entered. Nina was still trembling and needed to sit. Darius led her to the bed and handed her down to it. He bent down to unzip her boots and tugged them off.

He urged her to lie down gently. When Nina was lying down comfortably, Darius pulled the lilac comforter over her. Then he knelt down beside her to hold her hand.

"It would be prudent for you to go now even though I don't want you to go. Be careful Darius, don't go straight home. Someone will be following you so go to the church and stay there for at least a half hour before you go home. Then call me." Nina advised him.

"Why would anyone follow me?" Darius asked slightly puzzled.

Nina sat up to stare at him. "Honey I've just announced to the world that you are the man in my life, you've just become interesting. Be assured that someone is going to approach you for an interview. It will be up to you to agree to one or not," she informed further.

"I don't know if I'm ready for all of that, Babe. Can you teach me to come on like you've just done without the shaking of course?" Darius asked with a small smile on his handsome face.

Nina smiled back. She wasn't trembling anymore. "It is funny how hard it had become to do that. It has been a while since I've had to concentrate to pull the Diva out, as my aunt would say. It was something that was so ingrained in me that it was natural to be it. My friends and I used to compete with each other to see who could out Diva who. Living simply with the people who truly love me is so much more wonderful. I can't imagine ever wanting to go back to that lifestyle."

"I was only teasing. I don't want to be in the limelight because I am your man. When I venture there, it will be for something pertaining to my ministry and not my private life. Baby I love you. Get some rest and I'll call you later," said Darius as he walked toward the door.

Nina threw back the covers to jump out of the bed and rushed to him. She hugged him close and kissed his neck. "I don't know what I would have done without you tonight. I don't know what I've done to deserve you and I won't question it. Right now I just know that I am grateful and I love you very much."

"I love you too Baby." Darius kissed her quickly and motioned for her to get back into the bed and then he left closing the door gently behind him.

Darius pulled the downstairs door firmly checking to make sure that it locked before he rushed to his car. Since Nina warned him, he didn't look around to see if anyone followed him. He got into his car and drove away.

He drove to the church then entered through the side door and closed it behind him. Again, as advised, he stayed there for a good half hour and found that he wasn't there idly. He did have some correspondence to take care off and he prepared them for his secretary. When he finished with his paperwork, Darius stood up to stretch. He pulled on his overcoat and left the church.

The lone reporter who followed Darius threw his little notepad down disgustingly and told his camera operator that they had nothing. "I don't know what I was thinking. Nina hasn't done a bad thing her whole life. She's finally dating and she picks a minister. I thought he was going to spend the night but he came out too quick to even suggest that they had been intimate. Come on let's go."

"We could come up with something," suggested the camera operator.

"Man, are you crazy? You don't mess with ministers unless you can prove stuff. That man has anointed written all over him."

"What are you, some kind of Christian?" the camera operator asked looking at the man he has worked with for over twelve years.

"You could say that. I grew up going to church and was even in the choir but when I started this job, I guess I changed. Some of the stuff I've seen just makes you lose your religion you know," replied the reporter.

"Man you are no fun. Take me back to the paper so I can edit the footage at the hospital and the house. Then I'm going home; you should too and maybe pick your religion up again," the camera operator said disgustingly.

The reporter started the car and drove off thinking that he just might do that.

Nina got out of bed to answer the house phone. The nurse who was caring for her aunt was on the other end. Nina had a little scare until she realized that the nurse was only calling her for kicks. The nurse told her that her aunt was fine and resting.

She brought the cordless up to her room in case it rang again and got into bed. It had been a long day and she felt very tired suddenly. The day started with her phone conversation with the filmmaker and then the meeting with the contractors and her lawyer. The meeting was successful in that she had a start date for construction to begin on the recreation center. She called to speak with Richard about perhaps flying to L.A to meet with the filmmaker. In light of her aunt's hospitalization and perhaps recuperation time, Nina thought she just might have to put the project on hold for a few more weeks.

Nina's cell phone rang and she picked it up quickly. "Darius are you okay?" she asked anxiously.

"I'm fine Babe. I don't think anyone followed me but then I've never had to think about such things before. I thought you'd have fallen asleep by now but you sound wide-awake. Are *you* okay?"

"Yeah, the nurse at the hospital called and I got the feeling that she was testing to see if I'd pick up. I hate when people play like that. She told me that Aunt Elaine was resting fine. Once she's out of the hospital, I'm going to change the phone number to something unlisted. She probably won't like that but I see no choice. Her number is now a hot commodity thanks to me. If things don't calm down soon I'm thinking I should move to my own place just to give her some peace," Nina complained.

"Baby, stop talking you're babbling. It has been a long and emotional day for you. What you need is a good night's rest and I guarantee that things will look better in the morning."

"I guess you're right. Good night Darius I love you." Nina said around a yawn.

"Sleep tight and I'll call you in the morning." Darius said and hung up.

CHAPTER ELEVEN

Sometime during the night, Nina awoke not sure what woke her up; and then she heard it. It was an unfamiliar noise. A loud crash downstairs convinced her that someone was in the house. She reached over for her cell phone to call the police and then she called Darius. He instructed her to lock her bedroom door and to get dressed. It wasn't hard to get dressed in the dark and she did so quickly. Nina tried to be as quiet as she could be and then tiptoed to her aunt's room through the connecting bathroom to lock that door.

Nina turned the lamp on to get her aunt's clothing for the hospital and then she returned to her room. The noises were getting louder downstairs. Whoever was downstairs didn't think anyone was home and wasn't even being careful not to be noisy.

It was another fifteen minutes before she heard the sirens. The noise stopped suddenly and then she heard running. Someone was coming up the stairs and she ran to the closet to hide in there. From what she could hear, the police were in the house as well.

Soon she heard a loud knock on her bedroom door. "Miss Bennett this is the police, open the door. We have a Pastor Fairchild with us."

Nina burst out of the closet and rushed to unlock the door. Darius and two uniformed police officers stood outside the door. She rushed into Darius' arms crying hysterically.

"Oh my God, someone broke into the house and I was afraid they'd come up here," Nina sobbed.

"It's okay Babe. The police caught them. They didn't even get a chance to run," he told her. He led her downstairs to the living room where there were more police officers poking about. They knocked the Christmas tree down and the ornaments lay broken on the floor.

Hand in hand with Darius, Nina walked around surveying the damage. She hurried into the award room and breathed a sigh of relief. They hadn't gone in there and everything was as she left them. The living room suffered the most damage. It occurred to Nina that since they hadn't known the layout of the house they couldn't very well know where to strike. Had they gone into the room they would have struck gold. All of her awards and some of her fathers were in there.

The police questioned her. She confirmed that nothing was missing other than the broken window and shattered tree. She answered all she could and then they informed her that of the two men they caught in the house, one of them was the one who snatched her aunt's purse. He must've seen the report on television and realized that he stumbled onto a gold mine, one police officer surmised. They even brought the purse with them. The police told Nina that they needed to hold on to it until after they booked the suspects. She'd be able to pick it up the following day.

The police thought to have someone board the window up and he was just finishing when the police were leaving. Darius closed the door behind the police officers and turned to face Nina who was shaking again. He took her hand, led her to the kitchen, and made her a cup of tea. He asked her if she was a diabetic and Nina admitted to suffering from low blood sugar sometimes.

"Have you eaten anything before I took you to the hospital?"

"No but then how could I eat when all I could think about was my aunt? When we got back here, I was too tired to eat. I went to sleep after I spoke with you." Nina replied.

"Do you test your blood sugar at all? Do you know how dangerous it is to go around like that? You have to eat something. Make yourself a sandwich and if you have soda drink it. With the front window broken, I don't feel comfortable having you stay here. Gather whatever you need for a few days and we'll go to my house." Darius said. He then escorted the men who had stayed behind to board up the window out of the house. Then he went upstairs to check and lock the windows.

Nina didn't even have the strength to argue. She was sweating and shaking. She obediently made the sandwich and sat down to eat it along with some orange juice. She thought she could bring her blood sugar to an acceptable level when she drank the juice earlier but it hadn't been enough it seemed. Darius was upset with her; she didn't know how to deal with that.

Darius returned with the case she packed for her aunt and asked her if she was feeling up to packing a bag for herself. Nina nodded and stood up. She wasn't feeling well but she wasn't about to give Darius any cause to be further annoyed with her.

Upstairs she quickly pulled out a small traveling case and packed for a few days. She took a deep breath and walked down the stairs to Darius. He was standing at the foot of the stairs talking on his cell phone. From what Nina could hear, he was trying to be very convincing.

"Thank you Sister, we'll meet you at the house," he said then hung up.

"Are you sure you have everything you need?" he asked her in a much calmer tone.

"Yes. I'd like to leave now, there are reporters outside again and I don't really want to make a statement at this time." She spied them from her window upstairs.

"I'll take care of them. Let's go," Darius said in an authoritative voice.

He opened the door and immediately bulbs were flashing in their faces. He held up a hand and spoke clearly. "Miss Bennett has had a really trying evening and would appreciate the chance to get some rest. As you know, the house was broken into and with her safety an issue, she will be staying elsewhere. Thank you for your understanding." Darius pushed Nina through the crowd and into his car.

"Miss Bennett was there any damage?" One reporter asked as Nina got into the car.

Nina looked at him and nodded. "Yes there was and now if you'll excuse me I need to get some rest."

Nina closed the car door and buckled herself in. She closed her eyes and wished she had thought to get her shades. She had a headache and felt sick to her stomach. "Darius could we leave now, I feel sick."

Darius didn't hesitate; he took in her pale features and her heavy breathing as proof that she wasn't feeling well and they took off.

When they got to his house, Darius looked around and was satisfied that no one followed them. He helped Nina out of the car and into the house then he went back for her bags. In the foyer, Sister Rachel and Jennifer were there waiting for them. Jennifer helped Nina with her coat while her mother and Darius took Nina's bags upstairs.

"Girl I wouldn't want to be in your shoes not for one minute. We saw you on TV earlier that's how we found out that Sister Elaine was in the hospital," she said.

Nina looked at Jennifer and tried to smile but the bile rising up her throat negated that. "Jen help me to the bathroom, I'm going to be sick." Nina said in a weak voice.

Jennifer quickly helped her to the bath off the foyer. She held Nina's hair out of her face while she was being sick and then helped Nina clean up. When they came out of the bathroom, Sister Rachel took over.

"You poor thing, come sit down while I make you something to eat."

Before Nina could take another step, her vision blurred and she blacked out. Darius caught her before she could hit the floor. With Sister Rachel's help, they laid her on the sofa in the living room. Jennifer got a wet cloth for Nina's head and tried not to panic. A few minutes later, Nina came to feeling extremely embarrassed.

"I don't suppose we could all pretend that this didn't happen huh?" She looked from Darius' stern face to the two women who watched her with concern. "I bet you're all wondering how I survived by myself this long aren't you?"

"Don't fret dear we know that there are extenuating circumstances. My God you've had a very bad scare." Sister Rachel said.

"We put your things in the room right off the stairs," Darius told her.

Nina tried not to look him in the eye for fear of finding disapproval in them. Because of her celebrity status, she inadvertently caused the break in at her aunt's house and now she worried that some overzealous reporter might print something about her staying here to bring Darius' wholesome reputation to ground.

"Perhaps it was a bad idea that I come here. It wouldn't be very hard for me to get a hotel room somewhere." She suggested looking into Darius' eyes for the first time since they walked into the house.

"Oh no, you can't do that we won't let you do that." Jennifer insisted looking from her mother to the pastor for confirmation.

"Could you give us a few minutes ladies?" Darius announced.

Jennifer grabbed her mother by the hand and they both left the living room.

"I brought Sister Rachel here so that our reputation wouldn't suffer. I don't see why you have a problem with staying here. Right now, I don't care to have you out of my sight. I am very afraid for you." Darius admitted in a low voice.

Watching him Nina could understand how all this looked to him. Ministering to families going through crisis, Darius was strong, but this was much more personal for him. She could understand his worry.

"I know you're afraid for me Darius but I'm more concerned for you and my aunt than I am for my own safety. Look what happened with that person who snatched Aunt Elaine's purse. As soon as he realized our relationship, he figured he could score big and break into her house. I'm afraid that something might happen to you too. I figure that if I go to a hotel, things will calm down for her and you. I wasn't even thinking about what the church folk will say or not say if I spend the night here," Nina said praying that there wasn't a bolt of lightning with her name on it for her half-truth.

Darius walked to the entryway and he called the women back in and they brought a tray of sandwiches. It was five am and no one was sleepy.

Nina wanted to keep the peace so she took a sandwich and nibbled at it. She wasn't hungry but common sense dictated that she eat something to bring her blood glucose level back to normal. They ate in silence for a few minutes until Darius spoke once more.

"Nina wants to go to a hotel because she's afraid that something might happen to me. She also blames herself for the break-in at her aunt's house." He told them.

"Girl you can't blame yourself for that. Do you know how many of those same break-ins has occurred recently?" They snatch purses and then with the information they get from the wallets, they know exactly where to go. You really are not to blame," Jennifer assured her.

"I know that you are trying to make me feel better, and you may even be right about the break-in, but I can't help feeling responsible. My stupid face was all over the news and then those reporters were no help following me to Aunt Elaine's house. I became an easy target for them." Big fat tears streamed down Nina's face, which she wiped away angrily.

"Look it is late and you are in no shape to go anywhere. Why don't you spend the night and then in the morning, you can rethink the situation? Jennifer drove me here and I for one won't be happy if it was for nothing," Sister Rachel said.

Nina stood up. "I'm sorry. I feel blessed to have friends like you. Sister Rachel I apologize for not being more appreciative of what you're doing for me and Jen I know that you'd rather be in bed than staying up to hold my hand.

You are right; it is late and I guess we should all get some rest and perhaps in the morning things will look better." Nina then crossed the few feet between herself and Darius. She threw her arms around him and hugged him close.

"I'm sorry. Thank you for being there for me," she murmured into the crook of his neck.

Darius' arms tightened around her. "Why don't you go upstairs and get some rest. Sister Rachel is going to stay with you while I make sure Jennifer gets back home safely." He released her then and beckoned to Jen.

"I'll see you later Mom, get some rest Nina," Jen called out as she followed the pastor out of the house.

Nina followed Sister Rachel up to the bedroom assigned to her. She entered it and found it to be the same room she mistook for Darius' bedroom that other evening. There was a bed in it and this time, made comfortably for her. These walls were a stark white with yellow trimming. The curtains were yellow and white stripes, the carpet a vile butternut yellow, but as rooms go, it was pleasant enough to sleep in.

"I can't thank you enough for going out of your way like this for me. As you can see I am not very good at receiving care," Nina began.

"Oh you stop it right now. You are part of the Christ Tabernacle family now and we take care of our own. Get in bed before Darius gets back or he'll be mad at both of us instead of just you. That man loves you and he needs to protect you, so let him," said Sister Rachel.

Nina fluffed the pillow and smiled at the woman standing at the foot of the bed. They had an understanding between them. Under the gruff manner she sported, Sister Rachel was kind. Her aunt had a very good and caring friend in Sister Rachel.

Darius returned and knocked discreetly on the door before entering. He looked tired and Nina felt a pang of guilt once again. It was her fault that he hadn't gotten any rest, she knew he had to leave for work in few hours.

Rachel left the room telling the pastor that she was going to her room and would see them both later.

"Are you feeling better?" he asked as he came to stand beside the bed.

"Much. You look tired. Are you going to be able to go to work later?"

"I've already called in only to find that I had the day off anyway. I forgot that I had it off." Darius sat down on the edge of the bed.

"In that case, you should sleep in today. As a matter of fact, have a fuzzy day." Nina suggested.

"What's a fuzzy day?" Darius asked with a smile on his face.

"It is a day you spend in your pajamas. You stay in bed the whole day and watch movies," Nina explained.

"I'll tell you what, one day after you marry me, we can have a fuzzy day."

"It's a date," Nina replied breathlessly.

Darius leaned over to capture her lips in a kiss. Nina clung to him kissing him for all she was worth. Just before it got too dangerous to kiss in bed, they came apart with a smile on both their faces. Darius stood up and walked to the door. He blew her a kiss and let himself out.

He went back downstairs to check on all the doors front and back and then he went into the kitchen for a glass of water. There he found Sister Rachel. She was sitting at the table with a cup of tea.

"Jennifer got home okay?" she asked.

"Yes she did. I asked her to call me to let me know that she was fine.

She called my cell just before I got back in. Is Nina still blaming herself for the break-in?"

"I don't know if I convinced her but she seemed less worried after our little talk. She's really a sweet child. I didn't expect that of her, her father did well raising her."

"She's got you hooked too I see. Her innocence makes you want to protect her. You and Jennifer were ready to cradle her in your arms. I'm in love with her you know." Darius admitted after a hesitant pause.

"She loves you too. I didn't trust her at first and she knew I didn't but she kept on staying sweet and that's what won me over. She worries that her being famous is going to bring you down. She needs to understand that no powers on Earth can do that." Sister Rachel stood up, rinsed out her cup, and placed it in the drainer. She wished him a good night and left him sitting at the table.

"*Father, watch over us tonight and send your healing touch to Sister Elaine who lies in a hospital bed. Send your angels to guard her house and protect it from further vandalism, in Jesus' name I pray, Amen.*" Darius prayed silently then he climbed the stairs up to bed. For the first time since receiving the bear for Christmas, Darius willingly reached out to hug it close.

Eight in the morning came too soon for some sleeping in the pastor's house. Sister Rachel was up making sure she had breakfast ready for everyone. She had bacon frying and the coffee brewing, filling the house with delicious aromas. Darius was the last to get up and he rushed to shower and to get dressed. He knew Nina promised to spend the day at her aunt's bedside and she was probably anxious to get going.

When he finally went downstairs, it was to find that Nina had already left the house. She informed Sister Rachel that he was going to have a fuzzy day.

Darius tried to stay calm as he questioned his housekeeper on how Nina was able to leave the house since his car was still in the driveway.

"She had this scary looking gentleman pick her up. She asked me to inform you that she was going to the hospital and that you shouldn't worry about her." Sister Rachel conveyed.

Darius looked extremely angry. Worry and anger warred within him, finally, worry won and he calmed down long enough to eat his breakfast and call Nina's cell phone. He hung up after a man answered the phone. Confused and curious as to who answered Nina's phone, Darius quickly made his morning calls and then informed Sister Rachel that he was going to the hospital as well.

As he drove Darius tried to calm down, he was angry again. He was afraid at the same time as well because he was convinced that Nina because she was famous had become a target of some sort. When he got to the hospital, Darius parked quickly and entered the building. He ignored the elevators to take the stairs instead.

Sister Elaine's room was on the sixth floor and after two flights; Darius decided to take it easy and took the elevator the rest of the way. He didn't want to appear winded when he reached Sister Elaine's room. He didn't want Nina to see how anxious he was.

Darius entered Sister Elaine's room cautiously. Sister Elaine was sitting up in bed and Nina was sitting beside her. As soon as he was inside the threshold, he spotted him. Darius stopped to stare at the man. He stood up and Darius fought to stand his ground. The man was huge.

"Oh Darius you're here! This is Theo, Richard sent him to me last night but we had already left Aunt Elaine's house. So this morning he called me then we came here." Nina explained quickly.

Theo was six feet ten inches of solid muscle. He was a clean-shaven black man with a trimmed goatee. He was dressed all in black and he came to stand beside Nina. He had a menacing look about him. His stance alone spoke volumes. No one was going to get to Nina but by him first. Nina touched Theo's arm gently and smiled up at the nearly seven foot tall giant beside her. "Theo, this is Darius my boyfriend, Darius this is Theo my bodyguard." Nina said quietly.

"Pleased to meet you, Pastor Fairchild," Theo said in a very surprisingly gentle tone.

"Pleased to meet you too Theo," Darius replied as he shook the man's hand.

Darius pulled his hand away quickly embarrassed by how little his hand looked in Theo's hand. Apparently, Theo already knew who he was since he addressed him as Pastor Fairchild.

"Theo, would you wait outside the door while we visit please?" Nina asked the giant.

Theo nodded and left the room. He closed the door behind him, no doubt standing guard and causing all kinds of alarms with anyone passing by.

"Sister Elaine, how are you this morning?" Darius asked ignoring Nina for a few minutes. He chatted with her aunt until he felt that he was calm enough to speak with her.

"Don't you think that Richard went a little bit overboard sending you a bodyguard?" he asked her when he could bring himself to look her way.

Nina shrugged her shoulders, "Richard means well. He was worried and thought I needed protection. He called me early this morning to let me know that he'd sent Theo for all of us."

"All of us?" Darius asked turning to face Nina fully.

"Yes all of us, you included. Last night I told you that I'd felt that I was endangering you too. You don't know the lengths some people will go to when they think money is involved. Theo is a bit much but he really is very nice. He's been with me for about as long as Richard has."

"He's worked for you before?"

"Theo traveled with me when I worked. He kept me safe," Nina, elaborated.

The look on Darius' face was grave. He didn't know what to say. To say that Theo was a bit much was an understatement. The man brought more attention to Nina than he did shielding her he thought and Darius didn't think she needed that much protection.

The purse-snatcher couldn't have foreseen that the bag he took would get him anything more than a few dollars and even if it was part of a bigger plot like it turned out to be; connecting Sister Elaine's address to Nina was coincidental. They didn't need Theo's services. How could he make her understand that without sounding as if he had a bruised ego?

"How long is he staying?" Darius asked finally.

"I think it will be until Aunt Elaine gets better. Richard thought that if there were a few shots of Theo guarding us that whoever means us harm would think twice. Then he could go back to California." Nina didn't seem overly concerned having the big man around.

"Well I certainly would think twice before I tried anything," Aunt Elaine blurted out. She was enjoying this very much. At first, she was shocked when the big man entered her room ahead of Nina. Her niece quickly assured her that Theo was a friend. While they ate breakfast, Theo kept watch at the door.

Soon someone from administration came up to see what was going on because the nurses started to complain about the big man. Nina had to explain first who he was and why he was there. The administrator come up to speak with her and to assure her that while Nina's aunt was in the hospital, he was responsible for her safety, that a bodyguard such as Theo was too intimidating for the staff.

Nina explained what happened during the night and he backed down. However, she was to keep him out of sight. They asked him to stay inside the room and that was why Darius found him there.

"Honey I don't really think Theo is necessary. Your aunt is perfectly safe here and I know that she'll be much more careful from now on. Those people who broke into the house last night hadn't known that you were there. They thought only your aunt lived there. A couple of days ago the same thing happened at another location and last night the cops got lucky and caught them."

"Could we discuss this later? I've only just gotten Aunt Elaine to calm down about what happened last night. I don't want her upset." Nina implored him. She darted anxious looks toward her aunt who was sitting up looking very interested in their conversation.

"You're too late, I'm already upset. Here I am in a hospital bed and some low life breaks into my house. What kind of damage is there Nina?" Sister Elaine asked.

"Oh Auntie there wasn't that much damage. The police arrived much too soon for them to take anything. The front window is broken and they knocked the Christmas tree down but everything else is fine. As a matter of fact, I have to meet with someone to fix it this afternoon." Nina assured her.

"I was there Sister Elaine and Nina is right. The police got there before they could do any damage. I was going to suggest that you get a security system installed to prevent anything like that from ever happening again," he told Nina.

"That's a good idea. Nina did you get a chance to call my job yet?" Sister Elaine asked. She was looking calm again.

"I called to speak with your supervisor this morning. He saw the news last night and insisted that you needn't worry. You are to call him when you get out of the hospital," Nina replied.

"Praise the Lord!" her aunt exclaimed. "That man is getting really mellow in his old age. He's let people go just for calling in. I tell you the Lord is watching out for me."

"Now you can stop worrying and just concentrate on getting better. I've brought you your clothes so when the nurse comes to help you wash later you can change into them and be more comfortable," said Nina.

"The nurse should be coming around very soon. Why don't you go on and let me get some rest before she gets here. If I didn't believe the doctor before about my broken hip, I do now. They have to move me a certain way to prevent pain and I tell you it hurts whichever way they try." Aunt Elaine told them.

Nina looked stricken as she patted her aunt's hand. "Oh Auntie I am so sorry you have to go through this. I wish there was something more that I could do for you."

Sister Elaine patted her niece's hand in return. "You've done enough already child. I really enjoyed breakfast and I am looking forward to dinner. So why don't you go see about getting the broken window fixed and then you can come back and surprise me with something good to eat?" she suggested.

"Okay, call me if you need me to come back sooner." Nina told her aunt. She stooped down to kiss her cheeks and straightened to look at Darius. "Would you like me to ride with you and have Theo follow us?"

Darius walked over to the bed, took Sister Elaine's hand, and said a small prayer. When he was done, he took Nina's arm and led her to the door.

"Sister Elaine, we'll see you later." Darius said at the door.

When they reached the elevator banks, Darius turned to Theo who was following them.

"Is it okay with you if she rides with me?" Darius asked the big man.

"I'll follow you in Nina's car then. Are you going to her aunt's house or back to yours?"

"We'll be going back to her aunt's to see about the repairs." Darius told him.

As soon as Nina buckled in, Darius took off. He kept an eye out for Nina's SUV and found that Theo was either behind them or in front of them. Darius supposed he kept changing positions to keep a better eye on them.

"Baby is there any way we can come to a mutual agreement about Theo? I mean I understand that Richard felt that you might've been in some kind of danger but once we get the security system installed, he really won't be necessary."

"Richard worries about me Darius. He feels that I have been too sheltered to be out on my own. Moving out here has been very hard for him and I think he feels even more responsible for me since my dad passed. I don't think I need Theo either but if he stays just for a few more days, then Richard will be satisfied. He's been calling me ever since Aunt Elaine got hurt. I know that he is being really good by not saying he told me so."

Darius stole a glance at Nina. She had a reserved expression on her face. He supposed that she felt protected and perhaps cared for if not loved by Richard.

"As your bodyguard, Theo is expected to be with you wherever you go. When you lived in California, did he go to church with you too?" asked Darius.

"Theo went with me after my dad got sick and couldn't make it. Usually he is with me mainly when I worked and especially if I had to go on location and such. If you are worried about him causing a stir in church on Sunday, you don't have to worry. He'll make sure that I get there and pick me up afterwards." Nina answered. She reached out to lay her hand gently on his shoulder. "I promise he won't be a nuisance and I'll send him away as soon as the house is secure, okay?"

"Do you think I'm making a big deal out of his being here?" asked Darius.

"I understand that you want to be there for me and I want you to be there for me too, but this situation is not ordinary. Please understand that I don't doubt that you can protect me either. It's just that I feel safer knowing that when I go to sleep tonight that I won't feel scared. You have a job and you can't be with me all the time." Nina told him.

She hoped that she wasn't giving too much away. She was terrified the other night when those men broke into the house. It really didn't have anything to do with her being a celebrity. She was just plain scared. Back in California, she didn't have to worry about her home being broken into because measures were in place to prevent that. She had alarms and security cameras so that if anyone had been bold enough to make it to her front door, he would have tripped all kinds of alarms.

New York was a wonderful place and its dangers were no different from those in California. Her aunt lived in her house a long time and the people in the neighborhood looked out for each other too. Because the house didn't have any alarms, she almost got hurt. Spending the night at Darius' house was fine and all, but she couldn't sleep just thinking how close she came to being hurt or worse.

Darius parked the car in the drive while Theo parked Nina's SUV in front of the house. Shortly after going in, the doorbell chimed and Theo went to answer it. The people she had scheduled to put the security system in arrived to install it. While they worked, the window people came to put the new window in.

The installed window and the security system left only the tree to redecorate and she decided to take it down instead. A repairperson was there to repair the holes the security people put in the walls, so that by the time he was done, the house looked just like it did before the break-in.

Nina busied herself preparing lunch for them and they sat down to eat. For Theo, she made sure he had a double portion. He smiled when he saw his heaping plate.

"Nina you always look out for me, thanks," he said.

"Now that we've got all the unpleasantness out of the way, you haven't told me how your family is doing," Nina replied with a smile.

"My sister is doing great. She has a little girl now and she is the apple of my eye. My son has a playmate now," said Theo.

"That's great, how is Jason doing?" Nina asked him.

"Jay is wonderful. He is in kindergarten now and that's a load off my mind. He's adjusting and loves it," replied Theo.

"That's too cool." Nina said then turned to Darius to fill him in. "Theo's a widower and he's been taking care of his son since he was just a little thing. They travel with me many times. You should see him Darius he is adorable."

"Who's with your son now?" Darius asked.

"My sister and her husband are caring for him. I tell you I miss the little guy so much," expressed Theo.

"I really think that you should go home Theo. I have the security system in place and the window is fixed. Richard didn't really have to send you. As you can see, I am fine and I have Darius to look out for me," Nina took the opportunity to say.

Darius watched Theo and held his breath. He didn't dare say anything to mess this up. Nina was being supportive of him and brave too.

Theo's eyebrows shot up. "Do you really feel safe? I mean I know that the house is secure and all but will you feel safe when you go out alone?" Theo asked.

"I was fine before the break-in and I don't think it had anything to do with me personally. There has been a similar crime reported a few weeks ago with the same set of circumstances. A woman had her purse snatched and then a few days later, her apartment was broken into so, you see it wasn't me they were after. I don't even think they connected me to my aunt," Nina explained.

"It really is not up to me Nina. You have to convince Richard that you don't need me. I'll tell him whatever you want me to but he's paying me to make sure that you are safe and you know that I take your safety very seriously."

"Don't worry about Richard I can handle him. You need to go home to your son, besides I'll be in Los Angeles in a few weeks to do a film on my parents. We'll see each other then. Is Jason still crazy about cars?" Nina asked him.

Theo nodded his head enthusiastically. "That boy has a thing about cars that is unnatural, and you don't make it easy for me when you keep buying him those remote control cars."

"You don't fool me Theo. I've seen you sit on the floor with him arranging them so that you can race each other," laughed Nina.

"Well then it is settled. You just let me know when you are leaving and I'll give you a ride to the airport." Darius added.

"Thank you sir, I really appreciate this. I am not usually away from him longer than a few days. I took this assignment because Nina and I go way back."

"So where are you staying?" Darius asked him. He felt more comfortable now knowing that the big man was leaving.

"I'm staying at the Clarion on Rockaway Boulevard. Do you know where it is?"

"Sure, it is not far from here," Darius, answered.

"I think that I'll stay just one more day and then go home. I don't know about you but I don't think I can get used to the cold," Theo informed Nina.

Nina laughed aloud. "You should have seen me when I first got here. I was bundling up something outrageous. Aunt Elaine teased me for days about it. You know it is not so bad now. I have gotten acclimated to it and it doesn't bother me anymore."

"Well more power to you. I love the warm weather and always will." Theo vowed.

"Are you a California native then?" asked Darius.

"My family is originally from Barbados. My father was a journalist and he traveled all over but he and my mom fell in love with California and stayed," he explained.

Nina got up to clear the table and quickly washed the dishes. She pulled open the freezer to see if there was anything to cook for her aunt's dinner. It looked like she might have to make a trip to the grocery store. The telephone rang and it was her aunt. She told Nina that she didn't have to bring dinner after all because Sister Rachel was bringing it.

"I'll still come to visit with you so I'll see you later," Nina told her aunt.

The men went to inspect the work done on the window and Nina joined them in the living room.

"Aunt Elaine said that I didn't have to bring her dinner because Sister Rachel was going to. I told her that I would visit with her later," Nina told them.

"Good why don't you go up and take a nap? I know that you didn't get much rest last night. I heard you tossing and turning most of the night," Darius suggested.

Nina nodded and headed up to her room. It was true that she'd had a restless night. It wasn't because she couldn't rest it was mostly because she was reliving the break-in. She didn't know how she was going to sleep in the house all alone.

She pulled down the covers and got into the bed. With the assurance that Darius and Theo were downstairs, Nina fell asleep.

CHAPTER TWELVE

Theo took a late evening flight back to Los Angeles two days later. Darius was well acquainted with him and thought that he would feel comfortable knowing that when Nina flew out there to do the film, Theo would be there to keep her safe.

Sister Elaine was doing so well that the doctor thought that she might be able to go home earlier than he had originally thought. No one was more relieved to hear that news than she was. Nina was glad as well because she was accustomed to having someone in the house with her. She had gotten over her fear and settled down. Meetings with the architect and contractors kept her busy until she left for California. They came up with a scaled model of the center she wanted to build. Nina was satisfied and was grateful that Darius was able to go see it with her. He was impressed. The other surrounding businesses scheduled a meeting once they received notification of the intent to build. Nina expressed to them that their businesses would certainly benefit from the center because their services were services that anyone using the center would enjoy because of its proximity to them.

Sister Elaine was finally home and she took a few days before going back to work. Her boss was glad to have her back and she enjoyed the notoriety she attained from the whole incident until people started asking her to introduce them to her niece.

She got a standing ovation her first time back to church and she cried. Pastor Darius made a special mention of her at the beginning of the service. Nina felt encouraged by the love her aunt received.

Late February Nina finally boarded a plane to California to do the film. While away, she called her aunt and Darius every night. The production took more than the six weeks projected but Nina was able to fly home twice during it. While she waited for her aunt to recuperate, they did a lot of the filming. She found that she missed her aunt and Darius more than was imaginable. The work was easy and she found that the director's vision brought her parents' work to life in the most becoming fashion possible. The last day of filming was bitter sweet because she came to care for the people she worked with. Richard was true to his word. He hadn't once tried to convince her to come back. He told her that he truly believed that she was happy.

Nina got a surprise when she got off the plane in New York. Darius was there to meet her. She couldn't stop crying once she saw him. He even thought to bring her car. The weather was warm and she raised her face to the sun when she stepped down from the car. Her heart swelled in her chest when she looked up to see her aunt at the front door of their home.

Nina rushed up the steps and into her aunt's open arms.

"You're finally home," cried her aunt.

"Oh Auntie I missed you so much." Nina said through fresh tears.

Darius hustled them into the house and closed the door. The neighbors were coming out of their homes to see what the fuss was. Both women were loud.

"I can't believe how wonderful this place looks. And you look great too," Nina said hugging her aunt close once again.

Darius went back to get her luggage from the trunk of the SUV and after three trips counted no less than eight pieces.

"I can't believe you have so many bags. I don't recall you taking this much with you," he stated.

Nina turned from her aunt to face Darius and replied, "Most of the clothes in it are clothes I wore in the film. I figure that if it makes it to the award shows, I can auction them off to benefit the center. Construction starts in a few days you know," she reminded him.

"Yes I know," Darius replied with a smile.

"And that means that you have a few days to rest up before you get busy again. I can't believe that the center is finally going to be a reality," Elaine commented.

"I can't believe it either and I am very proud of you. When you first came to me about the center I didn't quite believe that you'd stick around to make it a reality, but you made me feel ashamed that I had even thought that of you. Baby you are amazing." Darius told her.

"Thank you. It really wasn't that hard to bring about and I didn't do anything by myself. I believe God saw the need and He used everybody I encountered to make it a reality. Just imagine that in a few short months, the youth in this community will have a place that will be positive and supportive to them," insisted Nina.

"It still sounds like a lot of work to me. I prepared a welcome dinner for you and I know that it is a little early but I figure that you can get to bed earlier to rest up from your long trip. Why don't you go upstairs to freshen up?" Aunt Elaine suggested.

"I think I will do just that," Nina agreed. She waved at them and hurried up the stairs to her room.

It was good to be home she thought as she washed her face and changed into a black skirt and tan top. She was getting tired of hotel rooms, dressing rooms, and make-up people. It was fun but nothing beat sleeping in one's own bed or sitting at a table with loved ones.

Nina joined her family in the dining room and was surprised to see Sister Rachel and her daughter Jennifer. They got up to hug her and Nina tried hard not to cry again.

"You guys are the best friends a girl could ever ask for," Nina exclaimed.

"Girl things had gotten so boring when you left. I'm just glad that you are back," Jen said brightly.

"I'm glad too. Pastor was driving me crazy with his sighing. He pretended to be okay but we all knew that he missed you," Sister Rachel said.

"Oh gee, I missed him too and all of you. I am glad that I have people to miss me," Nina replied tearfully.

"Okay that's enough now. This is a celebration. Sit down and eat and tell us what you did out there," said Aunt Elaine. She shooed Nina to the seat beside the pastor and then everyone clasped hands. Darius said a prayer, and they began to eat.

"How was it doing the movie?" asked Jen.

"I'm really proud of it. I think it is worthy of an award. It was fun to do and I saw some of my parents' old friends. Everyone had wonderful things to say about them and I am really glad that I hadn't passed it up," Nina admitted.

"Where did you film it?" Darius asked. He couldn't stop looking at her he missed her so much.

"Mostly in Los Angeles, but we traveled to Chicago, Detroit, Louisiana, and Paris." Nina could see that they were impressed.

"It must've been exhausting going from one place to another like that, especially if you were there only to work. Didn't you get to shop in Paris?" Jen asked.

Nina swallowed a mouthful of cornbread stuffing and nodded. "Yes it was tiring but fun in a way. I did have some time to myself and I got some shopping in too. Theo was a great help." Everyone nodded because they all remembered Theo.

"Now that's what I'm talking about. If you are going to fly from place to place like that, getting to shop is the only thing to make it worthwhile. Good for you," Sister Rachel said.

A look from Elaine kept the questions to a minimum. They could all see the dark circles under her eyes. Nina was tired.

After dinner, Nina insisted that Darius help her bring her bags upstairs. Only when they had gotten all of them in her room did he understand why she was so insistent. She had gifts for all of them. Darius helped her bring them down and she presented each of them with wrapped boxes or packages.

"I prayed every time we traveled that I would get some time to shop. Shopping for you guys made me feel less lonely," she explained.

Nina watched expectantly as they opened their gifts. For her aunt she got a cookbook from Louisiana, gospel music from Detroit and a pair of boots from the windy city. Sister Rachel got a sweater from Chicago, an original recording of Mahalia Jackson from Detroit and a Cajun cookbook from Louisiana.

Jennifer opened her gifts to find a scarf from Chicago, autographed greatest hits CD by Billie Holliday, and from Louisiana Nina got her a boxed CD Jazz collection.

Darius opened his gifts and found that Nina got him a Concordance from Chicago, a gospel CD containing some of Detroit's greatest gospel pioneers. From Louisiana, she got him a tie with colorful pictures of musical instruments. From Paris, Nina got everyone bottles of perfume for the women and cologne for Darius.

Nina was so happy that they loved the gifts she got for them. Because they were close friends she had been able to guess what would appeal to them, and she had guessed correctly.

"Nina I can't wait to listen to this CD, thank you so much for everything!" Jennifer exclaimed.

"My mouth is just watering just looking through these recipes. As soon as I master them, you will be the first person I'll cook them for," promised Sister Rachel.

"Nina I know that you won't admit it but you are tired. We are leaving so you can get some rest. I'll catch up with you later. Come on Mom." Jennifer said standing up to gather their gifts.

Aunt Elaine made noises about getting the kitchen sorted out and soon only Darius and Nina were in the living room.

"Not very subtle are they?" Nina asked him.

Darius shook his head. "No they are not, but I am grateful that they are giving us some alone time," he said as he took her hand in his. "I really missed you Babe."

"Oh Darius I missed you too. I especially missed you on Sundays. I made it a point to go to church, but being recognized made it almost impossible to enjoy the services. And when I came for your birthday it was so hard to board that plane again."

Darius pulled her close for a kiss. His arms clasped her tightly to him and Nina gave in to the emotions swirling inside her. She wrapped her arms around him as well, enjoying the kiss and the rapid beating of their hearts. Darius was the first to pull away; they were getting close to the danger zone.

"Wow that was some kiss," Nina murmured softly. She laid her head on his shoulder and held his hand.

"When we get married, I don't want us to ever go away without each other," stated Darius.

Nina pulled away to see his face. "I thought we agreed that we wouldn't talk marriage again."

"We aren't. I was just saying what we aren't going to do when we are."

Nina eyed him suspiciously and shook her head. "Whatever. Doing the movie has taught me a few things I didn't know about my parents. For example, I didn't know that my mother had a miscarriage a few years after I was born. It would've been great to grow up with a sibling. It was in the newspapers but Dad never told me."

"Do you think he didn't tell you deliberately?" Darius asked her.

Nina shook her head. "Knowing dad, he probably didn't tell me because it was painful for him. It took him a long time before he could talk about mom comfortably. Although he was sad about dying and leaving me behind, he talked about being with mom again. I think he made himself believe that so he could go peacefully."

"Was your mother a Christian?" Darius wanted to know.

Nina's features scrunched up in thought, "I have memories of us together in church and I would like to think that she was. I guess I will have to wait and see."

"Babe you do know that there won't be the same types of relationships in heaven don't you? Up in heaven we are all going to be worshippers."

"I know but just in case we can recognize each other, it would be nice to spot people we know," Nina insisted.

Darius patted her on the shoulder and suggested that she should take her aunt's advice and get some rest. He left after extracting her promise.

The next few days, Nina did nothing but rest. She realized that she had been out of practice. Moving to New York changed many of her habits. She very rarely exercised anymore and getting up early to work had been outdated. Running the center just might be what she needs to keep her occupied if not trim. She gained a few pounds and Richard commented on the fit of her clothes. He was gentle about it, but Nina had felt self-conscious afterwards and started using the hotel gym most mornings before going to the set.

She promised herself that she would get back to her regimen of exercise and diet once again. Darius has been talking marriage more and more these days especially while she was away. Should she start to feel more confident about being ready for such a step, Nina thought she might want to slim down to fit her dream wedding gown. She hadn't even thought of one yet but if she did, she'd like it to be her regular size four.

The second week in May, ground was broken for the center. Nina hadn't really thought that it was newsworthy but it was. Darius and a few of the trustees from the church were there. A reporter for the community newspaper was present to interview her and to take pictures.

The weather started to warm up in earnest and Nina was glad to shed her heavy clothing. Jennifer and Brother Jonas announced their wedding date and surprised Nina by asking her to be their maid of honor. The date was set for the third weekend in July. Jennifer and her mother, Nina and her aunt went into a planning frenzy. They had two short months to have everything done. Sister Dorothea was Brother Jonas' only relative in the United States and she joined in as well.

The recreation center was coming along nicely, with the foundation and framing done. The two men who sold the property to Nina turned out to be invaluable assets to the construction company. They both became supervisors in their fields. They routinely thanked her when they saw her and she routinely invited them to services at Christ Tabernacle.

About a month later, they surprised her and showed up with their families. They kept coming until finally during one powerful service, all three of the families asked to join the church. It turned out that they were Christians attending another church and found that the Lord was truly with the pastor and the saints at Christ Tabernacle.

At Sunday brunch afterward, Aunt Elaine commented on how the Lord used Nina to bring more souls to Him.

"Auntie I didn't do anything. They were already attending services elsewhere," she argued.

"No child you heard their testimony. These people were stagnating where they were. They were just going through the motions and not progressing, much like you when you were in California. I believe that God placed you in their paths for this particular reason. Because of your kindness to them in getting them jobs, you gained their trust. And seeing that you were honest and didn't cheat them, they were open to your ministering." Elaine insisted.

"Well Praise the Lord then, I am glad He could use me this way. That's thirteen people added to the congregation. While we are on the subject, this has been on my mind for some time now. Every so often, I hear Trustee Worthington announce that the mortgage payment is short. He has to take in a special collection to make up the difference. Why?" asked Nina.

Aunt Elaine looked at her niece and shrugged. She wondered when Nina was going to notice that. Lately it's been happening a lot and she prayed about it. Nina was generous to a fault, but she hadn't known how to approach her niece.

"Well Honey if you look around you on Sundays you'd see why tithes and offerings are short. Most of our congregation are either elderly and on a fixed income, or too young to bring in anything decent, and then there are some who just don't tithe or give an offering. It's a shame that our church is lacking."

"I have noticed the congregation Aunt Elaine and I never really thought about it until Bro. Worthington started taking in those separate offerings. Darius always seems to clam up when I talk about church business. I think he feels that he shouldn't ask me to help. Perhaps I should talk with the trustees without Darius; that way I could get a straight answer. I really wouldn't mind helping with the payments. I feel that it would be a privilege for me to do so. After all, this place has become a home to me," Nina explained.

Aunt Elaine came up from her seat to hug her niece. "I am so glad that you feel that way. There's going to be a business meeting next week and I think you should attend. You are a member now and are entitled to sit in. I'll go with you so that it won't seem too obvious. I know what you mean about Darius not talking with you about the church's financial affairs. I declare that man takes on the whole load onto his shoulders."

"Good. I know that we probably will argue about it but he can't stop me from making a donation. My old church in L.A never had that problem and I guess it was because there were many influential people who attended. It was a show place and every Sunday was like a parade," Nina told her aunt. Perhaps that was why she never really felt the Lord there. There had been too much interference for Him.

The following Wednesday at bible study, the subject was about souls and where they go after death. Nina suspected that Darius chose that particular lesson with her in mind. She'd already read up on the subject and understood that when the Lord came, they would all change in the twinkling of an eye into spirit beings. As such, their old lives on Earth would be a lost memory.

She did extensive research on the subject, reading different views on what happens to people after death. So she sat and listened to Darius teach. She allowed her mind to wander after a while and started daydreaming about being his wife. She tried to imagine what their everyday life would be like and thought that it would probably be busy.

Darius always seemed to be visiting, officiating or teaching. The man hardly rested and even though he denied being tired, she knew that he was. It was a secret pet peeve of hers. When they married, she intended to insist that he rest often. It only made sense; otherwise, the congregation would end up with an overworked, burnt out shell of a man who would be of no use to anyone. She knows that he desires to pastor for a long time.

Someone tapped her on the shoulder, startling Nina back to reality. Everyone was staring at her. She was the only one still seated as everyone stood up for the final prayer. Nina quickly stood up knowing that her face and ears had turned bright red. She staunchly refused to look to the front of the church because she could feel Darius' eyes on her as well.

"Are you okay Sister Nina?" someone asked her. Nina looked up and found that it was Sister Dorothea. There was a worried expression on her face. Nina smiled brightly to quell her fears.

"I'm fine Sister Dorothea. I'm embarrassed to say that I had been daydreaming. Please excuse me," Nina murmured.

It was an exercise in futility as she tried to exit the sanctuary. Everyone seemed concerned about her. She had to give her explanation four more times before she finally made it to the parking lot. Just as she was inserting her key into the car door, she felt Darius' hands on her shoulders.

"So you were trying to leave without saying goodbye?" he asked her.

Nina turned to face him. She felt her face get warm again and knew that she would have to tell him the truth.

"You caught me," admitted Nina. Darius opened the car door and she sighed.

"Did you enjoy the lesson this evening? I put it together with you in mind." Darius clasped her hand to entwine their fingers.

"I thought it was great. I learned a lot," Nina, answered vaguely.

"So you understand that when you die, that when you awaken to the trumpet's call that you will be different?" Darius asked pressing on.

"Yes I do."

"Good. Would you like to get a coffee with me?"

Nina's hope of escaping was getting scarcer and scarcer. "I would love a cup," she acquiesced.

"I'll follow you to your aunt's house and then we can ride in my car," Darius told her and turned to go to his car, parked two cars to the left of hers.

Planning to get out of the lot and doing it were two different things. Being the pastor meant that someone was guaranteed to stop him every step of the way. It was twenty minutes before he could actually get into the driver's seat. By then Nina felt resigned to the lecture she was sure she was going to get from him.

Sure enough as soon as they had given their orders to the server at the coffee shop, Darius pounced.

"Wasn't the lesson interesting enough for you? I kept looking toward you and you weren't taking notes like you usually do nor were you even paying attention. I thought I had done a good job giving the lesson and it seemed that everyone else was getting something out of it. Where did I lose you?" Darius wanted to know.

"You didn't lose me Darius, I confess to not paying attention because I had started daydreaming. After you left the other day, I went and did my own research on the subject. So I got a little bored because I felt that I already knew what you were going to say."

"What were you daydreaming about?" asked Darius.

Nina squirmed a little and took several sips of her coffee to think of a good answer. It wasn't that she didn't want him to know that she daydreamed about them married. It was because she knew that if she confessed to it, he would continue to pursue the subject. She still thought that they haven't been seeing each other long enough. One can't possibly learn all there is to learn about a person in that time frame to make an informed decision, especially about marriage.

"It really wasn't important. I feel embarrassed that I allowed it to happen in church. If I gave you the impression that I didn't care for your lesson, I'm sorry," Nina said and hoped it derailed him from wanting to know what she was daydreaming.

Darius eyed her suspiciously, "All right keep your secrets. I wanted to tell you that I caught the trailer for your film today. I think it is going to be very interesting. I almost didn't recognize you in the wig. Your mother was a red head; that explains the green eyes. You don't see many Italians with red hair or green eyes."

"My grandfather was Italian and my grandmother was Irish. It is a weird mixture but then so were my parents. I didn't think the film was going to be released until after the private screening." Nina answered. She was grateful that Darius wasn't pressing her about daydreaming.

"Are you interested in going to see it?" he asked.

"I was going to ask you to go with me. The viewing is in two weeks."

"I'll make a note of it. Where is the viewing anyway?"

"In Los Angeles, we'd have to be gone a whole weekend. Is that possible for you or not?" Nina asked. She realized that since this outing with him will be totally for pleasure and not at all about the Lord's business, Darius might have some problem with it.

"Where would we be staying?" he asked unconcerned.

"I stayed at my house while we filmed in L.A, but we can stay at a hotel in separate rooms of course," Nina replied with a red face.

"I suppose one of my assistant ministers could preside over the services on that weekend. I can see by your expression that you thought I'd say no," he accused her.

Feeling convicted, Nina looked down at her hands. "Okay I didn't think you'd want to go, so sue me," she said agitatedly.

"Baby I love you and I'm going just to support you. Didn't you sell your house?"

"It's been on the market ever since I left. Theo's been keeping an eye on it for me while it's empty. It's still furnished so I thought why spend money paying for hotels when I can get a good night's rest at home and be comfortable." Nina explained.

"Why is the house not generating any interest, is there something wrong with it? Are you asking too much for it?" Darius wanted to know.

"The house is in mint condition and the real estate agent showing it thought that it was worth 10.5 to about 15, so I left it up to her. I think that once the film is out, the price could easily go up. I could probably ask for 20 and get it." Nina answered. She didn't seem concerned.

"Are you talking about millions?" Darius choked out.

"Yes and before you go weird on me remember that my parents were in show business and they had been famous and making money before I was born. The house is relatively small by Hollywood's elite's standards but Hollywood Hills is Hollywood Hills," explained Nina further.

"I don't recall you ever saying that you lived in Hollywood Hills. You always talked about L.A." Darius said. His eyebrow shot up in surprise.

"It doesn't matter now does it? I'm selling the house and once it is sold I was thinking of investing in real estate out here."

Darius whistled and smiled at her. "You are already on your way with building the center. You are so business minded; I look at you and see someone who should be out there throwing money around but not you, you are an old soul."

"You have my dad and Richard to thank for that. Ever since I started earning my own money, they made it their business to see that I didn't waste it like my contemporaries. Some of the young people I worked with are broke or close to it especially if they aren't working steady. The 'Where are they now' show turned me down because I didn't fit the criteria they were looking for," replied Nina.

"What were they looking for?" he asked recalling seeing at least one of those shows.

"They were looking for someone who had real tragedy in their lives like a drug problem, children out of wedlock, down on their luck and out of work. Since I was successful and still in the business, they didn't want me. I wasn't a Drew Barrymore who had that drug problem at a young age, or a Todd Bridges. There weren't any skeletons in my closet," Nina explained.

"Praise the Lord for that. Now tell me, when will it air and do I have to wear a tuxedo?" There was an excited gleam in his eyes.

Nina laughed. "It can go two ways. I for one don't think that it will generate that much interest to merit coverage, but then again I didn't think anyone would feel that my parents' story was worthy to tell either so to be on the safe side I'd wear one. I'll know something soon."

"So what were you daydreaming about?" Darius asked once again.

Nina threw her head back and sighed, "I was daydreaming about you if you must know. I was wondering about what our future would be like. You are always busy and I was trying to figure out how to get you to rest and relax," Nina told him, it was partly true.

Darius looked at her and smiled. It was a knowing smile and Nina pretended to be interested in what was in the bottom of her coffee cup. Any minute now, he is going to say something about marriage she thought.

"In this daydream of yours, are we married?" he asked, proving to Nina that she at least knew this about her man.

"We'd have to be in order for me to find ways for you to relax." Nina replied not quite answering the question.

"How would you feel about getting engaged this summer?"

Nina looked up at him through wide eyes and with her mouth parted slightly she presented a pretty picture to him.

"I thought we agreed that we weren't going to talk about marriage anymore Darius."

"This is not about marriage, it's about the promise *to* marry," he replied succinctly.

"Well I don't think I'm ready for that either Honey," Nina said.

"I'm beginning to think that you want us to date indefinitely. I want to marry and have a family. Isn't that what you want too?"

"I love you Darius and I want us to do all that in a timely fashion. Right now five months hardly seems enough time to make a commitment that serious. Believe me when I say that I am looking forward to marrying you and having a family with you, but I don't want us to make a mistake that's going to hurt your career or your standing in the community."

"So you still think that we are a mistake?"

"I never thought that. Darius I take what you do very seriously and I would feel awful if our relationship were responsible for tearing it down. I love you but I love the Lord more." Nina said. Her eyes were filling up with tears because she felt that Darius wasn't being patient enough with her.

"I love the Lord too, but baby I've been alone for a long time and I have been patient and I have waited on the Lord to provide the perfect mate for me. He sent me you. That dream you had suggested that supernatural forces had a hand in us getting together as well and yet you freak out every time I suggest that we make things permanent between us. What are you really afraid of?"

Once again, Nina looked down into her now empty coffee cup. She didn't have an answer for him. She knew that she loved Darius and she also knew that she wanted to commit to him one day, but she wasn't sure if now was the time.

"Can you take me home now please?" Nina asked in a small voice.

"We are having a discussion Catalina and I'd like to finish it." Darius said tersely.

Nina stood up. "I don't want to talk about this any longer. You can either accept it or take me home or I can call a cab," she told him. She used every ounce of Diva she had in her to convey her point.

Darius slammed some money on the table and stood up as well. He signaled the waiter and pointed to the table. He took Nina's arm and led her toward the door. Neither said a word on the drive back to Nina's house. When Darius finally parked the car in front of the house, he turned to the quiet woman sitting beside him.

"I'm giving you some time to think things over. I won't call you so I suggest you use that time to figure out what you want. I want a wife and I want children. I want you. You know what I have to offer and I hope that it is enough." Darius stated. Then he depressed the button to unlock the door for Nina to get out.

"Thank you," Nina murmured and she stepped out of the car. She never looked back as she entered the house. As she leaned on the door feeling miserable, she heard his car as he drove away.

Nina tried to be very quiet as she opened the closet to hang up her light jacket. Although it was June, the evenings were still a little cool. Her aunt hadn't called out to her so Nina supposed that she was upstairs asleep.

Nina walked up the stairs on wooden legs. When she reached the top, she knocked on her aunt's door to let her know that she was home. Her aunt murmured sleepily and Nina left it at that. Besides, she didn't want to talk with anyone. She wanted to cry.

Her bedroom was the only place where she could examine the weight crushing her heart. Darius had given her an ultimatum. She had to either agree to be engaged to him or what. Did he want to break up with her if she didn't want to accept his ring? That dream she had so long ago was haunting her now. Did God really have something to do with her and Darius getting together?

As Nina got into bed sometime later, she realized that her face was wet. She had tears streaming down her face and once she realized it, she cried freely then, feeling a pain, she couldn't describe. Was she on the verge of losing this man she loved? What was she going to do about it?

Sleep took a long time in coming and Nina alternately thought about the ultimatum Darius gave her and crying. She truly didn't know what the best thing to do was. She wished she had been the frivolous type and had had some type of experience to compare her relationship with Darius. There was something about experience. Darius had been in love and been married once before, so he felt confident in his feelings. She hadn't dated much and the one boyfriend she'd had was short lived. They hadn't progressed from the getting to know you stage when they broke up. After that, Nina had gone out with friends in groups. She hadn't felt the need for a relationship instead; she had concentrated on her career and her dad.

Just before sleep overtook her, Nina said a brief tearful prayer asking God for guidance and for God to soften Darius' heart. She loved him and didn't want to lose him.

CHAPTER THIRTEEN

During the remainder of week, Nina tried to act as if everything was fine in her world; that was until she attended the business meeting in church the following week and saw Darius. He looked so good and the sound of his voice made her heart quiver. Her own voice broke a few times when she asked questions pertaining to the financial status of the church. She asked about the mortgage and its payments. Bro. Worthington was quick to give her the answers she was looking for. The mortgage payments were sometimes more than what the church was taking in, just as she thought.

Nina was also right in assuming that Darius was putting his pay back into the coffers to make up for the deficiency. Darius who had been trying to affect nonchalance, perked up at her questions. He tried to catch her eye but Nina was not cooperating. She wouldn't look at him.

After the meeting, and with the bank information in hand, Nina and her aunt made to leave. Darius caught them in the parking lot. Nina didn't want to be rude so she rolled the window down as he approached them.

"Good evening Darius," Nina said politely when he was near.

"Good evening Nina. How are you this fine evening Sister Elaine?" Darius asked looking past Nina.

Aunt Elaine leaned forward to see his face. There was a puzzled expression on hers as she answered him. "Fine Pastor, just fine," she replied.

"That's good. Do you mind if I steal Nina for a few minutes?" he asked and didn't wait for an answer as he pulled the car door open to practically yank Nina out.

"What are you doing?" he asked her in a deceptively calm manner.

"I don't know what you mean," Nina said looking up at him.

"Woman, do not play games with me. Why were you asking the type of questions you were asking?"

"I was just curious about the reason there was problems in meeting the mortgage payments. As a member of Christ Tabernacle I am entitled to know what is going on, after all I do pay tithes," was her explanation.

"Why did you want to know the amount of the monthly payments?"

With her chin up Nina puffed up bravely. "You cannot stop me from helping with the payments Darius. It is not up to you."

"Why?" Darius asked with his eyes filled with pain and sadness.

"Because this church feeds my soul and its pastor has a special place in my heart. If it is within my power to ease his burden then I am glad to do it."

Nina walked away from him, got into her SUV, and drove off. She left him standing there knowing that it was the hardest thing she had done to date.

Elaine threw curious glances at her niece as she drove. Finally when Nina offered no explanation as to what was going on, she plunged in. "Is there a problem between you two?"

"Leave it alone Auntie." Nina replied a bit brusquely.

"If this ain't something my brother would do, girl you had better step down from that pedestal you're standing on and tell me what's going on." Aunt Elaine said and she had that no nonsense look on her face but Nina wasn't fazed.

By this time, they had arrived home and Nina parked. She got out and went over to the passenger side to help her aunt step down from the car. Once they were inside the house, she continued to ignore her aunt and went up to her room.

No sooner had she sat down at the foot of her bed did Elaine barge full of righteous indignation into her room. "Catalina Bennett you had better remember that this is my house and that I will not have you disrespect me in it. Now I asked you a question and I expect an answer. Have you and Darius broke up?"

"I'm sorry if you felt that I was disrespecting you Auntie, I would never do that. Darius and I haven't spoken in a week. We are going through a power struggle at the moment and so we aren't speaking." Nina tried to explain.

"What exactly is going on?" asked her aunt.

Nina looked up at her. "Darius and I are having a disagreement about marriage. He wants to us to marry and I think that it is too soon. We haven't even reached the six months mark yet. I feel pressured and I won't talk about it any longer." Nina stated.

"Darius wants to marry you now?" Aunt Elaine asked. Her face was full of rapture.

"Not exactly; he asked me to get engaged this summer and I told him that it was too soon. I told him that I didn't want us to make a mistake that would harm his career. Auntie I love that man with all my heart but I really think that jumping in now would be a mistake. There is still so much to learn about each other. In my opinion we haven't even scratched the surface yet," she argued.

Elaine went to sit beside Nina on the bed and took her hand.

"Sweetheart, your uncle and I were married for twenty-nine wonderful years and we were still learning things about each other. You are worried about what people will think and not about what you feel in your heart. That man loves you to distraction and I know you do too. Who cares what people think? What matters is what you two feel for each other. I for one don't think there should be a time limit put on love. Either it is there or it isn't. The other thing you have to understand is that engagements can be long too." Elaine stood up and left the room just as abruptly as she entered.

Nina launched her body to land on her back onto the soft mattress. Perhaps her aunt was right. There should be no time limit on love and perhaps she shouldn't care that people might think it was too soon for them.

Most of all, perhaps she should put her fears aside and commit to the man. Just the thought of them married made her heart race. It didn't matter if people thought they did things a little fast. Darius and she are the only important people in the whole equation. No one was going to live their life but them and no one would suffer the consequences if any but them. So why was she afraid?

Nina sat back up. She changed into a comfortable pair of sweats and a tee. She packed her overnight case, put sneakers on and left her room. She knocked on her aunt's bedroom door and waited for her aunt to call her in.

"What's the matter child?" Elaine asked. She sat up in bed to watch her niece. She noted the clothes and waited for an explanation.

"I think you made a lot of sense and I am going to speak with Darius. I wanted to let you know that I wasn't coming back tonight. I'm going to stay in his spare room after speaking with him."

"Godspeed then, I'll be praying for you both," Elaine said with a relieved smile as she reached for her dog-eared bible.

Nina walked over to her aunt to place a kiss on her cheek then left the house. The drive took twenty minutes but Nina felt that it might've been longer. She was afraid and excited at the same time. She had never done anything like this before and it was somewhat exhilarating. It had only been an hour and a half since she left him in the parking lot and knowing from experience, he may have not gotten home yet. It would be problematic if he wasn't home and it would certainly put a damper on her plans, enough for her to turn chicken and go back home.

Darius' car wasn't in the drive but it was coming straight at her. Nina eased her SUV into the parking space in front of his house and waited for him to park in the driveway.

Darius passed her car slowly as he coasted into the driveway and when he had done so, he took his time getting out of the car. Nina waited for him to go to the front door before she gathered her courage to join him. With bag in hand, she waited for him to unlock the door.

Darius looked her up and down and then did a double take when he saw the bag. His gaze went back up to her face questioningly as he stepped back to allow her entry into the house. He leaned on the door after he locked it staring at Nina.

"Well aren't you going to say something?" Nina asked breathlessly.

"No this is your show," Darius answered then he pushed away from the door. He walked away from her and into the kitchen.

Nina dropped her overnight case on the floor in the foyer and followed him.

"Would you like something to drink?" Darius asked politely.

"I'd like something hot please," Nina, told him.

"Coffee then," he suggested.

"No, I'd like some herbal tea if you have it." Her stomach was full of butterflies.

"Sure."

While he fixed the tea, Nina sat down at the small table by the open window. The cool breeze filtering through the curtain made her shiver. She watched him silently. All her bravado was gone and she didn't know what she going to say to him. She supposed she could start with an apology but she didn't feel that she owed him one.

Darius placed the steaming cup in front of Nina and took the seat across from her with a mug of his own. He took a sip and waited for Nina to say something.

"I suppose you are wondering why I'm here," she began, "I was all set to let things go as they were until Aunt Elaine talked some sense into me. She said that there shouldn't be any time limit on love. She also said that she and my uncle were married for twenty-nine years and were still learning things about each other, kind of makes what I felt foolish. You see I thought that I needed to know everything about you before I marry you, but that's dumb isn't it. It would take a lifetime to know everything about you or you about me." Nina looked down at her cup and picked it up to take a cautious sip.

"So now that you've had a revelation, you don't think I'm rushing things?"

"I still do but that's only because I have nothing to compare our relationship with. I've never had one before you and you at least have experienced one and been married. I feel that you have an unfair advantage over me. I thought that maybe tonight I'd at least get to glean something about you before we marry."

Darius stood up suddenly, something about what she said didn't sound right. "What are you planning on learning?" he asked anxiously.

Nina stood up too and went around the table to stand in front of him. Her heart was beating so fast she could hardly catch her breath.

"I know what it feels like to kiss you and I know what it feels like to have your arms around me. Tonight I want to know something more intimate. I'm asking you to do something with me that we've never done before. I want to sleep with you," Nina said simply.

"Does your aunt know what you've planned?" Darius asked in a trembling voice.

Nina smiled and closed the space between them. She threw her arms around his neck and gave him a little peck on the lips.

"Relax Baby, I just want to sleep with you, not *sleep* with you. We'll both have our clothes on and we'll just sleep. Okay?"

"No it is not okay. Nina what were you thinking as you drove here? Did you really think I'd let you come into my home and allow you to sleep in the same bed with me?" Darius wore an incredulous expression on his face.

"Yes I did, because we love and trust each other."

"Woman, why are you doing this to me?" Darius asked now with a pained expression on his face.

"Honey, we don't have to go to bed we just have to sleep together and it doesn't matter where. If the bed makes you uncomfortable, we can sleep on the couch. All I want is to fall asleep in your arms. Let me have that experience and then you can go ring shopping," Nina said trying to bargain with him.

"You are certifiable you know that don't you?" He didn't know if he was giving in or not. She appeared to be so sure of herself, he thought.

"And that's what you love about me right?" Nina asked smiling endearingly up at him.

"Yes that's what I love about you." Darius agreed giving her a little squeeze.

Nina pulled away then and headed toward the living room. As she eyed the couch, she smiled and turned to him.

"Before we go to sleep, I want us to discuss the church building's mortgage. Why are you so upset about me helping?" she asked him.

"Catalina you just can't do this. It would seem that I used you."

Nina walked aimlessly around the room, "It would seem that you've got paranoid issues as well. Darius the mortgage on *this* house is your responsibility, the one on the church building isn't. Why would it bother you so much if I helped with the mortgage?" Nina asked spreading her arms wide.

"You are my girlfriend and you are rich. As a man I can't have you paying my way." Darius admitted.

"I don't see why your ego is involved in this at all. You know that the payments aren't your responsibility alone. That's the reason the church receives tithes and offerings. It's to support the ministry, the church building and its upkeep. Besides, I only meant to ease the burden a little. To pay the whole thing would be selfish on my part. And no one need ever know what I've done."

"What do you mean by no one will know?"

"Exactly that, I go to the bank and put a payment through and only the trustees and you will know. There needn't be any announcements or acknowledgements. Then on Sundays, you just do what God put you on this Earth to do. You preach and know that there won't be any more special offerings to take in to make ends meet and you can take your pay home," said Nina.

Darius had such a surprised look on his face that Nina almost laughed. Did he really think no one realized that he wasn't taking his pay?

"How did you know?"

"Because my darling that's the kind of man you are. You will do anything to make things easy on the church even if it means you go without. I bet you and Rebecca argued over that plenty of times. That's why you have an outside job isn't it?"

"Sometimes you are scary do you know that?"

"And that's another thing you love about me isn't it?" Nina asked with a relaxed smile on her face. The crisis was over she thought.

"Now about our sleeping arrangements, what did you have in mind exactly?" Darius asked not quite convinced.

Nina looked around her. The light blue couch was deep and if she removed the pillows, it would be even deeper. The matching loveseat was deep too and if they pushed them together, it would be perfect. Nina told him her idea and he went to work pushing the furniture around.

"Perfect," said Nina when he was done. "Now all we need is some bed linen and we'll be all set for our slumber party."

"Yes and no. You see Nina you need to know one tiny little fact about me," Darius said putting up a finger, "I sleep in the nude; otherwise I won't be able to fall asleep," he said.

Nina turned red in the face and shrugged. "For tonight you will have to be clothed much like the night I spent here when my aunt's house was broken into."

"I was teasing you Babe," Darius laughed weakly, "was there anything else you wanted?"

Nina shook her head. "I'm going to change my clothes while you do the same. Then we can meet back here. Most nights I do my own bible study and I have a few questions for you." Nina told him. Then she walked out to the foyer to get her overnight case and then rushed up the stairs.

Nina returned to the living room wearing a pair of silk pajamas in pale lavender. She put her hair in a low ponytail and waited for Darius to bring the linen.

When Darius returned he was wearing a full pair of red and blue stripped pajamas, which he buttoned to the top. He was loaded down with the sheets, pillows and a comforter, which he dropped into her outstretched arms. He watched as she deftly made the couch and loveseat into a bed with the loveseat serving as the foot of the makeshift bed. It was going to be a tight fit for Darius who was taller than Nina's five foot five frame, but he was game.

She got into the makeshift bed, sitting up in it with her back supported by the back of the couch then she smiled up at him. "Come on in Darius, I won't bite."

"I'm going to plead the blood all night because you are not well Nina," Darius warned her.

"You are doing this because you love me and want to please me,

Darius. I know you are off tomorrow, so stop worrying and focus on what I'm going to ask you. I've been reading all over the Bible and the book of Revelation fascinates me. How literal should I believe the end time is going to be?" Nina asked.

They spent the next hour and a half discussing the passages in Revelation that she wasn't clear on. Darius got out of the bed to get concordances and other reading material to help her better understand the meaning behind the book. By the time, they both felt that she'd had a good grasp on the subject; Darius had removed his pajama top, as he had gotten hot. Nina and he had relaxed enough so that she was leaning against him as they were discussing the Word.

It became less awkward as they wound down to lie beside each other talking quietly. Nina eased her body to lay her head on his chest. This was nice she thought contentedly. His heartbeat was even telling her that he wasn't anxious anymore.

"Darius, thank you for allowing me this special time with you. I know that it is hard for you and I appreciate it," she murmured softly.

When he hadn't answered, Nina lifted her head from off his chest to see his face. She smiled. Darius was praying. She laid her head back down and felt his arm enclose around her. After a few minutes of silence, she realized that Darius had fallen asleep so she closed her eyes as well and soon she too was sleeping.

For Darius, calm and a sense of well-being had suddenly enveloped him and he knew that he could sleep with his woman in his arms and not succumb to anything sinful. This was love at its purest. He thanked God in his prayer for giving him a small glimpse of what married life with this woman was going to be. He knew the Holy Spirit was responsible for the peace he felt, and accepting that, Darius pulled Nina closer and slept.

They both slept so deeply that neither heard when Sister Rachel came in the following morning. The woman was puzzled as she entered the house. She recognized Nina's SUV and the pastor's car was in the drive, yet after entering the house, she couldn't find either of them. Nina wasn't in the spare bedroom upstairs and Darius wasn't in his room. She checked the office, the basement and then the kitchen.

When she entered the living room, she beheld something wonderful. The pastor and Nina were asleep in each other's arms. Sister Rachel hadn't felt that there was anything wrong with what she was looking at. They were both fully clothed and the Holy Bible was resting between them.

"I suppose I have to make breakfast for three instead of two this morning," she said loud enough to wake them.

Darius was the first to awaken and he jumped off the couch so fast, Sister Rachel was tempted to laugh but she didn't. Nina moaned and stretched before she opened her eyes. Once her eyes connected with Rachel's, she turned beet red.

"Good morning you two," she said cheerfully, enjoying their discomfort immensely.

Nina was the first to recover. "For Pete's sake Rachel, stop enjoying this so much," she said and got up slowly. She walked around the couch and stood beside Darius to clasp hands with him.

"Why shouldn't I? If I wasn't a good person, I could hold this over your heads for a long time," she said with a big smile.

"You know very well that all we did was study the Bible and go to sleep. The evidence is all around you," Nina said waving her hand toward the couch. The Bible was on the couch and several of Darius' concordances were on the floor beside the couch.

Darius took in a deep breath and spoke. "Sister Rachel I believe that you were asking about breakfast?"

Rachel sobered up. She looked him in the eye. "I wanted to know if I was cooking for three this morning."

"I want everything!" Nina exclaimed turning to face Darius. "I want strawberries with whipped cream and coffee," she said. She held both of Darius' hands smiling angelically up at him.

Darius looked down at her and held his breath for a moment. He couldn't believe how beautiful she was. Her eyes sparkled like emeralds and her cheeks were rosy. Standing in front of him smiling sweetly like that, she was breathtaking and he thanked God hard that she was his.

"I was wondering why I had this urge to buy strawberries this past week I don't usually buy them you know." Sister Rachel said. She turned and left them muttering to herself about breakfast feasts.

Darius pulled Nina close after Rachel left them. "Good morning Catalina."

"Good morning Darius, please don't kiss me I have morning breath." She warned him.

Darius kissed her closed mouthed and hugged her tightly to him. "I have had the best night's sleep and I have you to thank for it. I love you so much," he said into her hair.

"I feel wonderful Darius and I love you too." Nina admitted to him. "I'm going to brush my teeth and then help Rachel with breakfast."

Darius watched her leave and sighed. It had been a strange evening the night before and an even stranger morning thus far. Sister Rachel finding them in bed in each other's arms wasn't even embarrassing. He even enjoyed her teasing a little bit. He was confident that she wouldn't gossip about them because there just wasn't anything for gossip. He sighed once more before pushing the furniture back to their proper places again. Because he was feeling good, he gathered up the bed linen and put them away. By the time he had the living room back to rights again, he could hear the women in the kitchen. That was his cue to go up to shower.

"You know I didn't know what to think when I got here. I saw your car and his car and thought that maybe you had come to have breakfast with him. The house was quiet and when I went upstairs to let him know that I was here the bedrooms were empty. I began to pray because I wanted things to be right between you two. My heart started pounding in my chest and I was afraid that something had happened, but when I turned the corner and looked in that room and found you two sleeping, I was relieved. If you don't mind my saying so, I saw peace and tranquility in his features for the first time in a long time. You two are so right for each other." Rachel told Nina.

Nina watched the woman in awe. This was the longest conversation she had ever had with her and to hear her say such positive things to her made her eyes fill up with tears.

"Rachel I love that man so much I could burst. I think I scared him silly coming over here last night. All I wanted was a closeness we'd never shared before and I think I got it. I feel good this morning." Nina said and suddenly felt shy. She blushed and went back to rinsing the strawberries. Rachel smiled at her back.

"I've been a widow for eight years now and I still miss waking up in my Frank's arms. You don't even have to say it I see it in your eyes. It is the most wonderful feeling in the world. You are lucky to have a love like that and you should cherish it."

Darius returned to find the dining room table set for the three of them. Nina changed into a flowered sundress and she appeared to be spring personified.

Breakfast was really a festive affair. They had eggs, bacon, grits of which Nina tasted a small bit and the strawberries Rachel didn't usually buy. Recently Nina surprised Darius with a few pounds of flavored gourmet coffee and this morning they had French Vanilla.

Since Darius had the day off, he dressed casually and wondered what else Nina planned for them. Sister Rachel went about her regular duties and Nina sat at the table smiling at nothing in particular.

She turned to him suddenly fixing those beautiful green eyes at him. "I need to check on my aunt and then I want to spend the whole day with you."

"I have a few errands to run but you can tag along if you like. We'll have lunch and then see what else we can do together later." Darius replied.

"Good. I'm going to call Aunt Elaine right now and then I'm all yours."

Darius cleared his throat and thought privately that her choice of words lately, have been pregnant with connotations he didn't want to examine. He got up to go check his appointment book and compared it with his palm pilot. His morning was surprisingly light. He needed to return a long distance call to Bishop Elias Smalls of South Carolina who would be presiding over the PAW council this year. Darius suspected that they were going to ask him to preach on one of the event's services.

Darius felt that it would be an honor if the call were about his preaching. Bishop Smalls has visited Christ Tabernacle a few times to preach and Darius had always felt in awe of the anointing on the man. He witnessed twenty baptisms after one of the bishop's powerful sermons.

Darius checked his watch and found that it was almost time to make the call. After the call, he planned to visit mother Woods who had heart surgery and then he would be free.

Darius sat at his desk, had pen and notepad ready, and then picked up the telephone. He took a deep breath before he dialed the long distance number. Bishop Smalls' secretary answered and put him on hold for twenty minutes before the bishop took the call. They exchanged pleasantries for a few minutes before the bishop spoke what was on his mind.

"Now Darius I hear wonderful things are happening at Christ Tabernacle. I always knew that you would do well there. As you know, the council is convening in a few weeks. Your name came up to preach and it is my honor to inform you of it. Will you be able to make it son?"

"Bishop Smalls it would be an honor to preach at the council this year. Just let me know which service and I'll be there." Darius answered.

"It isn't that simple son. You are also required to teach a leadership seminar. Now can we count on you?" Bishop Smalls reiterated.

"Yes sir you can count on me," replied Darius, his fingers drumming silently on the desk. He couldn't explain the sense of dread he felt, but it was growing.

"There is something else too. It would be a treat if we could have Miss Bennett sing at the council as well," said the bishop.

Darius frowned and was at a loss of what to say. He felt the set up coming the minute the bishop said that there was something else. Nina brought in the crowds and that meant money. He was associated with a commodity everyone wanted. He's been fielding appearance requests from the area churches because the first thing they wanted was for him to bring her along.

"Sir," Darius began, "I cannot answer for her but I will ask."

"It would be one of the highlights of the council to have her sing son. Why don't you ask her and then get back to me sometime today; we have programs to print up and such, you know." The bishop hung up after that not giving Darius a chance to make any replies.

Darius placed the receiver back onto its cradle. If by some miraculous act, he could reach through the phone lines to throttle the man he would have. How dare he place him in such a position? He'd been upset with Nina for wanting to help pay the church building's mortgage because he'd felt that she was being used and now the bishop was asking him to do the same thing.

Bro. Worthington has suggested several times that he approach Nina for financial help but Darius resisted. He knew that Nina wouldn't feel put upon but he felt it for her.

The other night he caught only a glimpse of how much money she had and it boggled his mind. To her it was completely natural. Of course, he's come to terms with his financial status compared to hers and knew that their relationship wasn't about money, or its gain on his part. It was purely love.

He felt insulted every time someone came close to talking about her money. When he looked at her, he didn't see the famous star or her bank account. He saw the woman he was going to marry and the future mother of his children. He now understood her anguish at the tabloids' unforgiving stories about her. She complained about people not seeing her for who she was and now he understood that perfectly.

To have the bishop put Darius in this position was cruel indeed. His tone suggested that if Darius couldn't get Nina to sing at the council then his preaching gig was gone too. Was he wrong in his assumption? Darius closed his eyes and prayed. He asked forgiveness for his ill feelings towards the bishop and rebuked any more such thoughts.

Nina came looking for him and found Darius sitting at his desk wearing a disgusted look on his handsome face.

"What's that look for?" she asked him. Nina went to sit on the edge of his desk.

"I've just had a conversation with Bishop Elias Smalls. You don't know him but he and the other bishops have elected me to preach this year at one of the council's evening services."

Nina slipped off the desk to hug him. "Congratulations Darius, that's a fantastic opportunity." She didn't understand his lack of enthusiasm. "Why aren't you happy about it?"

"Well that would be because he suggested that you come as well. They want you to sing," was his reply.

Nina frowned. "Is that a bad thing?"

"It is if they are using your fame to attract the crowds. I've been trying to shield you from that sort of thing, much like when you warned me about talking with reporters. And what's worse is that they will hit you up for a hefty donation." Darius told her.

"So you don't think I should sing?" Nina asked him.

"Baby, that's entirely up to you. I feel that they are using me to get to you and using you to bring more people to the council and not to mention soliciting money from you." Darius had that disgusted look on his face again.

"What do you want me to do?" Nina asked again.

"You see it is situations like this that makes me upset. The PAW (Pentecostal Assemblies of the World) is a worthy organization and I am proud to be part of it. Then you have Christians who act so mercenary, you wonder where their loyalties lie. This man's motto is 'By Any Means Necessary.'

I truly feel that he means to use you to make this year's council a success. By success, I mean attendance and revenue. To him it won't be a gathering of Christians to exchange ideas and to fellowship. The council normally convenes in one area and usually in Upstate New York. This year it will convene simultaneously in two separate states. New York and South Carolina will be hosting them. Suddenly it has become a competition to see which will bring in more crowds and revenue," he explained.

"Honey I get it. My question to you is this, if I wasn't in the picture, do you think that they'd invite you to preach anyway?" The man was so correct that he was stiff with it she thought.

"I don't know, I guess so."

Nina smiled brilliantly at him. "Then you also have your answer. If indeed this has turned out to be a competition of sorts, they've asked you to preach because they know that you'll do a great job. They are looking to impress so they need the best out there. I don't mind singing at the council, but as far as a donation is concerned, let me be the judge of how much. They cannot make me give any more than I am willing to give. I'll make a donation because it is for a good cause, not because I want to impress anyone," Nina told him.

"Are you sure you want to do this? We will have to attend every night for the better part of a week," Darius warned her.

"You are going to California to support me and it would be retarded of me if I didn't go to support you," reasoned Nina.

Darius stood up to take her in his arms. "Did I tell you that I loved you today yet?"

Nina giggled. "I don't believe you have."

"I love you," Darius murmured softly before he kissed her.

Nina was glad she had an opportunity to witness Darius at work. He entered Mother Wood's room at the rehabilitation center where she was recuperating from her surgery, like the man of God that he was. He greeted her with a kiss on her weathered cheek then sat down on the chair next to her bed.

He then introduced Nina before getting down to business. Just before entering her room, he inquired after her progress. Mother Woods was progressing slowly considering her age. He sung a few hymns Nina barely knew and then read from the bible. When he prayed, he placed his hands over her heart, hips and finally her knees. That was why he asked about her progress at the nurses' station. Mother Woods had heart surgery, and she had had hip replacement months before as well. Mother also had bad arthritic knees that ailed her constantly.

As they drove away from the rehab center, Nina asked him about the hymns he sang. Darius told her that Mother was old and didn't know the new songs so he sang songs that she knew.

Nina felt that his capacity to minister in that manner was also part of his anointing. Every event that the pastor of Christ Tabernacle was a part of was flawless. Lately the services were so powerful that Nina was afraid to miss any of them. The church was growing rapidly with either new converts or baptisms happening practically every Sunday. Darius

190

was probably oblivious to the phenomena because he was at the center of it. As modest as he was, he would insist that it was entirely God.

The rest of the week, Nina was busy with meetings on the other projects she had going. She was working on her gospel album and wanted to work with musicians in New York. Choirmaster Jonas was instrumental in introducing her to several with whom she could work. Nina preferred to work with Christian musicians because she wanted Gods' blessing on it.

She wrote seven songs and thought she could fill the rest of the album with the less familiar hymns she heard Darius sing with Mother Woods. She went online to find the music and lyrics. She decided that she could revamp them just a little bit so that they would flow with her other songs.

Once she picked the musicians, she called her lawyer to set up contracts and such so that everyone received compensation accordingly. Her record label was eager to do business and granted her free reign. Nina decided that she would begin rehearsals after the opening of her movie and the PAW council. Preparing for the album meant resting her voice so she was not singing with the choir for a while.

Sunday morning dawned sunny and very warm. Nina decided that she wouldn't wear a suit; instead, she chose a pale green eyelet skirt with matching quarter sleeve blouse to wear. The skirt fell to just below her knees and she wore white high-heeled sandals. When she stepped out of her bedroom, she met Elaine just coming out of her own room.

"My, don't we look cool this morning," she commented cheerfully.

"I thought that I'd be prepared this time for another hot service. The Lord can do whatever He wants today. I am going to be cool and dry," Nina replied.

"Oh child I know just what you mean. Lately the Lord has been working wonders in the church, the Holy Ghost just moving all up and down the sanctuary."

"I want to get to Sunday school a little earlier today so I was thinking that we'd have a light breakfast. Is that alright with you Auntie?"

Elaine nodded, "I agree wholeheartedly, it is getting too hot to eat a heavy meal. Summer is going to be hotter than normal it seems and it is only June."

Nina quickly prepared two fruit cups, toast and tea for her aunt and coffee for herself. Before long, they were getting into the SUV and heading for the church.

CHAPTER FOURTEEN

Nina sat next to Elaine during Sunday school. This morning Darius taught the adult class and she enjoyed it immensely. She watched him struggle to hold back from preaching. Sometimes he forgets and this morning she felt his struggle. She wondered if he knew that sometimes teaching and preaching were the same things in certain circumstances.

This morning, the subject was on temperance and he was practicing it relatively well. He taught that a Godly life produced temperance. Nina thought that he was speaking directly to the new converts who attended in record numbers. It is especially important to them that they learn how God wants his children to live. How in so doing, they can overcome their old selves to put on the new. Darius also stressed that Christians should appear different from the secular world as well, which was what putting on the new was all about. He went on to point out how by giving examples. He explained that the way we speak, act in public and privately, and the ways we dress were a few.

Nina was glad he mentioned those points because she had begun to notice that quite a few of the young converts were still dressing inappropriately. It was a touchy subject and she wondered if maybe Darius would have a separate class on the subject. Perhaps she was a little strict about how people should dress when they come to church, but she felt that at the very least God's house demanded reverence. So perhaps once these new Christians learned that they were a light onto the world they left behind, that appearing different would make sense to them.

Once Sunday school was over, Nina went to greet Darius in his office and then joined her aunt in the pew. Having the body of Christ grow was wonderful except for when one's regular seat was taken and one had to smile and be gracious, ever conscious that one was in the house of the Lord.

Nina excused herself from singing with the praise team because she didn't want to tax her voice too much. Rehearsals for the album were going to be on the same night as the choir and praise team rehearsals. She was content to sing along with the rest of the congregation.

As the church building filled up, the praise team set the atmosphere for worship. Nina's ears picked up a couple of good voices in the crowd behind her. The song that the praise team was singing was a popular song from Fred Hammond so the younger set new it well. As a church grew so should its choir, she thought. She intended to inform Brother Jonas about them. Although the choir was a good size, there wasn't anything to prevent it from improving.

To begin his sermon, Darius read from John. He relayed the story of Jesus healing a man who had been sick in his body for thirty-eight years. The Bible doesn't say that the man was thirty-eight years old, but that the man was sick for that many years.

Darius further developed his sermon on the subject by pointing out that this man lay near the pool of Bethesda. At a certain time of the season, an angel would come down to this pool and trouble it. At that particular time, anyone who went into the pool received healing of whatever ailed him or her. This man lay beside the pool for a long time. He had no one to help him into the pool when the angel came to trouble the water. If he got near, he wasn't fast enough to get in and someone else beat him to it.

"Jesus was in town during that season and he knew about the man and his illness. Jesus also knew that this man was sick for a long time. He knew about this man, and God meant to send his son Jesus at that specific time to heal this man. You must understand that God had a plan.

Jesus approached the man and asked him, "Wilt thou be made whole?" In other words, do you want to a healing? The man answered describing his plight. He told Jesus that he had no one to help him into the pool when the angel came down to trouble it. Perhaps because of the nature of his illness he couldn't get to the pool fast enough. His answer to Jesus was yes.

I don't know about you but thirty-eight years is a long time to wait for a miracle. The Bible doesn't tell us how long the man waited by the pool and perhaps he came to the pool soon after he got ill nor does it tell us how the man got there, but this man knew that he could be made whole, and knowing that he held fast onto his faith that one day he would.

Jesus looked down on this man and I imagine that he looked on this man with all the compassion of our Heavenly Father. He looked at the man and commanded him to take up his bed and walk. The Bible tells us that as the man obeyed, he was healed. He took up his bed and he walked. The rest of the passage said that it was also the Sabbath. The Jews were a little bit miffed that this man was doing work on the Sabbath. Carrying his bed was work and the Law of Moses clearly stated that they do no work on the Sabbath. They asked him why he was carrying his bed and the man answered: "He that made me whole, the same said; Take up thy bed and walk."

"The Jews then asked the man to point out this Sabbath breaker and Jesus was nowhere to be found. The Bible tells us that Jesus and this man met later on in the temple. Jesus said to him, "Behold, thou art made whole, sin no more lest a worse thing come onto thee." (John 5: 1-14 KJV)

"Church of the living God I tell you today that the Bible says the man who was made whole departed. I would like to think that he went and didn't sin anymore. Now, I could say more but my message to you this morning is that the Lord wants you to know this: He knows about you and he cares for you. He may not do what you ask when you ask, but when he does it, it is always on time. You must understand that God always has a plan. You may wonder why it took so long for this man to get his miracle and the reason is that the timing was not right. Jesus had not yet been in place. You see, my dear friends there was a lot going on by that pool that day.

First, it was the Sabbath, the seventh day. The day the Jews know to be sacred. Secondly, there was a man that was waiting for his healing.

Thirdly, there were those who were lying in wait for Jesus to accuse him of breaking the law. I tell you dear friends that all at once the timing was right.

The man needed a healing on the Sabbath to glorify the Father. The Jews needed to accuse him to glorify Jesus. He told his accusers that he did nothing the Father wouldn't have done. Jesus told them to search the Scriptures because they speak of him. In other words, it was a revelation to them. Jesus revealed himself to them saying that he was the Son whom the Father had sent, the one they'd been reading about in the Scriptures. (John 5: 46 KJV)

As I read the passage further, I received a revelation myself. It is this: Jesus commanded this man to take up his bed and walk. The man obeyed and picked up his bed and he walked. That was the nature of his miracle. He couldn't pick it up before Jesus came along but after meeting the Savior, he suddenly could. Now I don't know about you but I would have gotten up and ran away as fast as I could from that bed. The bed represents the man's sin and Jesus commanded him to take it with him. That bed was his testimony, his proof that Jesus and forgiveness had come into his life. He got a healing but he could always look on the thing that had him bound and rejoice that he was whole in spite of it.

For some of us it has to be this way. You see some of us are so hardheaded that we need a reminder. So don't think that God slighted you, He is doing you a favor. Sin had you bound and now you are free. You are free to look back at what had you bound and rejoice. As long as you have that reminder, you will always remember that but for the grace of God, you could've still been messed up, sick and wretched.

Church of the living God stand up on your feet and praise God for his Grace and his mercy. Shout Halleluiah and thank him for his love!"

Nina and those who could stand did to praise God. The spirit moved and blessings flowed. The praise team got up to sing as Pastor Fairchild announced the altar call. So many went up that the rest stayed in the aisles. After the prayer, two more souls had come to the Lord and asked for baptism.

After the baptism, the pastor announced the offering. It was first Sunday and the building fund was due, that meant the mortgage. Nina tried not to feel anxious but she was anyway. A short time later, Bro Worthington and one of the other trustees asked for an additional offering to fill the difference for the mortgage. They were short six hundred dollars. Nina gave three hundred and some others came up with the rest.

By the time the building emptied, Nina gave up waiting for Darius. She went to find her aunt and left. On the drive home she vented to Elaine about the problem, the church had paying its bills.

"There are close to three hundred people sitting in the pews and more are joining every week. I still don't understand why we are having so much difficulty receiving enough to handle business?" she asked frustratingly.

"Honey I thought Darius explained the situation to you. Although the church seems packed from week to week, the people aren't actual members and they are not obligated to pay any tithes. Some give a generous offering but tithes are another thing," Elaine explained.

Many years ago, her husband had been treasurer and he explained the business side of the church to her. She could understand the frustration Nina was feeling. It didn't seem right that the house of the Lord should want for anything.

"Didn't you discuss your plan to help with Darius?"

By this time, they had arrived home and Nina was helping her out of the SUV. Nina waited until they were inside before she answered.

"Auntie, Darius and I discussed my plan to help and he wasn't happy about it, but he understands why I'm doing it. Evidently, he is very uncomfortable with my being rich," Nina told her aunt remembering how disgusted Darius was with the bishop for asking that she make an appearance at the council.

She followed her aunt up to her room and sat in the rocker her aunt had beside her bed. It occurred to Nina that her aunt might've bought that rocker with the intention of rocking her own child in it. Her aunt and uncle never had children.

Elaine changed and turned to Nina clothed in a flowered housedress.

"Child even I'm uncomfortable with your money. You are not just rich, you're filthy rich and that is intimidating to a man." Elaine wore a kind smile on her face, softening her words.

"It is not something I can help Auntie, that's just way it is." Nina rocked a few times then got up to go to her own room.

Nina undressed and because it was hot, she pulled on a mint green halter-top dress. Her arms and shoulders were bare and she could see the tan lines. Absently, she thought of getting a tan to even out the pale areas. Because she was so fair, she didn't tan very easily but she realized that just being out in the sun bronzed her skin quite nicely. She especially liked the contrast of her skin against that of Darius' skin. She decided that she would take a walk after Sunday brunch.

As she descended the stairs, Nina could hear her aunt in the kitchen. She hurried to go help but before she could get to the kitchen, she detoured to answer the door.

Darius changed out of his sweat drenched preaching garments into a short-sleeved tan Polo shirt and dark brown pants. He really was a fit looking man Nina realized. She blushed just as she thought it. Darius ignored her as he too suddenly acknowledged how beautiful she was.

"You know time doesn't stand still when you two see each other, there are some of us who are hungry and would like to eat, namely me," Elaine announced breaking the trance holding Darius and Nina.

Nina coughed and turned to her aunt. Her face was flushed crimson and she hurried into the dining room ahead of them. She could hear her aunt snicker and say something she didn't hear to Darius.

Darius sat next to Nina at the table with Elaine across from them. They clasped hands and Darius said a blessing over the food.

"That was a fine sermon this morning Darius. I know my soul was edified." Elaine said breaking the silence.

"Thank you Sister Elaine. I usually don't agonize over a sermon as I did this one. I kept trying to go into one direction, but the Lord had other plans. Most of what came out wasn't on the official sermon. Sometimes I just have to let the Lord have His way," he explained.

"And have His way He did. I don't believe that there wasn't anyone who wasn't blessed." Nina stated finally getting a hold of her emotions to join in.

"That was the whole point. If I preach and no one gets it, I believe that I preached in vain," Darius stated. He spooned some collard greens onto his plate and some onto each of the women's plates too. "Sister Elaine one of these days you are going to give me this recipe. Rachel's is tasty too but I like yours the best."

Elaine's smile got wider on her face. "I will give it to Nina after you guys get married. I do believe that a woman should be able to make her husband a fine meal every now and then."

Nina ducked her head to hide her blush. *What was wrong with her? Lately she hasn't been able to look Darius in the eye without blushing it seemed. She didn't need Elaine's teasing.*

"See that you do. So Nina, were you able to get a morning flight for us?" Darius asked suddenly turning his attention to her.

"I did and Theo is going to meet us at the airport so that I don't have to rent a car," she replied in a composed manner she didn't feel.

"Good old Theo," Darius murmured to no one in particular.

"The service won't be the same without you come Sunday morning," stated Elaine.

"Minister Aldridge is a fine evangelist and he has done a fine job in my absence before and I believe that he will this time as well," Darius told her confidently.

Nina looked to her aunt anxiously, "Do you believe that everything will crumble if Darius isn't there for one Sunday? I mean we'll be gone for only four days. Darius could probably be back in time for Monday night prayer service."

"Relax child I was only teasing. You've been so touchy lately, what with the preparations for the album and checking on the building construction; I do believe that you need a vacation," Elaine stated.

"And you say that I work too hard? Baby you are out of the house all day four out of seven days and when I went with you to the studio, I saw a whole different side of you. You work very hard and you rule that studio with an iron hand. Rehearsals haven't even started yet," he said.

"I want to put out a quality product and to do that one has to strive for perfection." Nina said in her defense. She felt that Darius was criticizing her work ethics instead of praising them.

Darius stood up to help Elaine clear the table. Nina sat where she was watching them. She could hear them laughing in the kitchen enjoying whatever joke they were telling each other.

"I'm going for a walk," she announced loud enough for them to hear.

By the time Nina went upstairs to brush her teeth and come back down again, Darius was by the door waiting for her.

"You didn't think I was going to let you go by yourself did you?" he asked as he swung the door open for them to pass through.

"No."

Darius clasped her hand as they cleared the front steps. "What's troubling you Baby?"

"Nothing, ooh I don't know. I'm just nervous I guess."

"What are you nervous about?" Darius asked giving her hand a little squeeze.

"I was thinking that perhaps we should stay at a hotel instead of my house. I've been watching the trailers for the movie and I can see Richard and his PR people all over it. I don't think it would be wise for us to be alone in the house. There'll be reporters following us everywhere and I don't want them to print something ugly about us," she replied.

"Is that what has been bothering you these past few days? You know nothing is going to happen between us out there. You really don't have to worry. Besides, it doesn't matter where we stay because we are a couple and you are a star. Those reporters are going to say what they want to say because they want to sell papers," Darius said.

"Okay. Maybe Theo can pal around with us while we are out there. Do you have a problem with that?" Nina asked looking up at him.

"Theo will be great fun," Darius said finally.

"Good then it is settled. I'll call him later."

Darius caught her to him suddenly in a hug so comforting she wanted to cry. Nina held onto him and breathed in his scent.

"I know we haven't walked a full block yet but I need to kiss you. Let's go back to the house," he whispered in her ear.

Nina nodded and when they came apart, her smile was brilliant. "I need to kiss you too," she whispered back.

They laughed when they realized that they hadn't gone very far. Still laughing, and with Nina in a better mood than she had left in, they entered the house.

Darius didn't give her a chance to close the door before he caught her lips in a needy kiss. Nina nudged him against the door as it shut behind him to kiss him back for all she was worth.

"You know when you two finally marry and Nina moves out of here, I am going to bronze the whole front foyer. I'm going to put up a plaque that immortalizes the site of your embraces," Elaine said behind them causing them to break apart suddenly.

"Sister I think that we will have a wax figure of you just where you are standing to further identify this famous site," Darius replied playfully.

Nina pulled him along behind her and as she passed her aunt, she winked at her. Elaine shook her head and continued on her way up the stairs, murmuring to herself.

When they were safely in the living room, Nina released her hold on him and sat down on the loveseat. Darius folded his long frame to sit beside her. Nina had that worried look on her face again, cluing him in to the fact that Nina had other concerns besides what the reporters might write about them.

"Okay Baby, what else is bothering you?"

Nina looked to him and smiled out of pure nervousness. "We've been seeing each other long enough to discuss anything without fear of judgment right?" Nina asked quietly.

"Of course Baby, you know that." Darius pulled her closer to his side. "What's on your mind?"

"Lately things have changed and I thought that I should let you know," Nina suddenly jumped to her feet to pace the length of the over-stuffed tan sofa across from him.

"You've had your times when it was difficult to be near me and I've been strong and talked you through them, it's been my turn for some time now and I really need you to help me. I'm afraid of what I might do once we are alone in my house, where there won't be anyone to see us."

Darius stretched out his hand to her, "Come here," he beckoned.

Nina walked slowly back to him and sat beside him once more. She couldn't look at him feeling too ashamed of what she'd just revealed to him.

Darius took Nina's hand then cupped her chin so that he may see her face. "How long have you been feeling like this?"

"Long enough to plot your seduction; I feel so ashamed." Nina confessed.

Throwing caution to the wind, Darius took his woman into his embrace.

"Baby I love you very much but I don't think it would have worked. Remember that the Holy Spirit lives in us and no matter how much temptation we encounter, the God we serve is abundantly merciful. It is natural to have those feelings but remember we have a well that we can draw from when those feelings overwhelm us. Just know that I fight those feelings too and I pray constantly for the strength to resist."

Nina smiled brilliantly at him. "I feel better but I still think that we should have Theo and his son stay at the house with us. They are great fun and I'd feel more confident."

"That's fine with me. Just out of curiosity, how were you going to seduce me anyway?" Darius asked playfully.

Nina pulled back and smiled deviously. "I can't tell you that. I think that it is something for when we are married."

Darius cleared his throat lightly and took her hand again. "Those feelings that scare you and scare me are the reasons why I think we should get engaged and set a date for marriage. We already know that we love each other and we know that we love the Lord and we are good for each other," he reasoned.

"I know that you don't feel that it is too soon for us but I do know that once the news gets out about our engagement it will cause a stir. I realize that the longer we know each other the stronger those feelings will get, but I trust you. So, go buy your ring." Nina had a sweet smile on her face and her eyes darkened a shade deeper causing Darius to lose his train of thought.

"I think I will. Would you like to tag along or do you trust me to pick out something nice?" Darius asked quickly.

"I want what you feel I deserve. Jewelry is not that important to me and you've seen my collection. It's not very big and it's very modest," said Nina.

"Baby exactly how much *are* you worth?" Darius asked with an uncomfortable expression on his face.

"Are you sure you want to know? I mean it is quite a bit. I won't ever in my lifetime be able to use it all," answered Nina.

"Tell me," Darius insisted.

"The last meeting I had with my accountant and lawyer they informed me that my net worth was one hundred and ninety-five million, not counting the money my dad left me."

It was Darius' turn to stand and pace. He just couldn't grasp it. This woman had all that money and she was content to live a regular mundane life? He wasn't a very promiscuous man, but if he had all that money, he surely would be living better.

He turned to her and tried to smile. "Catalina I love you but that is a lot of money and it makes me feel so inadequate."

Catalina jumped to her feet as well to stand in front of him. Eyes that were dark with emotion before were now flashing at him.

"Money isn't everything Darius. Look at all those who have it. They are out there everyday spending it on things they don't want or need. They are not happy and they use the money to try to buy it. I've found something that is worth more than what is in my bank account and you feel justified in saying that you feel inadequate? You are worth more to me than all the money in the world. I would gladly give it all away if I it means forever with you."

Darius hung his head in shame. Once again, he allowed Nina's financial status to shatter his confidence. He nodded to her.

"Forgive me I am just a bit awed that you don't flaunt it. I know that you don't look down on me because I don't have as much as you do. I confess that my ego sometimes gets in the way and I feel just less manly. One thing I want to ask of you before we go into an engagement. Once a year I go on vacation and the church usually pulls together a trip for me. I truly appreciate it, but this year I want to go somewhere really exotic and I want to go with you," he stated.

"Oh Darius I would love to go on vacation with you but don't you think that we should wait until we are married first?"

"Of course I meant after we marry. What I'm trying to ask is that you pay for it. What I have in mind is too costly for me."

Nina smiled and nodded at him. "Honey, where would you like to go?"

Darius took her hand and pulled her close. "The vacation I mean to have is our honeymoon. I want us to have a honeymoon we will both remember for as long as we live. Where do you want to go?" Darius asked.

Nina laid her head on his shoulder and hugged him tight. "Darius you don't play fair, you are trying to---, if I tell you, you would trap me into planning it right away. I want to marry you but not right away. I don't mind being engaged because it won't be so hard leaving you when I go on tours and such, but once we are married, it'll be harder."

Darius tilted her head back to see her face. "What tours?"

"Well I am working on an album if you recall and once it is done, I'll probably go on tour for a little while to promote it. Since it is a gospel album, it'll probably be less involved than a secular one. A couple of concerts in certain cities and then I'm done," she answered.

"We will have to discuss going on tours in detail one day soon. Now it seems to me that every time we talk about marriage you put all kinds of obstacles in its path. Why?" demanded Darius.

"I don't understand what you are talking about. Of course, I want to marry you. I was just pointing out that although I won't be doing the Hollywood actor thing, I have started something entirely different. I don't know how the gospel genre operates and how much traveling I'll be doing, but I'd rather travel as an engaged woman than a married one. I would want to be near my husband," she explained.

"Okay I'll make a deal with you. You will set a date for our wedding soon after our engagement. I'll give you a few months to get used to it, but I want us planning our wedding in the meantime. Is that a deal?"

Nina pulled away from him hating that she had done so. It's been getting increasingly difficult to be away from him. She looked at him and wanted to rush into his arms and get as close as she could, but that was scary in itself. What Darius was proposing was wonderful and she couldn't understand her hesitation.

"I knew the minute I said yes to an engagement you'd be planning a wedding. There isn't any danger of you buying a ring so soon but I bet that you already have it picked out. It probably is just a matter of rearranging your finances to get it, and knowing how tricky you are, a few months could mean that the wedding would be around the corner. I foresee you locking in a wedding date for some time next spring."

"So what is your answer?" Darius asked. He wore an eager expression on his face that told her that she was right about his plans.

"How did we get onto this subject? We were discussing my going on tour not getting married."

"What is your answer Catalina?" pushed Darius.

Nina took a few more steps away from him to think. *This was such a big step she thought, one that would be life changing for both of them. He was so eager to do it and yet she was afraid. Why was she so afraid?*

Nina closed her eyes tightly to hold back the tears she felt filling her eyes. Suddenly she knew why she was afraid, the reason she feared marrying Darius.

Somehow sensing that she was struggling Darius came to her pulling her into his embrace. "I'm sorry if you feel that I am backing you into a corner Nina, but I love you and I don't to live without you any longer. Because I love you, I'll do anything to make you happy. Stop crying and tell me why marrying me is so scary."

Nina pulled away reluctantly and wiped at her face. "Loving you and having you in my life is wonderful, but somehow in the back of my mind I've had this feeling that it could all go away and I'd be alone again. You see after my mom died, dad made sure that I was okay physically as well as mentally. I had some sessions with a counselor. They helped me to understand first that my mother's death wasn't my fault and secondly that it was okay to let people into my life even if they go away after a while.

I was afraid of letting anyone in for a long time after her death. I clung to my dad and I guess I performed with him because it was one way of keeping him near. It wasn't until I was sixteen that I was able to feel comfortable having friends and being with them without fearing that I could lose them. It just dawned on me that I've feared forever with you because it might not be. Losing my father was so hard and I don't think that I could survive losing you."

Darius pulled away to see her face. "Baby short of the rapture happening, where we'll both be going to the Lord, I won't be going anywhere. I promise you that I'll always be here for you." Darius pulled her close again.

"So you don't think I'm being neurotic?" Nina asked finally.

"No I think that you are human and that's fine with me. Now that we both understand that we are going to be together forever, will you marry me?" asked Darius.

"Yes, I'll marry you," Nina answered with a big grin on her flushed face.

"Good. Now what looks better against your skin, white or yellow gold?" asked Darius.

"Yellow. Darius tell me that you aren't going to over extend yourself to get my ring. You aren't going to mortgage your house, sell it, or borrow money to buy me a ring that you feel is worthy of my financial status. Tell me you won't do anything foolish like that." Nina stared intently into in his eyes waiting for his answer.

"I promise you that I won't be doing any of that. I may not have the kind of money you do but I do have some. I have some investments that have done nicely. I don't see why I couldn't use some of the returns to get the woman I love a ring that is worthy and expresses the love I have for her."

Nina smiled shyly at him. "In that case then, you'll want to know that I don't want anything pretentious. I don't want anything that I'll be afraid to wear when I go out alone. I also want you to make sure that whatever ring you get that you get it insured."

"Is there anything else?" Darius asked playfully.

"Yes there is, I love you." Nina stated simply.

The kiss they shared was so intense Darius pulled away to say a silent prayer for strength. He left quickly after that. He told her that he would call her later and didn't even wait for her to acknowledge that she heard him.

Nina smiled to herself as she climbed the stairs to her aunt's bedroom. She knocked and entered the room. Elaine was sitting in the rocker with a photo album in her lap. Nina rushed to her quickly and knelt on the carpet beside her. It was an album she never saw before and her eyes devoured the pictures she saw in the page her aunt held open.

"You must've been about four in this picture. I couldn't believe how much you'd grown when I saw it the first time," she said of the picture.

"Did Dad send you pictures of me all the time?" asked Nina.

Elaine nodded. "I would get an envelope full every few months. Sometimes he'd send me a tape with you singing in it. You've been singing since you were just a little thing. Your father wasn't sure he wanted you to go into show business at all. He wanted you to have a normal life. Your mother insisted that he allow you to sing if you wanted. That was why you had those lessons to perfect your talent. Your mother was very proud of you," she explained.

"That's what he meant." Nina said to herself. On his deathbed, her dad told her that she should sing.

Nina and her aunt looked through three albums that chronicled her childhood. Both aunt and niece had tears in their eyes by the time they finished. Elaine cried because she missed her brother and Nina cried because she missed her dad and because she realized that her aunt had not missed much of her childhood even though she was far away.

CHAPTER FIFTEEN

Thursday morning, Darius and Nina boarded a plane for Los Angeles, California. Darius noted the preferential treatment Nina got because she was a celebrity. He decided that he would wear his clergy collar to fly and that gave him a little edge as well as being her traveling companion.

As pre-arranged, Theo met them at LAX after their plane landed. Darius and Nina were seasoned travelers so they weren't tired. At the airport however, there were tourists who recognized Nina and if it weren't for Theo, she would've had difficulty getting away from them. Darius realized that in New York, the fans were a bit tamer than this lot.

By the time, Theo drove them to Nina's home she had relaxed and pulled off her sunglasses. Darius was looking forward to seeing who her neighbors were and tried to hide his disappointment when he couldn't see any other home nearby. Apart from being exclusive, her neighborhood was quiet and not very exciting he thought.

He couldn't believe how much land surrounded the property. The long winding drive that led up to the electronic gate and then further up to the house proper was impressive. Theo was very professional in his duties as he held the car door open for them. He then proceeded to unload the trunk while Nina led Darius to the front door.

The foyer was elegant with marble columns and flooring. The floor plan inside was circular and spacious. Nina led him through a door off to the right into a room which she informed him was once used as the family room. The furniture was black leather. Nina dropped her purse onto a chair and then took his hand once more and led him to the kitchen.

The kitchen had red tinged marble flooring and stainless steel appliances. The island was a massive structure cut in the same marble as the tiled floor. Nina opened the refrigerator to pull out a pitcher full of what appeared to be lemonade.

"Would you like a cool drink?" she asked him.

"Yes please. I thought you said the place was empty?" Darius queried.

"It is. I had Theo stock it up for our stay. We can either stay in for dinner or go out. Theo has to go pick Jason up and then he'll join us later. Would you like a tour of the house?" Nina offered as they drank the refreshing drink.

Darius nodded. He allowed Nina to take his hand once more as she showed him the other downstairs rooms. She showed him the empty room her dad once used as an office, the family room and the dining room. There was a state of the art gym in the lower level. Toward the back of the house were the sauna, Jacuzzi and pool.

Her dad built a recording studio in the lower level and Nina showed him that too. Finally, she showed him the six bedrooms upstairs three of which were ready for them. There was a connecting bathroom between the bedrooms Theo and Darius would be occupying.

"Did you have Theo stock up and make the bedrooms up for us too?" Darius asked.

Nina shook her head. "No, I had a maid service come in to air the place out and to stock up and such. Theo only had to let them in and lock up afterwards." Nina came to stand in front of him and casually threw her arms around his neck.

"What do you want to do now, rest or what?"

Darius wrapped his arms around her loosely and drew her close for a kiss.

"I think we should rest and plan dinner. I'm sure Theo wouldn't be up for going out with us and have his son along."

"Perhaps you're right. Let's go see which bedroom Theo picked out for you and then you can change. My bedroom is down the hall from you. I'll change also and meet you back here."

The first bedroom they came to had two twin beds in it and Darius surmised that Theo probably claimed it for himself and his son. The next one was obviously for Darius as his luggage was sitting on the floor in the middle of the room. Darius walked into the room and told her that he'd meet her downstairs as agreed.

Nina nodded and left to go to her room down the hall. She hesitated briefly by the door of her dad's old bedroom and with a deep breath, hurried into her room.

She unpacked quickly and changed into a pair of shorts and tee. Flat sandals covered her feet and she was ready to meet Darius.

Darius also unpacked and changed into a pair of tan slacks and short sleeved shirt. It was warm out but comfortable in the house. He surmised that it had central air. The house was a showplace indeed and with all the extra touches Nina and her father added over the years, he could imagine it going for the amount she quoted a few days ago.

He noted that Nina's presence changed the closer they got to California. She transformed into the star that she was just like when the press accosted them when her aunt was in the hospital. She was confident and in control. Her surroundings didn't impress her as it did him because she was accustomed to them. He recalled her saying that she and her dad lived simply and now he had to question what she thought simple was.

Out here, people catered to her and it was clear to him that she was accustomed to it. He wondered how hard the transition was for her when she first moved in with her aunt.

He wondered how hard it was for her to leave all this behind and live without all of what he saw in her house. As much as she tried to downplay her past lifestyle, Darius questioned how truly committed she was to leaving it behind. After all, she had no trouble falling into old routines and habits. Her whole demeanor changed and she got and expected preferential treatment as soon as they touched ground. Once they were married, was she going to want to live a pampered life? That was something he planned to discuss with her.

Darius left his bedroom, which really was a small suite. He had oak, queen sized bedroom furniture and a very comfortable sitting room. The bathroom that connected Theo's room with his was spacious. It had a Jacuzzi bathtub and a shower stall on the other end. His and hers sinks were of deep blue enamel. The light blue shag carpet on the floor matched the blue and white tiled walls.

Nina came to meet him at the foot of the winding stairs. She was smiling and held her hand out to him.

"You look cool. Come on let's go see what's in the freezer." She grabbed his hand and pulled him along.

The fully stocked kitchen had everything they could possibly want. He asked her what she intended to do with what they didn't use. Nina told him that she was donating the food to a women's shelter in Los Angeles. She already arranged for someone to come pick it up.

The freezer held gourmet meats that were individually packaged and pre- cooked. They really didn't have to cook anything. Whole dinners were already prepared for them and it looked like they had more than enough for the duration of their stay. Nina suggested they wait for Theo to decide on dinner. Since it was only a little past five in the afternoon, she further suggested they go for a walk on the grounds.

During their little walk, Nina pointed out the home of a celebrity in the distance. On their way back, her cell phone rang and it was Richard calling to inquire about her.

Richard wanted to know if she arrived and if she wanted to have dinner with his family. Nina declined dinner telling him that Darius flew out with her and they had plans for dinner. Nina hung up to take his hand again.

"It feels funny being here again." Nina admitted to him.

"What do you mean by funny?"

"Well it feels like I never left but different somehow. The house is familiar but it doesn't feel the same. I guess what I'm trying to say is that it doesn't feel like home anymore. I keep thinking that Aunt Elaine is going to show up any minute now or I'll wake up from a dream."

"Perhaps you've acclimated to New York and the life you're living there," replied Darius.

"Very soon this will all be a distant memory," Nina elaborated spreading her arms wide to encompass all to which she been accustomed.

"I've been wondering about that myself," Darius began. He stopped walking to face her. "You say that you and your father lived a simple life and I find that hard to believe. Your home is worth more money than I'll ever see in my lifetime. I cannot equate simple with a recording studio, sauna and pool in one's home. Your neighbors are superstar celebrities and you can pick up the telephone from thousands of miles away to have your home cleaned, stocked and ready for your arrival. Baby what kind of life are you expecting us to live once we are married?"

Nina took a deep breath and insisted that they continue their conversation inside the house. Darius nodded and they walked past the tennis court and around to the front door.

Nina led him to the only room she hadn't shown him. The living room was spacious as was every other room in the house. A grand piano complete with candelabra dominated one end of the room on a raised platform. The furniture was pristine beige and ultra-modern. The paintings on the walls were originals of her father and herself as a young girl. The beige Berber carpet had flecks of brown in it. There were areas of the room that were bare and she explained that those pieces were in storage. The real estate agent handling the house suggested that she leave some furniture in place to show the house.

Darius looked around him and it only reinforced his summation that Nina would have trouble leaving it all behind.

Nina sat on the love seat and patted the cushion beside her. "Sit down Darius. In the beginning of our relationship, I was the one who was afraid and doubtful. I see you looking at the house and the conversation we had the other day about how much money I had is still an issue with you. You have a very expressive face and just by watching you take all of this in, I can tell what is going through your mind," she said spreading her arms wide.

"And what do you think is going through my mind?" asked Darius as he sat down beside her.

"Well for one thing, you doubt that you can give me a life I'll be happy with. You have to understand that what you are seeing my past, not my present or my future. Baby I love you and even though I've been dragging my feet about us getting married, I am happy. My life before was full of stuff that didn't make me happy; they kept me occupied but not happy. I sang, danced and made movies but I wasn't as happy as I am now with you in my life. I am excited and looking forward to becoming your wife and partner. I think my life will become complete once I feel our child growing inside me. I will be happy cooking and cleaning for you and even spending sleepless nights with a colicky baby. Nothing I've done in the past can compare to what we will have together in the future. So stop scaring yourself. You are what I want and need in my life." Nina told him and before she could stop herself, she got up to sit in his lap straddling him. She caught his lips in a kiss that was so full of emotion Darius quickly put a stop to it, slid her off his lap and stood up.

They stood there staring at each other afraid to move. Darius knew that Nina was feeling overwhelmed. She was breathing hard and her eyes were so dark he couldn't tell what color they were. Her cheeks flushed crimson and all he could think of was how beautiful she was. Besides, he wasn't doing so well himself.

"Catalina you need a cool drink and some air. Why don't we go sit by the pool? We can finish our conversation later," suggested Darius.

Nina seemed to have come to herself to realize what happened between them. She covered her face and couldn't look at him. "Oh my goodness I did it again!" she exclaimed miserably through her fingers.

"You didn't do anything." Darius was quick to assure her as he covered the few feet between them to pull her into his embrace. "Baby you did nothing wrong."

Nina pulled her hands away to look up at him. "If I didn't do anything wrong then why did you push me away? I only wanted to kiss you, I needed to."

"It was just a little too intense that's all. It might've gotten out of hand because you were sitting my lap." Darius explained.

"You're right about us needing to get married soon. It is getting harder and harder to be proper with you," She made an impatient gesture. "If we are going to talk about this then we may as well lay it all on the table," she stated. She pulled away from him to pace the floor, trying to gather her thoughts. "I have never understood what was meant by wanting a man until recently. All those clichéd words make sense now. I want, I ache and I need. They all apply when I'm with you now. I don't know if I should enjoy feeling this way or pray for them to go away. Why is everything so complicated now?" Nina asked him in a shaky voice.

"I wish I could say that it is a phase or that it will pass. I certainly hope that we feel this way the entire length of our life together but for now that's just the way it is. However, I can say that it will get better after we are married because there won't be any restrictions between us. It is natural to feel this way about the person, you love and I guess God made us man and woman for this particular reason. Without attraction and love, this feeling would be meaningless."

"That's all well and good, but what do we do about it now? How do I enjoy being in your arms and not think about other stuff?" Nina asked flushing once again.

Darius smiled at her. She was so cute he thought. "When I hold you in my arms I tell myself that one day very soon I won't have to let you go and I won't have to hold back."

"I guess I can tell myself that too," Nina answered with a much-relieved smile. Darius didn't reprimand her or make feel sinful. How she loved him.

The doorbell chimed and Nina hurried to answer it even more relieved that they now had a delightful distraction in the form of Jason.

Jason endured the hug he got from Nina and the minute she let go of him, he ran ahead to the living room. He didn't stop until he got to the piano to hop onto the bench.

Nina and his dad joined him leisurely catching up on his antics. He expressed an interest in music so Theo started him on his way with a small piano at home.

"Auntie Nina, come hear me play," he urged her eagerly when his dad and Nina finally entered the living room.

"Okay, but before you wow me with your talent, I want you to say hello to someone special," she replied.

Darius stood up and for the first time Jason acknowledged him in the room.

"Jason I would like you to meet Pastor Fairchild. He and I are going to be married," Nina said liking the ring of what she said.

"Hi, can you play the piano too?" Jason asked as he stuck out his hand.

"I don't think I can play better than you can. Show us what you've got." Darius replied pleasantly. His smile widened when Nina introduced him as the man she was going to marry.

Jason who jumped off the piano bench to shake Darius' hand, hopped back on. He fingered the keys and then played 'Twinkle, twinkle little star' for them.

The adults clapped while Jason got down from off the bench to bow at the waist just like his piano teacher taught him. Nina laughed and scooped the little boy up in her arms to hug him close.

"I am impressed. You have been practicing and that means that you will get better and better. Very soon you can participate in recitals like I used to do when I was a little girl," Nina told him.

"What's a recital?" Jason asked wide-eyed.

"It's like a concert only you play the music instead of singing.

"Cool. Daddy, can I go in the pool now?" Jason asked.

"Not so fast sport. We have to have dinner first and then we can hang out at the pool. And have to ask your Aunt Nina first," Theo told the little boy.

Jason was hopping from one foot to the other in his excitement. "Auntie Nina, can I go in the pool?"

"Your dad is right honey, we have to eat first. Why don't we go see what's in the fridge?"

Jason led the way to the kitchen with his dad following close behind him. Nina and Darius brought up the rear.

"I take it he's been here before. He is a cute little thing." Darius said of Theo's son.

"After Theo's wife died, Jason traveled with us all the time. I didn't have the heart to fire Theo and get a new bodyguard so I hired a nanny to care for Jason when we traveled. Jason and the nanny would stay at the hotel while Theo accompanied me to wherever I had to be. It worked well and Jason and I became pals."

"I understand the loyalty now. It was very nice of you to do that for him. Are you his only client?"

"No. We just clicked that's all." Nina answered easily. By this time, they had reached the kitchen to find Jason and his dad setting the countertop up. Theo arranged four stools around it from somewhere because Darius couldn't remember seeing them before.

"I hope you guys don't mind sitting at the counter. Jason insisted and I didn't think to ask." Theo explained.

"Oh no, this is fine. What can I do?" Darius asked.

"You help the guys and I'll get dinner," suggested Nina.

Darius nodded and proceeded to help with the dishes and silverware, while Nina pulled three platters of crab stuffed sole, three different platters of vegetables, and wild rice from the refrigerator. While she tossed a salad, she put the fish in the oven. She asked the men to choose which vegetable they wanted and carrots won easily which she steamed.

For dessert, they had ice cream. Theo led Darius and Jason to the back of the house where the pool was while Nina cleared up in the kitchen. After loading the dishwasher, she joined them. The sun was just setting and the floodlights went on automatically as soon as it was dark enough. Jason asked about getting into the pool again and Theo led him to the changing room to suit up.

When they came back out, Jason ran headlong into the pool and for a moment Darius thought that he had gotten away from his dad until Jason who had gone straight down came back up laughing. He asked his dad to race him. It was then Darius realized that Theo had also changed into swimming trunks.

"Do you swim Darius?" Nina asked him.

"Of course I do, but I didn't think to bring a suit with me."

"No problem Dad kept different sizes in the changing room. Let's see if any of them will fit you." Nina suggested. She stood up and beckoned him to follow her to the changing room.

Darius didn't know what he was expecting, but the room had shelves with different sizes and styles of swimwear for both men and women. Nina eyed him up and down then reached into a cubby to pull out red trunks for him.

"I think these will fit you," she said handing them to him. "I'm going to change in my room. We can race Jason together."

Darius nodded and closed the door behind her to change. Once again, their conversation came to mind about the luxuries she would be leaving behind. She would no longer be able to entertain on this scale once they were married; he thought at least not if they lived on his salary and budget.

Nina thought about propriety as she chose a suit. She couldn't wear a bikini so she chose a one-piece suit in black and hoped it was good enough. She stuffed her hair into a massive swim cap and threw on the matching cover up then went down to join the men.

The three of them were playing with a beach ball that probably was Jason's in the pool. Nina approached them, untied her cover up, and then dipped a toe into the pool. Theo was the first to see her and smiled up at her.

"Come on in, we need a fourth so we can play properly."

Darius looked up and his mouth fell open. Nina was so beautiful, he thought. Black certainly did enhance her looks. He smiled a little nervously up at her. She had beautiful shapely legs, which he couldn't help notice since she had changed into shorts earlier. The next thing he noticed about her was how pale her skin was.

"Baby you need some sun," he said simply.

Nina jumped in beside him and splashed him in the face. "Maybe if you aren't so busy this summer we could go to the beach and I could get some."

"I tell her that all the time. Have you ever seen anything paler?" asked Theo.

"Just for that I'm going to get you. Jay, help me teach your dad not to sass me." Nina said. Jason was very eager to 'help' Nina try to pull his dad under water.

At the deepest end, the water reached up to Theo's shoulders so it was an exercise in futility to get even with him. Nina gave up and supervised Jason's progress to less deep water and then she joined Darius.

"Do I need to teach you a lesson too?" she asked him playfully.

"You've got great legs." Darius told her.

"Good answer." Nina giggled.

Jason showed signs of being tired and they decided to call it a night. Theo carried his son piggyback to the changing room where they showered before going up to their room.

Darius and Nina followed suit and went into the house. She smiled to herself as she showered. The evening turned out just as she hoped. Theo and Jason's presence was what both she and Darius needed to stay safe. It was a narrow escape earlier and she'd learned that Darius talked a good game but she found out that he wasn't as in control as he appeared to be. She scared him when she sat in his lap. He moved her off him so fast that she almost didn't notice the change in his body. It was an impulsive move on her part and she wasn't thinking. She vowed to be more careful being with him.

Even now, thinking about how she felt in his arms brought a blush to her face. Perhaps getting married as soon as possible wasn't such a bad idea after all. It was a sin to lust and right now, that was where she stood. She murmured a little pray then got out of the shower. With God's help, they were going to be strong and not succumb to sin.

Theo and Darius met in the living room once more. Jason was fast asleep Theo told him. They sat opposite each other talking about the only thing they had in common. Nina was special to both of them.

"Sir I want to take this opportunity to tell you how happy I am that Nina has you in her life. She doesn't think I knew how lonely she was but I did. I haven't seen her happy like this since before her father passed. His death took all her joy away. Seeing her smile again is a beautiful thing."

"Thank you Theo. I love her very much and while we are on the subject, I wanted to take her out to celebrate after the viewing. Do you know of any place that's decent that won't bankrupt me?" Darius asked the young man sitting across from him.

"As a matter of fact I do. My family is in the restaurant business, well my brother-in-law is. I think he would feel honored to host a special dinner for you two, but I must warn you that Richard and Ms. Rubinowitz have plans for after the show. Nina might not be able to get away until very late."

"How late are we talking about?"

"Those events usually last far into the night. If I'm not mistaken, the viewing will be held in a banquet room, so food will be served.

Richard gave me a schedule for the duration of your stay. The viewing is Sunday, but he has her booked to do several interviews and promotional appearances before that. Tomorrow morning she has to do a morning show. She has to be in the make-up chair by 6 am sharp. After that she's appearing in a talk show."

Darius whistled. "Does she know she's booked that heavy?"

"Who's booked heavy?" Nina asked at the door.

"You are. Did you know that Richard has you booked solid to promote the movie?" asked Darius.

"Of course I know. He emailed me the itinerary last week. And since you both know that I have to be up early you'll understand why I have to say good night," Nina said.

"Baby will I be in the way if I tag along with you in the morning?" asked Darius.

"I was hoping you'd come with me," replied Nina with a big smile.

"Good then I'll say goodnight as well," said Darius.

"My sister's house is on the way and she'll be waiting for me to drop Jay off to her, I guess I'll call it a night too." Theo pointed out.

Nina jumped out of bed almost before the alarm went off. She showered quickly and dressed in a pair of jeans and tee. She knocked on the doors as she passed them to let them know that she was up.

She went down to the kitchen to brew a pot of coffee and made some toast. She was tired but she also felt a quick thrill. She hadn't done any promotional appearances in a long time and she was excited. There was a frown on her face when Darius joined her later.

"You are either not a morning person or you are still sleepy," he told her. He placed a chaste kiss on her cheek then turned to pour himself a cup of coffee.

"Neither. I was just thinking how excited I feel to be doing this sort of thing again. I want the excitement but not the work it entails," she said.

"Baby of course you're excited. You've done a movie about your parents and now it is your job to get people excited about it too."

"Oh so I shouldn't worry that Richard might've been right all along? I mean he did warn me that I might miss it." Nina reminded Darius.

"Do you still want to marry me and have my children?"

"Of course I do, I could never change my mind about that."

"Then stop worrying about it and just enjoy it for the moment," Darius suggested.

Nina smiled brilliantly at him. "I do love you!"

"I'm afraid there isn't much time for the mushy stuff, we've got to get going," Theo said interrupting their intimate moment.

"We're ready!" Nina declared.

Theo carried his sleeping son in his arms. They filed out of the house with Darius wondering what lay ahead.

Universal Studios wasn't what he was expecting either. They didn't go to a super luxurious office suite, nor were there a buffet table laid out for them to feast. Instead, Nina and company were ushered onto a back staircase where a woman whom Darius assumed was the make-up person took hold of Nina and led her away. Someone showed him to a seat off to the right. From where he was sitting, he was able to watch the woman work on Nina.

As fascinating as it was to watch his woman transform into a beauty, Darius was bored out of his mind. He alternately watched Nina and the various workers do their jobs. Obviously they were backstage of the Los Angeles' version of a morning show. He could hear an announcer announce the show and then he heard applause.

Nina stood up and waved at him to follow her. Another person clasped her arm and led her to a dressing room where she changed. Darius waited just outside the door for her.

Then it was to a staging area where both Nina and Darius waited for her turn to go on set. Richard appeared out of nowhere to greet them. He offered to stay backstage with Darius while Nina did the interview.

Nina looked gorgeous and she held out her hand to Darius. They squeezed hands and he let her go. He watched her walk through a doorway out onto the set. The live audience clapped for a long time and Darius' heart beat hard in his chest.

He could hear the questions and the answers she gave. Richard brought him to an anteroom where they could see the show themselves. Darius watched Nina smile and be entertaining. She was humble; he thought she was going to cry when she answered questions about her father.

One of the hosts on the set asked a question that made Darius hold his breath.

"We've heard rumors of romance in your life. Is it true? Are you seeing someone in New York?"

"Yes it's true. I'm in love and it is very serious," Nina replied with a smile.

The co-host joined in eagerly. "All you guys who have been drooling over Nina these past few years are out luck. She's out of circulation now. So are you going to keep the world in the dark and not tell us who this mystery man is?"

Nina giggled. "I think I'd like to keep it private for as long as I can."

"Too late, we've got footage of you announcing it already in that incident with your aunt. Roll the tape!" the woman called out.

Nina covered her face as the tape played. It was the short comment she gave the press just before she entered her aunt's house, hours before the house was broken into. She uncovered her face to see Darius' face on screen for the world to see and hear her say that he was the man in her life.

"Wow he's hot!" the female co-host announced. The audience clapped and called out good-naturedly.

Nina was starting to feel uncomfortable. She tried to catch the woman's eyes to signal to her to stop, but she was having too much fun.

"He's a minister too. I want to go to his church," she continued.

Nina was about to say something to let the woman know that she wasn't amused when the signal for commercial break came.

During the break, Nina told them off microphone that she didn't appreciate the inappropriate jokes about her boyfriend. Both hosts promised that it wouldn't continue. Nina calmed down to plaster a smile on her face when the show went live again. She finished the interview, waved graciously once again at the audience, and then walked off stage.

Richard got to her first and she glared at him. "I hope you're happy. You gave them that footage didn't you? They didn't have to say those things Richard."

"Come on baby-girl, lighten up. They were just having a little fun. No harm done." Richard cooed at her.

Darius came to her then and took her in his arms. "It's okay baby, it wasn't too embarrassing," he assured her.

"It was so undignified. They had no respect for your collar," she complained.

"Remember that well I told you about? Draw from it and keep going. We're going to get through this okay."

"So," Richard said rubbing his hands together, "I'll see you next door in a few hours," and he turned on his heel to leave.

Darius looked after him and shook his head. "Where to now?" he asked.

"We have a few hours so we can go somewhere quiet to have breakfast, I am starving." Nina told him trying to be cheerful again.

Nina led the way outside to find Theo waiting for them. "Hey I caught the show. That was way brutal," he said.

"It sure was. Take us somewhere for breakfast. As disgusted as I am, I find that it hasn't messed with my appetite." Nina told Theo.

"I know just the place." Theo ushered them into the rented SUV and soon they were off.

He drove them to a diner. Theo informed them that his brother-in-law owned it. They were able to enjoy a full breakfast without interruption. Theo's brother-in-law was polite and after breakfast, Theo took Nina and Darius back to the kitchen to introduce them to his sisters' in-laws. They owned the diner and a West-Indian restaurant that was doing very well in Beverly Hills.

His brother-in-law was soft spoken and shy. He asked if Nina would take a picture with him for his collection of celebrities. She consented and one of the cooks took the picture.

On the road again, Nina leaned back against the seat and closed her eyes. Darius knew she was tired; even though they hadn't gone to bed late, the rest she did get wasn't sufficient. Richard booked her to do two morning talk shows and then there was a taping of the George Lopez Show later in the evening.

On Saturday, she had the morning off, but was doing a late night interview on the Tonight Show. Sunday was the lightest day for her. She had to sit through the private viewing and then attend the after party later.

Darius had to give credit where credit was due. Celebrities did work hard. They worked strange hours and endured a lot with a smile. He was certain that he could never in his weakest moment want to live like that. How Nina did this for so long was a mystery to him. Theo dropped them off at the studio once again and promised to return for them later.

Nina's make-up was touched up and she changed her outfit. They allowed Darius to wait with her and then escorted him to another room where he could sit and watch the show in comfort; that was until Richard joined him.

"She looks good out there. She's even enjoying it. Perhaps some time off was what she needed after all," commented Richard.

Darius stared at the man and shrugged. How could Richard think that? Didn't he see that Nina was acting? Nina was making every effort to appear relaxed doing this didn't he see that?

Darius turned to watch the monitor screen as Nina did her stint. Once again, she pulled the diva out to entertain the crowd.

"May I ask you a question?" Darius asked Richard.

"Shoot," Richard answered studying Darius with unblinking eyes.

"What do you see looking at her now?" Darius asked pointing to the monitor.

"I see poise and confidence. She isn't even rusty. She's enjoying herself."

"There must be something wrong with your eyes then. She is a professional doing what she must to make the movie a success. She is tired and she is enduring not enjoying." Darius told him.

"You fail to understand the nature of this business Pastor Fairchild. These people thrive on the adulation and the more the better. Nina is one of these people and she may get tired sometimes but as you can see, she bounces back."

Darius was about to disagree strongly when the hosts' next question caught his attention.

"This movie was a chance for you to flex your acting skills in a whole new direction. Your image thus far has been squeaky clean, but this movie has shown us that your range has broadened. Have you given any thoughts to doing movies with more adult situations? When can we see you doing something X-rated?"

Nina dropped her smile to look down at her folded hands in her lap. Darius could see her gathering her thoughts.

"I had a lot of fun stepping into my parent's world. I gleaned firsthand how hard it was for them to start their careers. It is true that they'd seen many unsavory things and I really couldn't tell you if they indulged or not. I quit acting because I had grown disenchanted with it. I consider myself very lucky to have had the upbringing I've had. My dad's philosophy was that drugs would ruin you in ways that you can't fix. He also taught me about self-value.

We live in a world where we don't teach our young about morality anymore. Our young people do anything and everything without fear. I am proud to tell the world that I don't drink nor smoke. Until I marry, I will remain a virgin. There isn't enough money in the world that will make me forget who I am to degrade myself on screen and call it acting. I don't call it range and knowing that as a Christian I have a greater authority to answer to, I would never allow fame and fortune to dictate how I make a living. If I seem old fashioned in my views then that's just the way it is," Nina answered quietly.

The applause following Nina's statement was deafening and surprising to the host. Apparently, he wasn't expecting anyone to agree so strongly with her views. His smile when it came was late and phony.

"Well there you have it ladies and gentlemen, the last living dinosaur. Go out and see the movie which will premiere in two weeks," he told the audience.

Nina stood up to more applause and then walked off the set. She rushed into Darius' arms as soon as she saw him. She hugged him tight and let the tears fall.

"It's over Baby. We can go home," Darius, told her stroking her hair Nina pulled away to smile up at him. She turned to Richard who stood up to greet her. There was a big smile on his face.

"Richard I won't do any more of these. He called me a dinosaur. I don't care because for once in my life what I do matters." Nina squeezed Darius' hand and smiled.

"I thought the interview went well overall. The last question was a bit much but it wasn't that bad. Did you see the standing ovation you got, it was fantastic!" Richard gushed.

"I'm tired Richard. I'll see you later tonight?"

"No, I was hoping you'd have dinner with us tonight?"

"Sure before the taping, I need some sleep." Nina replied.

"Great. Agatha will be thrilled to see you."

"I will be happy to see her too. Does she still like those pink roses?"

"Yes she does. Then it's settled, we'll see you tonight and Pastor you're invited as well," Richard said.

"Thank you." Darius said and nodded to him.

Nina clasped Darius' hand and together they left the studio. Theo met them outside for which Nina was eternally grateful. She got into the SUV and sighed heavily.

"Your announcement on is going to be major fodder for the media. The George Lopez Show is going to be the beginning of a lot of ridicule," said Theo.

"I know the jokes are going to be flying all over the place but I don't care. I think it's time the world knew where I stood. I have never really spoken out for or against anything before and this feels great. Many people out there still believe as I do and they are the ones that matter to me. I've always seen myself as a role model and I will continue to be one for as long as I am in the lime light," Nina said.

"Not to mention that the gospel album you are putting out is going to be a great success thanks to your public views." Darius pointed out.

"Hey I didn't think of that, yes this should boost my image in the religious world and I wasn't even trying. How good is God?" Nina replied.

"Very good indeed," added Darius.

Back at the house, Theo slowed down when they got to her turnoff. No more than three news vans from various stations and magazines parked outside the gate.

"What now?" Nina asked as she pulled on her sunglasses. She stepped out of the SUV before Darius or Theo could react to stop her.

Reporters flung questions at her from every direction. She fielded, as many as she could and answered the ones she thought would benefit her movie and the album. She smiled for pictures and then waved at the reporters before she got back into the SUV.

"Duck now!" she warned Darius.

She helped him put his head down and told Theo to open the gate. Theo who was up on the game quickly drove the SUV through and closed it via remote before the reporters could get back into their cars. Nina was confident that no one took pictures of Darius.

"What was that all about?" Darius asked when they were safely inside the house.

"I've figured out Richard's game plan. It clicked suddenly as soon as he told me that he wasn't going to be at the Lopez Show. He usually isn't around when he's the one who tips reporters off. As soon as I saw those reporters out there I knew that I was right," Nina clarified.

"What was the point?" Darius wanted to know.

"Do you remember what you told me about the bishop? By any means necessary is Richard's motto too," replied Nina.

"You mean this is all staged publicity? Weren't the interviews and the shows tonight and tomorrow enough?" he asked feeling confused.

Nina shook her head. "This is an independent film which means that the big studios didn't back it. The people who are responsible for the movie don't have deep pockets. The more publicity we get the better the chance the film has of making money. People are curious about me now and Richard probably told them that I was staying here," Nina explained.

"Why did you have me duck?" Darius wanted to know.

"I didn't want them to have any new pictures of you. I've just announced to the world that I am still a virgin. The big question will be what kind of man are you that you haven't done me yet?" Nina replied agitatedly.

"Oh I see," was all Darius could say.

"I don't want to interfere with your stimulating conversation but I suggest that you guys eat something and get some rest. The Lopez Show taping is at 10pm and you have to stay on stage for the duration." Theo reminded them. He also told them that he was going to check on his son and would be back for them later.

Nina headed for the kitchen with Darius following behind slowly. His head was reeling from the day's activity. He felt confused by it all. He couldn't understand all the ins and outs involved. What Nina faced just to promote what she loved doing was brutal to put it lightly. Dog eat dog was truly in force here. Her own manager went behind her back to create a sensation to keep her in the public eye and she just took it in stride.

They opted for a late lunch after which Nina suggested that they relax indoors. Nina surprised Darius with a request that he come to her bedroom to talk and watch television. She told him that it was the only room in the whole house with a television set.

She changed out of the outfit she wore for the talk shows to wear her shorts again. She explained to him that Richard took care of what she wears during the interviews.

Nina's bedroom was lovely. She had a queen sized sleigh bed. There were pictures of her and her dad on the pale lavender walls. The carpet was a plush lavender pile and the white lampshades broke the lavender from one side of the bed to the other. The sitting area was a shade deeper with the biggest chaise Darius had ever seen. She had pillows of every shape and size on it. She went over to the chaise and casually brushed the pillows to the floor to sit down.

"Come sit beside me Darius. I want to snuggle and watch TV," she said picking up the remote to turn the television on.

Darius walked over and sat down. It was only two in the afternoon and he was tired too. Maybe just relaxing wasn't such a bad idea after all, he thought.

"Nina what's with all the purple?" he asked looking around the room again.

Nina, leaned against on his shoulder, sighed softly. "When I was a little girl my father read me a story from a children's bible he bought me. I don't remember much about the story except that it said that the royal colors of princes and princesses were purple. Dad used to call me his little princess back then so I asked him if I could change my room to purple. He agreed and my room has been lavender and purple ever since," she explained.

"I see. I thought it was just the whimsical side of you."

"Darius I want to apologize for whatever flak will be coming your way for the comments I made and the ones the hosts made. Apart from not feeling any satisfaction from what I was doing, it was what people said to me or about me that made me quit. The only thing I will be doing from now on is the gospel albums. I might be lured into doing a gospel film, but no more secular stuff," Nina vowed.

Darius looked down at her and found that she was half-asleep. "Hush now, go to sleep Baby." He said a quick prayer and closed his eyes as well. The television set was the only sound in the house for several hours.

Nina was the first to awaken and she was glad. She found that she liked waking up in his arms. Somehow, they wound up lying down on the huge chaise holding each other.

She tried to disengage gently so she wouldn't wake Darius but the minute she touched his arm to sit up his eyes flew open.

"Hi, I was just getting up it's almost time for us to leave," Nina told him breathlessly. She was still feeling fuzzy from being in his arms.

"I cannot wait to marry you." Darius said. It was apparent that they were feeling the same thing.

Nina got up then cleared her throat, found that she couldn't speak and practically ran into the bathroom. Nina leaned on the door taking deep breaths. Across from her, she caught her reflection in the mirror. Her cheeks were red and her eyes sparkled. She didn't have to tell him she realized. He could tell just by looking at her to know what she was feeling. Wow she thought. She shook herself and undressed quickly to shower. The directions her thoughts was leading her was too dangerous to continue.

When she came out of the shower, Darius had already gone to his room. She dressed casually in a white flared knee length skirt and a pale yellow cotton blouse. The color enhanced her own eye color causing her to smile at her reflection. She put on a pair of white high-heeled sandals and went to find Darius.

She met him downstairs in the living room; he changed also. This evening he was wearing a pair of black slacks and a white short-sleeved shirt. The sleeves seemed too small for the powerful arms bulging through them. He was holding two ties in his hands looking confused.

"Which one of these two, do you like best?" he asked her when she came to stand in front of him.

"Why do you want to wear a tie?" she asked eyeing his neck.

"We were invited to dinner at Richard's house and I want to make a good impression."

Nina reached up to unbutton the top button of his shirt and for the first time noticed that he had chest hair. She unbuttoned the second button and sighed softly as her world shifted. "I don't think you should wear a tie. The weather is nice and this look does wonders for me." Nina looked up quickly into his eyes and blushed crimson.

Lately their kisses have been different and this time it was even more so. Darius held her closer than before and she clung to him loving the closeness they shared. Darius pulled away all too soon breathing a little heavy.

"The Lord is good and his mercy endures forever," he said.

"Amen," Nina agreed and cleared her throat. "Would you like a snack before we leave?"

"No, I'm fine. I can wait to eat," he replied in a more normal voice.

"I must warn you that Richard and his family are not your typical Jewish family. They go to synagogue and all, but they do not practice their faith as strictly as they should. Agatha loves to cook and from week to week, they eat foods from different cultures. I should've thought to ask which it was this week but I forgot. I called ahead to have her favorite roses sent over so she should be in a great mood. Did I tell you that she was an artist?"

"What kind of art does she do?" Darius asked shaking his head.

"She's into erotic sculpture. She is going to give us a tour of her studio and I feel that you must prepare yourself for what she will show you."

"I am beginning to wonder about your choice of friends. I will keep that in mind and not preach at her." Darius said with a smile. He reached up to button up his shirt and winked at her. He went to stand in front of a window to put on the black tie he'd chosen to wear.

The doorbell rang and it was Theo. He was smiling and it cheered Nina up even more. The drive to Richard's house took less than an hour. Theo parked in front of a house that duly impressed Darius. The mansion was modest compared to most with only 16 rooms. The well-manicured lush and green lawn gave way to a tennis court on one side. The six-car garage on the other side of the house, held what he guessed was outrageously expensive cars.

Agatha herself let them in and Darius stood back to watch as Nina and their host hugged and kissed.

"Cat darling it has been too long. I worried that you weren't eating but you look great. I guess New York does agree with you," Agatha gushed. She turned to face Darius. "And who is this handsome young man?"

"Aggie this is Pastor Darius Fairchild. If you don't already know, he is the love of my life." Nina replied proudly.

"You are blessed I can tell, and you have such a beautiful name. Darius Fairchild. You two should marry and have lots of babies." Agatha said between shaking Darius' hand to eventually hugging him.

Nina groaned and Richard laughed when he joined them having caught the end of his wife's speech.

"From what I hear maybe this time next year they will marry and have at least one child," he predicted.

"Now that you've both thoroughly embarrassed me, where is Julia?" Nina asked their hosts.

"Julia is dating now and is out on one. Maybe if you stick around you might get to see her." Agatha said. She ushered them into the dining room and pointed to where they should sit.

Richard must've schooled her Nina thought because this was a tame Agatha tonight. Dinner was a surprise itself. Agatha had done well with a Southern favorite. She made fried chicken, collard greens, and rice and beans. Darius did justice to it.

"Aggie this was the best dinner I've had outside my aunt's house in a long time. Did you plan it just for us or are you doing the Southern states now?"

"This was just for you and your adorable beau. Now that you've eaten I know that you don't have much time before going on to the show, but you must see my latest piece," Agatha said standing up.

"Well lead on then," Nina, said gesturing that Agatha should walk ahead of them.

Agatha gave them a quick tour of the house confirming the tennis court, pool and the six luxury cars in the garage. The family car was the latest SUV of the Infinity persuasion.

Lastly, they came to the back of the house where Agatha's studio was and she unlocked the door with a flare. The studio was huge and along the walls were sculptures of various sizes and skin tones of the female and male physique. Her latest piece was of a young girl semi-nude posing in front of a mirror.

"Oh Aggie this one is fantastic! She isn't offensive and all her innocence is right there in that one pose." Nina told her.

"Yes that's it Cat, you hit it right on the nose. That is exactly what I was going for," Agatha exclaimed.

"Is it ready to show yet?"

"Almost, but I am so happy that you like it. What do you think of the piece Pastor Fairchild?" asked Agatha.

Darius plastered a smile on his handsome face and very diplomatically told her that the piece was pleasing to the eye and did convey an air of innocence.

"Spoken like a true man of the cloth," Agatha declared.

Then it was time for them to leave. Agatha handed Nina a take-away plate for Theo and waved goodbye at the door.

Theo was pulling up when they reached the curb. His smile was huge when he saw the plate. "Good old Aggie," said Theo.

"You know that she would never forget you. Anyway Nina the reason I'm not accompanying you tonight is because Aggie always insists that I be home when Julia goes out on a date," Richard said as he came around to open the car door for them.

"As a dad I think it is good practice just in case she's in trouble.

When will the show air?" Nina asked him as she got into the back seat with Darius.

"Sometime next week I believe but you can ask George, he can tell you," he replied.

"I will. Well thanks for dinner and I'll see you tomorrow okay?"

"Goodnight and have fun," Richard said as he stepped back from the moving car.

It was nine thirty and Theo had to drive a little over the speed limit to get them there safely and on time.

Nina endured the usual prep before they announced her to go on stage. Like the morning shows, the audience went wild when she came on. From the monitor, Darius could see the big smile she gave the audience and the chaste hug and kiss she gave her host.

The show lasted an hour and forty-five minutes. Nina closed out the show singing a song from the movie that her mother made famous. When she finally got off stage, Nina was still smiling. The show was a success and she had fun.

The following day, Nina slept in. She wanted to surprise Darius by taking him sightseeing. They rushed to leave because she still had the taping to do later. Nina had Theo bring the car so that she could drive Darius around.

They did all the touristy things she could do with him until she was recognized. Then she took him to the exclusive areas where she wouldn't be bothered as the other people frequenting the places were also celebrities.

Darius had fun spotting celebrities as they shopped. Nina bought gifts for her aunt and friends back home on Rodeo Drive's exclusive shops. Darius enjoyed the ambiance and preferential treatment Nina received. Some shops closed their doors because some big star was shopping there. Darius hadn't thought that it was true but believed it now.

They stopped for a snack and then headed back to the house. Theo came for them just an hour before Nina's final appearance. This one was an important show because Jay Leno was interviewing her and that was major. Nina wowed them and she sang again. Jay Leno was very enthusiastic about the movie as he was an avid jazz fan. He claimed to have all of her father's albums and some of her mother's as well. Nina warmed up to him after that and she laughed and interacted with the other guests as they came on. Overall, it was a great success as was the show from the previous night.

Sunday morning, Nina insisted that they go to her old church and when they got there, she asked that they not acknowledge her. However, her old pastor would not hear anything to the contrary especially when he realized that Pastor Darius Fairchild accompanied her.

Nina stood up to greet the congregation and they asked Darius to sit with the ministers on the pulpit. The service felt bland to Nina. Although she hadn't meant to compare the pastors, she did. Her old pastor was lacking in conviction that he was leading God's people. As he played up to the cameras trained on him, Nina realized that he had lost touch with God.

After service Darius and Nina made their exit as fast as they could. Neither cared to comment on the service and it was left at that. Theo picked them up and drove them back to the house. He was silent the whole ride that Nina noticed.

"Is there anything wrong Theo?" she asked her friend.

"I have something to tell you and ask you," he answered and followed them into the house.

Nina went to get them some cool drinks. She came back with a tray of lemonade and quickly served them.

"Now what's on your mind and what can we do to help you?" she asked him.

Theo fussed with his glass for a few minutes. He was ill at ease about something and he couldn't sit still. Darius smiled reassuringly at him to put him at ease.

"It's all right son, relax we are here to help you," he said quietly to the suddenly shy young man.

"Well you see it's like this, I've met someone and we have been dating for quite some time now. Our relationship is serious and I want to take it to the next level. Pastor Fairchild I was wondering if you would officiate at our wedding. I've already bought a ring and I planned to give it to her tonight but she canceled our date because she had an emergency at the hospital. You see she's a doctor and she's on call," Theo explained.

Nina stood up to hug her friend. "Theo you never mentioned a woman in your life. Why didn't you say anything? I am so very happy for you! How is she with Jay? What's her name?"

"Her name is Susannah Driscoll and they love each other. The other thing is that her family isn't happy with her choice. She comes from a very well to do family and although my family has a long history of journalism and some money, I am a bodyguard.

Her brother even insisted that I stop seeing her, but when Sue found out, she told her family off. She rarely sees them now and I feel awful about it. We want to get married as soon as possible but I also want to give her the wedding of her dreams. Her family will probably not attend but it'll be on them. I want you to marry us in a few months. I'll have to pin a date down but that's the least of my troubles."

"Does she know that you want to get married so soon?" Nina asked.

"Yes she does, as a matter of fact it was her idea." Theo said.

"I have no problem marrying you but I must know if there is any reason why you are rushing it. As a minister I must ask and counsel you on such matters," Darius told him.

"No, Sue is a very classy woman and I would never take advantage of her. We haven't slept together if that's what you're asking."

"You go boy!" Nina exclaimed, clapping him on the arm.

"Well I don't see why I couldn't marry you two. Were you planning on having the ceremony here or in New York?" Darius asked further.

Theo shook his head. "The reason I want to do it quickly is because I don't know how much longer this house is going to be empty, I wanted to do it here if that's okay with you Nina?"

"Oh boy that's just wonderful! You just let me know what you want me to move and I'll have it done. In fact, let me do this for you. Let me know when she says yes and the date and I'll take it from there," Nina told her friend excitedly.

"You are the greatest! I've got some money saved up from the insurance claim when Jay's mom passed and some of my own. I've planned a great honeymoon for us and with you doing the house, I can splurge some more on her." Theo said happily. He bent down to give Nina a hug and kiss. His worried expression was gone and to replace it was the biggest smile she had ever seen on his face.

"We have the viewing in a few hours and I wanted to get a little rest for it. Go home Theo and we'll see you later with some good news I hope," Nina said as she ushered her friend out the door.

She returned to find Darius sitting at the piano. He had a faraway expression on his face. She went to sit beside him and leaned gently against his arm.

"It is a nice thing you are doing for Theo. It brings to mind something I have been thinking about ever since we came up here. I've noticed something about you. You are accustomed to luxury. Look around you. The house you lived in and the things in it. It isn't a sin to have nice things Nina. You have the means to live like the princess your dad said you were and the queen I believe you are. I think we should go house hunting for something more suited to a queen. What do you think?" Darius asked seriously.

"Wow where did that come from? Don't you want to share the house you have now with me?" Nina asked quietly.

"It is too small. I want you to have your piano and your award room and anything else you want in your house. Once we are married, wherever we live will be your house. You should have what you want," he insisted.

Nina nudged him a little and nodded. "We can have two houses, I mean we can stay at the house you have now on weekends and whenever there is an event at the church that you have to be present for. Then we can have a house with all the things a king *and* queen should have. I won't be the only one to be happy and comfortable in our home. Perhaps a basketball court, a swimming pool would make it more palatable for you," said Nina.

"I suppose I could get used to those things, but if it had a recording studio I could be persuaded," he said with a big smile that did things to Nina heart rate.

"Then let's do it. The very first day you have off from work we'll go looking for it. Perhaps we can have our wedding there too. What do you think about that?" Nina asked getting into the spirit of things.

"God's good mercy endures forever." Darius said as he pulled in close to capture her lips for a kiss.

"Amen," Nina murmured at the end of the kiss. She stood up and wriggled her fingers at him beckoning him to follow her.

Darius stood up and shook his head. Nina insisted and held her arms out to him and before Darius knew it he was in her arms. Nina clasped him close and started humming. He recognized the tune and they began to sway to it. Nina took a deep breath and started singing. She sang the song Whitney Houston sang in *The Preacher's Wife*, the scene where the angel took her dancing and she ended up singing *I Believe in Miracles*.

Darius pulled her closer and closed his eyes. Nina sang with all the love she felt for him and when she finished the song, she was feeling very emotional. Darius gently wiped the tears that spilled onto her cheeks as she wiped the ones from his. This was a special moment for them; it was the one Darius was hoping for and he felt his heart swell within his chest.

Darius pulled away slowly and the expression on his face was very serious. He put a hand in his pant pocket to pull out a small black velvet box. When he was on one knee in front of her, he looked up.

CHAPTER SIXTEEN

The look in his eyes told her how much he loved her, the way his hand shook, how nervous he was. Nina smiled at him through fresh tears. She put her hand in his and waited.

"Catalina Anne Bennett will you marry me?" Darius asked seriously. He opened the small box and took out a two-carat pear shaped diamond ring. He slid it onto her finger and looked up once more.

"Yes Darius I'll marry you." Nina murmured and she fell to her knees before him to hold him close. The kiss they shared surpassed the danger zone but neither noticed nor cared. When they came apart, they started to laugh. They laughed until new tears fell from their eyes.

Darius got up bringing Nina up with him. "You promised that we would plan our wedding as soon as we got engaged and I am going to hold you to your promise. I want us married very soon."

"Was that the husband or the husband to be speaking?" Nina asked.

"I was a little forceful wasn't I?"

"You were but I'll let it slide for now only because I understand where you are coming from. Seeing this beautiful ring on my finger makes me want us to be married right away too. However, we need to sit and talk this through. Remember your schedule. You have Jennifer and Jonas' wedding and now Theo's; I would rather have our wedding sometime time next year maybe."

"Must you always be the voice of reason? In addition, you want us to wait a whole year. That's going to be torture, Baby. I don't know how I'll survive," Darius feigned sadness.

"Well you can tell yourself that it is just a little while longer and since I am wearing your ring now you know that it is going to be a reality. At night when you are feeling especially lonely hug holy bear and he'll comfort you," suggested Nina.

"I suppose you are right. Besides those weddings, we also have the center's opening ceremony coming up as well. We have a very busy couple of months ahead of us. Staying engaged for a little while longer makes perfect sense. I hear June is the month for weddings so how do you feel about being a June bride?" he asked her hopefully.

"I think June is wonderful. It is not too hot and people are less grumpy in the warm months. We can work out the exact date later. So did you plan doing this out here or were you feeling romantic because of Theo?" Nina asked eying the diamond as it sparkled in the light.

"Theo and I discussed it while you were resting upstairs and he was supposed to take us to his brother-in-law's restaurant to celebrate but then he reminded me that the after party could last into the wee hours of the morning. So I modified my plans to just this moment."

Nina clasped his arm and hugged it tight. In a few hours, they were going to sit through the viewing of the movie she did on the life and careers of her parents. Their engagement made her want to blow it off to spend time with her husband-to-be.

"If you don't mind I don't want to wear my ring tonight. There's sure to be press around and I want this just between us for now. When we go home we can celebrate with everybody but not with these people," Nina implored him.

"If that's what you want but you can tell Richard before we leave. I liked his wife and I would like her and Theo to know," agreed Darius.

"I love you so very much and my heart is so full right now I don't know what to do about it. I'll never stop loving you Darius. I'll love you even when you are old and gray. I hope that it is in my power to make you happy as I know you'll make me," Nina vowed solemnly.

"Our first night together is going to be wonderful and although you expressed that you want my children, I want us to have at least a year before we do," expressed her husband to be.

Nina blushed then and hid her face against his arm. "Darius I'd rather we discuss the house we are going to buy. I don't know where we are going to find a house with all those features you mentioned. We may have to hire a real estate agent to find it for us or perhaps it'll be more fun searching ourselves."

"I know that you are shy baby but there is something else isn't there?" guessed Darius.

Nina stood up suddenly to pace. Darius watched her pace and her nervousness grew. What could possibly be wrong now, he wondered. Whatever it was he wanted to give her his support and understanding.

"Darius, for a year and a half I've known that you were the man I was going to marry. When I moved to New York and saw you, I remembered the dream I'd had. Whether it was divine providence or what-have-you, I knew. I began to feel afraid of being with you after seeing you preach. There is so much power in you when you preach. As a man you may not know this but the passion you portray when you are up there on the pulpit is a turn on for women. Before we started seeing each other, I've watched some of the younger women watch you as you preach.

It is beyond charisma. It is virility in its rawest form. I began to think about what you must've been like in bed with your wife. As a virgin, I find it exciting to think about and scary to have to go through. I don't believe that you'll hurt me, but I worry that I won't be able to satisfy you. I fear that you are too much man for me to be any good," Nina confessed.

Darius stood up but he didn't approach her, instead he walked away from her to the window. With his back to her, he spoke about his first wife.

"On our wedding night, she cried and confessed almost the same thing. She too was a virgin and scared to death that she wouldn't be able to satisfy me. I must also confess that I hadn't been with a woman either so I was just as scared as she was. We relaxed enough our first night to find our way. We taught each other. I would like to think that we could do the same on our own wedding night. I don't know why women equate a man's charismatic behavior in his work to his performance in bed. But rest assured that I am just a man who wants to love his woman," Darius said. As he spoke, Nina walked up quietly to stand behind him.

Nina snaked her arms around him and laid her head in the small of his back. "I'm sorry, Darius. Perhaps that's the origin of groupies. All I know is that when you are on the pulpit, the power you give off makes women think about how powerful you probably are in bed. And for a novice such as myself, I couldn't help but feel inadequate in that department."

Darius turned suddenly and clasped her shoulders in a firm grip. "On our wedding night, the last thing I'll be thinking about is how good you are. It's going to be a time of learning and sharing. We will have a lifetime to enjoy our physical relationship and there will be no rush. Half the fun is in the learning. You'll see so stop worrying. I promise you won't disappoint me."

"Okay," Nina said shaking herself. "Do you want to eat now or do you want to wait for the party? These things are usually catered," Nina, informed him. She was glad to be talking about something else.

"I guess I can wait. There is one thing puzzling me about the movie. I don't know much about these things but I thought that the movie was quick from start to finish. Don't these things usually take time before they are shown?" He didn't mind at all that Nina changed the subject.

Nina nodded, "That's the case usually, but the cast was small and it was an independent film. They began filming the minute I said yes. By the time I came along to do my parts, they filmed half movie already. That's why it seemed so quick. I am curious how the finished product will look too because most of the time a lot ends up on the editing floor," explained Nina.

"Are you nervous?" Darius asked. He wondered what it was like to have to sit through one's work and have others judge it.

"Not especially. Tonight we'll be among friends and fellow cast members. They pick several test areas to show the movie before they release it nation-wide. Depending on the take on opening night, we'll know how well it will do. I'm keeping my fingers crossed that it at least grosses enough to cover the production costs."

"You don't sound very confident that it will do well. Don't you think it will do well?" he asked.

"I hope so with all my heart, but I just don't know. The other actors in the movie are seasoned. I was the only one who hadn't played these types of parts. If you recall the interview I did yesterday, they commented on the fact that I hadn't done anything like this before and they are right. I know I did a good job, but will the audience want to see me doing something unfamiliar?" asked Nina. She shrugged and shook herself.

"What are you wearing tonight?" Darius asked changing the subject yet again.

"I thought I'd wear something cool and comfortable. It's not such a big affair so I thought I'd wear something festive in off white."

"Good, I've decided against getting a tux and will be wearing a regular black suit and tie."

Nina smiled sweetly up at him. "We will be the best looking people there."

Darius looked at his watch and realized that they had a few more hours to kill before they had to dress. They talked about all the things he had planned on already and was glad that they were now on one accord.

It was then he realized that he just gave this woman his ring. Nina was going to be his wife and his heart double-timed it in his chest. His legs felt wobbly and he found that he needed to sit down.

"What's the matter?" Nina asked alarmed.

Darius looked up at her and smiled weakly at her. "I just realized that you are going to be my wife," he said quietly.

"I don't think it has sunk in for me yet so you'd better be ready to catch me. I may faint or scream or, or I don't know," replied Nina just as quietly. She was looking at the sparkling diamond ring on her finger.

She went to him and sat next to him on the arm of the sofa. "Tell me the story of this ring. Why did you choose this one?" she wanted to know.

Darius took hold of her left hand in his and gave it a little squeeze. "I walked into the jewelry store and looked around but nothing felt right. Then a sales clerk approached me to ask if I needed any help. I told her that I wanted a ring that would make my woman feel loved. She smiled and asked me wait while she went into the back room and came back with a black case. She also had her manager with her.

The manager unlocked the case and then stepped back. He said that those rings were more expensive and of better quality than what was on display. I knew the minute she recognized me because she clapped her hands and stepped back to whisper to her manager.

Three rings caught my attention. I pulled them out of their slots and asked her about the rings. The stones were round, square and pear-shaped. She placed each on her finger for me to see. She was light complexioned and I got a better idea how the ring would look on your finger. I asked her which she liked the best and she said that she liked the round one best. I asked her to put it and the pear-shaped one on and all of the sudden I knew the pear-shaped one was for you."

"How did you know she recognized you? She could've been excited that she was going to make a big sale you know."

"After I gave them your size and the deposit, she said that you would be very happy." Darius told her.

"How did you know my size?" asked Nina.

"You aunt let me hold a ring of yours."

"Oh. If the sales clerk recognized you, I guess word has probably spread about us already. When did you pick up the ring?"

"I picked it up Wednesday afternoon. Don't you think if she or her manager said anything that we'd know by now?"

Nina shrugged and reached into her pocket for her cell phone. She called her aunt to ask her if there had been anything in the news about her lately. Aunt Elaine was glad to hear from her but a little upset they hadn't told her about their engagement. Nina corrected her and told her that the news leaked before she could let her know and then she hung up.

"Well I guess the saleswoman or the manager have big mouths. Someone paid them very well for the tip I suppose. Are you upset?" she asked her fiancé.

Darius put his arm around her to pull her close. "I guess I should be but not really. I just have to get used to people knowing things about us. Are *you* upset?"

Nina nodded. "I wanted us to celebrate with our friends and family privately before everybody else, but now it is all ruined. I wonder why

Richard is so quiet about it. If the New York media know, it should be all over out here."

"I don't know, perhaps they are giving us some privacy. I guess we have to be ready for whatever tonight. Since the news is out, are you wearing the ring tonight?" Darius asked fingering it in his hand.

"How about we play it by ear? If we are asked about it, I'll magically slip it on, if not I won't wear it," she suggested.

"I just love your life; I would go crazy if I were you." Darius said in frustration.

"In twelve hours this will be over and we'll on our way home." Nina said. She got up and walked away from him to the kitchen.

He found her in the kitchen opening cabinets. She was pulling out canned goods and food items from them.

"Theo said that someone from the shelter was coming either tonight or early tomorrow to pick up the food. I thought I'd get the non-perishables out and ready for them. Are you sure you don't want me to fix you anything?"

Darius came to her and took her hand. "We could both use a little something so why don't you go sit by the pool and I'll whip us some omelets?"

Nina smiled brilliantly and nodded. "You are on, dear man I'll just go change."

Darius watched her go and shook his head. Surely, the Lord is merciful, he thought.

Nina sat on the pool chair and slipped her flip-flops off. She stared down at her legs and smiled to herself. Darius thought she had great legs. She frowned at the tan lines around her feet where the sun tanned around the straps of her sandals. She vowed to get an even tan soon. It just won't do to be so pale looking as Theo phrased it.

The sun reflecting off her ring as she moved her hands caught her off guard. She smiled again. *I'm so happy I could cry. My dad would have been so proud to call Darius son and so would mom.*

"I know that you can't hear me Daddy, but I wish hard that you could. The man you chose for me is wonderful and he is just what I need in my life. He loves me and he wants me to be his forever. If you are worried about me, don't be because I love him with all my heart and I am happy." Nina said aloud.

"I would like to think that you remembered our study and know that you are talking to the air and not your father." Darius said beside her.

"I know Darius. I talked to my dad while he was sick in the hospital. I continued for months after his death. It was comforting," explained Nina looking up at him.

"I know baby, I confess doing the same thing after Rebecca passed. I guess we are alike in how we grieve. I came to ask you if you wanted toast with your omelet."

"Yes please. Darius are we allowed wine, I thought we could have a glass to commemorate this occasion." Nina said waving her bejeweled hand in the air.

"All things in moderation, the Word says. I personally don't keep alcoholic beverages in my home because as a rule I don't drink. I decline it when it is offered to me at secular events," Darius explained.

"There's a bottle of non-alcoholic white wine in the refrigerator. It's been there since we arrived. It's also, what I usually drink here because I like the taste. Could we have a glass to toast each other? I don't want the after party the only celebration to remind me of our pledge today."

"We'll have a glass then," Darius said gently.

The doorbell chimed and Nina got up quickly to go answer it. Darius went back to the kitchen.

"It's all over the news. Is it true?" Theo asked Nina at the door.

"Why hello Theo, is what true?"

"That you are engaged, that's what."

"If you mean this beautiful ring Darius placed on my finger about half hour ago, then yes we are engaged," Nina told him as she waved her hand in his face.

Theo whistled. "That's a beauty. Why is it on the airwaves if it only just happened?"

Nina propelled him along to the kitchen. "That's what we were trying to figure out. Darius thinks that the jewelry store leaked it out," Nina explained.

Darius turned from the stove with a skillet in one hand and a spatula in the other. "Whichever way the media found out, we have no choice now but to flow with it," he added.

"Congratulations Pastor Fairchild, I know that Nina is good hands and I also know that her dad would be happy to know that his daughter is happy as well." Theo said as he shook Darius' hand once it was free.

Nina took over dishing out the huge omelet Darius made and then went to the cupboard to pull out three wine glasses. Theo nodded at her when she waved a glass at him.

She uncorked the bottle and poured for them. Nina shared her omelet with Theo and then they toasted each other. Theo showed them the ring he bought for Susannah.

"Oh Theo she is going to love it," Nina breathed. "Did you pick it out yourself?" Nina asked him.

"You and my sister both seem to think that I'm just this big hunk with no brains, of course I picked it out. As a matter of fact, Jason and I did it together." Theo told her proudly.

"Good job! I'm sorry I didn't mean to hurt your feelings Theo," Nina said a little subdued.

"I could never be mad at you, Nina. I guess I'm just a little nervous," Theo gave her hand a little squeeze. "Oh before I forget, there's a mob outside the gate. If you weren't big news yesterday, you are now. I had to gun it in."

"My goodness Baby, I don't know how you do this. When we get back home, I'm going to go speak with the jewelry store manager about his lack of tact. If we had been watching the news, it would have ruined my proposal to you." Darius stated.

Nina placed her head down on the marble countertop and groaned. She usually ran away from this type of madness. When would it all die down this time? They had the viewing and party to get through which would probably be crawling with paparazzi. The evening didn't seem to be going as she hoped it would.

New York was looking good right about now she thought. She only hoped that when they returned home that things would get back to the normal to which she had become accustomed.

"Baby, are you all right?" Darius asked.

Nina raised her head and nodded sadly. "Yes I'm fine. I just want to go home." She got up to go to her room.

Darius and Theo watched her go. Darius made to follow her but Theo clasped his arm and shook his head. When she was out of sight, he let Darius go.

"She'll be okay. Most celebrities live for this kind of publicity but Nina never had. She likes things to be quiet. When it is about work, she deals with it and hams it up for the cameras but when it is private like it is now, she withdraws. She just needs a little space," Theo informed him.

"How do you know so much?" asked Darius. He was still debating if he should go after her.

"You forget, she and I go back a long way. I've been there for her and I've grown to know her pretty well. You'll see, she needs to breathe a little and then she'll be okay."

A half hour later, Nina came back down to see what the men were doing. She found them in the family room talking quietly. She joined them and smiled reassuringly at them to let them know that she was feeling better. There was still a half hour before they had to leave and they spent it talking about Theo's upcoming nuptials.

"I really think that you should try to get her family involved. She may not feel that they are important now because of how they feel about you, but once you are married, she may feel differently," Darius said of Susannah's attitude toward her family.

"I tried reasoning with her, but she says that her family looks down on people who aren't of the same socio-economic background," Theo told him spreading his arms wide.

"Would it make any difference if they knew that I was involved?" Nina asked.

"They never expressed any interest in what I do for a living. I don't think they would care," Theo replied dejectedly.

Nina sighed and shook her head. This obsession with image and being seen with the right people and being in a certain tax bracket had always made her feel despondent. People were people and it didn't matter what their background was if they were worthy of someone's love. Susannah's family didn't even take the time to get to know her boyfriend. It would

248

be a disaster if they didn't at least try to tolerate him in her life, after all, grandchildren would change their whole outlook if they wanted to have a relationship with them.

"What time does Susannah get off her shift tonight?" Nina asked.

"She gets off around 10pm, earlier if it is a quiet night. Why?" Theo wanted to know.

"Well I think that we should get together tonight and perhaps make an effort to introduce you to her family."

"You forget that I haven't given her the ring yet," Theo reminded her.

"Okay then, how about we have brunch with them tomorrow before we leave. Are you up for an intervention of sorts?" She asked Darius.

Darius nodded his head and smiled. Nina was kind hearted to a fault. She would do anything for her friend.

"What exactly are we doing that's going to change how Susannah's family feels towards Theo?" he asked.

Nina got up to pace and think. There had to be something they could do to make sure that at least Theo's family and Susannah's meet and get to know each other before the wedding.

She whirled around suddenly facing them with a wide smile on her face.

"Okay, for this to work you've got to propose tonight. Are you sure she's going to say yes?"

"Of course she's going to say yes. What do you have in mind?" Theo asked leaning forward in the chair he was sitting in.

"Susannah has to be in on this as well. Does she have a sister?"

"She has two sisters and one brother. Her family lives in Los Angeles."

"Great. That's on the way to the airport so we can keep going after we are done. Wow, God works in mysterious ways Darius. Now come morning, we pack and leave as if we were going home only we are stopping to have breakfast with Susannah and her sisters. I'm sure that her sisters are going to be happy for her regardless of what their parents feel. I'll be your surprise guest and if you don't mind I'd like to tell them about offering the house and grounds for the wedding, okay?"

Theo nodded. "How did you know that Susannah has a great

relationship with her sisters? We hang out together all the time. It's her parents and brother who feel that I'm not good enough for her," Theo told them.

Nina clapped her hands in delight. "Wonderful this makes everything so much easier. I really hate using my influence like this but this is for a good cause. I am hot this week so I think I'll be able to use it to your advantage Theo."

Theo got up and he too started pacing. "Exactly what are we doing?" he asked.

Nina laughed. "Propose to Susannah and then have her and her sisters meet you for breakfast in the morning. You bring Darius and me to breakfast to meet them and I'll take over from there." Nina said counting on her fingers.

Theo looked to Darius who shrugged and agreed. He trusted Nina.

The viewing was at the Beverly Hills Hilton's ballroom. Gathered were the cast members, their agents, the producers and the director. Ms. Rubinowitz and her family, Richard and a number of movie critics were also present. The press had a table as well but not allowed to see the movie. About a hundred people sat at gaily-decorated tables.

Darius sat with Nina and a few of the cast members. He was nervous for her and couldn't relax. Nina held his hand and squeezed it during the parts she felt were critical for the film's success. The story unfolded with her parents just arriving to California. It chronicled their earliest beginnings in the business. While filming she learned that they took gigs surprisingly in less than desirable places.

Darius and Nina both were surprised that her mother sang in strip clubs and her dad played his beloved Jazz at those clubs too. There wasn't any nudity but of course, it was the music industry, there was a lot of drinking and drug activity going on. There was footage of her father with cigarettes smoldering between his lips as he played his jazz on the piano.

Nina's surprise was complete as she watched the footage of Catalina

Bennett's last performance in Chicago. The show was a great success. Nina purposely declined to see the scenes that she wasn't in so that the whole of the film would be new and as scenes of her, either of her parents unfolded on the screen, she expressed genuine emotion.

Nina felt a whole range of emotions. She was humbled and felt proud that her parents were who they were. The fatal car crash that took her mother's life was due to a drunk driver who lost control of his car. He drove in and out of his lane finally to crash headlong into the car in which Catalina was a passenger. She and her driver died instantly. The newsreels of the accident along with the funeral services were mercifully brief and Darius watched the silent tears running down Nina's face. He reached out to hold her hand. Nina didn't remember going but there were clips of her at the services.

The happy times in between, was a whirlwind of activity split between her dad's career and Nina's career. Darius got a kick out of seeing Nina as a kid singing on stage. He couldn't believe how talented she was. The clips that showed Nina's father in action were fantastic to say the least. He truly was a jazz great. The sounds he could produce on the piano were outrageous.

The last scene was of Charles Bennett at his beloved piano. That scene alone evoked emotions that ran chills up and down Nina's spine. She had a feeling that the movie was going to be a success. The applause at the end was also an indication that others felt the same. Nina forced herself to avoid looking toward the table the critics were sitting at because she was afraid that even though she felt that the movie was good, they might not.

One critic came over to her to shake her hand and to congratulate her. Nina imagined the grin her dad used to wear whenever he was pleased. She was overwhelmed as everyone stood to give her a standing ovation. She stood up to smile through her tears and blew kisses at everyone. Richard was grinning from ear to ear as well.

Hors d'oeuvres circulated throughout the viewing via servers who discreetly went around the tables. After the viewing, they served the main course while the guests talked and visited with each other.

"Nina you were the cutest little thing. I am so proud of you," a fellow cast member came to tell her. She performed with her dad on and off through the years.

"Thank you Julie. This is Pastor Darius Fairchild my boyfriend," Nina replied introducing Darius.

"Pleased to meet you Pastor. I know it is a little early but I'd like to be among the first to congratulate you two on your engagement. Nina is a wonderful person."

"Thank you," Darius answered, Nina was a beat behind him.

Nina quickly looked to her hand to make sure that she wasn't wearing the ring. Darius was to hold it for safekeeping.

"Oh I know it was secret but you know how these things get out. Be happy Nina." Julie said and walked on the neighboring table.

Darius watched her go and turned to Nina. "Was she fishing or is it really out there?"

"If she was, we just confirmed it. I wasn't even wearing the ring."

"Well no matter. I am so proud of you and I think this movie is going to be a hit. Your father was a great musician and if God hadn't taken your mother so early, she would have been a living legend," Darius predicted.

"Thank you Darius," she gushed.

The rest of the evening, Nina received accolades in lieu of her father and felt that they could call it a night, it was well past 11pm. Nina could not avoid speaking with the press who viewed only excerpts of the movie. She gave on the spot interviews along with fellow cast member throughout the evening. She was just wrapping one up when Theo came for them.

"Did you guys have a good time?" Theo asked once they were driving away from the paparazzi that had gathered around the car. He was in a good mood himself.

"Yes we did as a matter of fact. How about you, did everything go well?" Nina asked in return.

"She said yes, and she couldn't believe that that you wanted to meet her for breakfast in the morning. She didn't know that you were among my clients until tonight," he told them with wide a grin on his handsome face.

"Great, my plan is going to work, tomorrow morning is going to be so much fun," Nina said around a yawn.

"I think someone is tired," Darius teased.

"Yeah you know how it is," Nina said and then she yawned again.

Darius walked Nina to her room and bowed gallantly. "Good night fair lady."

"Good night to you kind sir," Nina curtsied and closed her door.

Darius walked to his room, packed his clothes and then undressed, all the while thinking what an experience these past few days had been. He completely understood why Nina felt the need to break away from that lifestyle. He watched the crowd at the viewing and was able to spot those who were trying to get attention. He recognized a few old time celebrities who participated in the movie. He hadn't seen them or heard about them in a long while. They were eager to take pictures with Nina and give interviews about how it was to work with her.

He recalled Nina telling him about the young man she once dated. She thought that they had a good rapport only to find that he was using her to boost his appeal. The world she left behind was so superficial that it was hard to tell who was genuine. He was looking forward to going home where it was quiet and calm and where everything was down to Earth.

In New York, Nina didn't have to defend herself. He knew that the movie would generate a few weeks of autograph seeking and press coverage, but she wouldn't have to be on. He was ready for family and friends to flock around them because of their engagement and he was confident that they wouldn't have to hide either.

Los Angeles was a great place to visit but he sure wouldn't want to live there. If by chance, Nina continued to do more projects that would bring her back here, he was sure that she wouldn't want to linger any longer than was necessary.

Darius fell asleep thinking that he would have to be the voice of reason at this breakfast meeting Nina planned to have. Although he was in complete agreement that Theo and Susannah's family should meet and become acquainted, he also knew that a relationship like that couldn't be hurried, or established in one day.

Nina knocked on Darius' bedroom door as she past it. She was up early and was just getting back from letting the people from the shelter in to pick up the leftover food.

Darius awoke to realize that he had overslept. He wanted to be up early just to make Nina her morning cup of coffee. Now it was too late. It was Nina's routine to get up early to make a pot of coffee before anything else. He sat on the side of the bed trying to will the sleep that still made him want to lie back down to recede.

By the time Darius showered and dressed, he could hear Theo downstairs with Nina. He was an early riser too it seemed. It takes a lot of discipline to survive the kind of schedule she had been on, on so little rest or sleep. Even though in New York she hadn't kept any particular schedule, he was impressed that she fell right back into it the minute their airplane touched ground.

"Good morning sleepyhead," Nina teased him. She kissed him full on the lips and handed him a cup of coffee.

"Good morning beautiful, Theo I see you're a morning person too." Darius said.

"Good morning Pastor. If you'll help me get the bags out to the car, we can get going." Theo said rubbing his hands together. It was clear to everyone that he was excited.

Darius nodded and hurried to get his bags and Nina's. Between the two of them, they managed to get Nina's bags and the gifts she and Darius purchased in the trunk. Theo made sure that the gifts were all boxed and wrapped. He then had them bundled into a tower of sorts so nothing would get lost.

Once they were on the way to the restaurant, Theo became more and more reflective and less talkative. Darius supposed that he was nervous about the plans for breakfast. He looked over to Nina who was sitting back with her eyes closed. She was serene looking and didn't appear to be worried at all.

It was just a little over an hour before they were parking the car in the restaurant's lot. Their flight was for 11am and it was just a bit past nine. They had a very small window to get anything accomplished but he was getting excited as well.

The waiter recognized Nina and he smiled brightly. He fairly strutted as he escorted them to their waiting table. Susannah and her sisters were waiting already seated. They got up to greet Theo who then introduced Nina and Darius to them.

"Oh my God, Ms. Bennett it certainly is a great pleasure to meet you. I didn't quite believe Theo when he promised to invite you to have breakfast with us. Nice to meet you too Pastor Fairchild," Susannah said excitedly.

"Good morning ladies. It is a pleasure to meet you too. Theo and I go way back and I felt that I couldn't pass up the chance to congratulate you and him." Nina replied. Darius waved and smiled at them.

Susannah's sisters immediately asked for autographs. They couldn't stop smiling. When the waiter came for their orders, they did it quickly because Theo warned them that Nina and her fiancée had to be at the airport quite soon.

Service was quick and Nina talked while they ate. "May I call you Susannah?" she asked pushing her plate away.

"Please," Susannah answered in awe.

"When Theo told me about your engagement, I was excited for him. I've known him for ages and he's been so kind to me. He's asked me to use my home for the ceremony and Pastor Fairchild to officiate at your wedding. Is that okay with you?" Nina asked the woman sitting opposite her.

"Oh my Gosh, Theo can we really get married in her house?" Susannah asked. Her sisters wore various expressions of shock on their faces as well. Her youngest sister couldn't stand it anymore; she whipped out her cell phone to call their parents.

Darius sat back to listen to everything that was going on. He gathered that Susannah's parents already know about the engagement because the conversation was more about the beautiful house and grounds Nina was offering them.

"You have to excuse my sister, she gets excited easily. Our parents were slow to accept Theo in my life. They are very protective of us. My brother is the eldest and as a lawyer, he is even more so. He is still on the fence," Susannah said by way of explanation.

"So you're saying that your family is okay with Theo?" Nina asked.

"Yes they are. I think that they weren't convinced that Theo was serious.

Your fantastic offers to use your home and for you to do our wedding will probably further impress them. They'll be thrilled actually," Susannah, gushed.

"We have a plane to catch, but we will keep in touch. Call Nina with the date and I'll be more than happy to marry you two." Darius told the couple.

"Ms. Bennett would you take a picture with us?" one sister asked.

Susannah pulled out her camera to get in the picture as well. They asked for several poses until they were satisfied. Theo put a stop to it reminding them that they still had to check in at the airport, that they had to leave immediately.

Nina hugged them good-bye as if they were lifelong friends. Theo kissed his fiancée longingly then waved at his sisters-in-law to be.

On the way out, Nina paid for their breakfasts and signed one more autograph before stepping into the back seat of the car.

Theo drove like mad to make it to the airport on time, but they made it with minutes to spare for check in. Even her notoriety couldn't excuse her from the check-in process which took a little extra time because she was a celebrity, she was signing autographs and having her picture taken.

Before boarding the plane, Theo hugged and kissed Nina's cheeks then clasped hands with Darius. He waved until he couldn't see them anymore and left the airport. He was happy and in love. Everything was right in his world. Susannah's family finally accepting him felt good. He hadn't felt right about it and worried that it would've ruined their marriage. Nina was a very good friend, he thought. Sue's sisters were going to be talking about meeting Nina for days. He couldn't wait to get back to them to tell them Nina gave him permission to take them to see the house when he meets with the cleaning service.

The flight home was long and Nina was finally able to turn off and be herself again. She was tired of being bubbly, of the phoniness and of being a diva. Although they were sitting in first class, other celebrities and executives thought they could engage her in conversation. After answering a few questions about the movie, she refused to answer anything about her personal life. Once they got the hint that she wasn't in a talkative mood, they moved on to someone else. Nina closed her eyes, linked her arm through her fiancé's arm and went to sleep.

The landing went so smoothly that it didn't disturb Nina. Darius shook her awake gently to let her know that their plane had landed and like the traveling pro she was, she smiled brightly at him and then stood up.

Darius had not rested the entire flight. Knowing that he was tired, Nina insisted that she drive them home. She parked her SUV at the airport and it was just a matter of retrieving it to drive home. The airport was only a thirty-minute drive from her aunt's house, but Darius kept asking her if she was okay to drive.

"Honey I slept on the flight, you stood guard over me like the knight in shining armor that you are so I am fine. It is late and although Aunt Elaine will be waiting up for us, I think I should drive you home first. You are beat," Nina expressed.

"My car is parked at your aunt's house if you recall, so I'm driving home." Darius told her stubbornly.

Nina shook her head, "How about I drive you home and then use your car to come have breakfast with you in the morning? You can drive me back later." Nina suggested.

"Are you sure?" Darius asked finally admitting to himself that he was tired.

"Perfectly, I'll leave everything in the car so can help me with the luggage tomorrow, okay?"

"All right Baby, you win. I am tired and I'd appreciate the lift home. Tomorrow is soon enough for your aunt to fuss over us and our engagement," he agreed with a smile.

Because the drive to Darius' house was a bit farther, that and traffic made it well over an hour before she was parking in front it. Darius had fallen asleep and she shook him awake gingerly.

"Darius wake up honey, we're here," Nina nudged him gently.

She watched him stifle a yawn and shake off the sleep. "If I didn't believe you before I believe you now. I feel like a wet noodle," he admitted.

"Promise me that you'll go straight to bed and not do anything until you've rested," Nina insisted.

"You have my word," Darius answered as he pulled his luggage from the trunk. It was too late for him to do anything anyway. Monday night pray service was over and he hadn't scheduled anything for afterwards.

He leaned over to give her a kiss and waved goodbye. He watched until the SUV was out of sight before entering his home. He hadn't experience jet lag like this in a long time, he thought as he wearily dragged his suitcase up the stairs to his room. He didn't even bother to unpack. Darius undressed and get into bed murmuring a quick prayer of thanks for their safe trip home and for divine coverage for Nina's drive home; afterwards, Darius knew no more.

Since Nina promised her fiancé that she would leave her stuff in the SUV, she parked in the driveway then closed the gate behind it. She entered the house carefully in an effort to keep quiet.

"Is that you Nina?" Elaine asked somewhere in the dark.

"Yes Auntie it's me. Where are you?" she replied.

"I'm in the kitchen child," she answered back.

Nina made her way to her aunt, feeling the rush of adrenaline coursing through her veins as she did so. She realized that she missed her aunt and wanted to rush to her arms for the hugs and kisses they were sure to share.

Elaine clasped Nina close to kiss both of her cheeks.

"Goodness child I missed you. How was your flight?" she asked.

"Oh Auntie I missed you too. The flight was too long but I'm so glad I'm home."

Elaine let her go and looked around her niece. "Where's Darius?"

Nina released her hand to sit at the table. "I dropped him off. He stayed awake the whole flight. He was so tired I was afraid of letting him drive so I drove him home so he could get some rest. I promised to have breakfast with him tomorrow so he could get his car back." Nina explained.

Elaine nodded. It made sense to be careful, but she was looking forward to seeing him to congratulate him and to welcome him into the family. She looked to Nina's hand, spied the engagement ring, and smiled. She took her hand to examine the ring more closely.

"I'm so happy for you I could shout. If your father was still alive I bet he would have been really proud," her aunt said.

Nina closed her hand around Elaine's hand. "You know getting engaged wasn't as scary as I thought it would be. Darius and I thought it would be better if we celebrated our engagement here instead, so I really don't feel it yet."

"That's probably because you had all that other stuff going on. You look tired too baby, go to bed and you can fill me in tomorrow." Elaine stood up and together they climbed the stairs to their rooms.

At her bedroom door, Nina blew her aunt a kiss then entered her room.

Just as she was taking off her sandals, Nina's cell phone rang. She knew that it was Darius calling and answered quickly.

"You were supposed to go to sleep," she accused him.

"I did. I fell asleep as soon as I got in the bed but I couldn't stay asleep. I realized that I had to hear your voice." His voice was velvety smooth.

"I love you Darius," Nina felt the need to say.

"I just realized something; this is one more night closer to us being together," he reminded her.

"I know and I can't wait. Tomorrow I am going to buy one of those huge calendars to start crossing off days. We have so much to clear out of the way first but I keep thinking once all those tasks are done, you are going to be at the end of it."

"You know that perfume you wore the other night, bring it with you when you come to breakfast. Holy bear's is fading fast." Darius said. The real reason he woke up was that he missed her. Those few days in California together were wonderful.

"I will and I'll bring my bear so you could douse him with your cologne too. Your scent is fading too," she told him.

"Baby I love you very much and I am so lucky you are going to be my wife. I was thinking that planning a wedding is a very long process, but finding a house is even more so therefore, I think we should at least visit a couple of real estate offices to see if there are any homes like what we talked about available. What do you think?"

"This week is not good for either of us honey, the recreation center is almost done and you promised that you'd help me furnish it. I have a meeting with the builders tomorrow for a walk through." Nina reminded him.

"Spoil sport, I remember. There is only a few days left of my vacation and then I won't have much free time either."

"Be patient my love, half the fun is in the looking," Nina told him. She yawned and shook herself. "Good night Darius sleep well."

CHAPTER SEVENTEEN

The following days were busier than they had originally thought for both Darius and Nina. Two teens from the church had been coming to him for counseling for tension at home. It really bothered him that families were going through trauma like this. These siblings had recently joined the church. Their parents haven't received Christ yet and were giving their children a hard time about participating in church activities.

Their father was an ex-gang member who experienced a lot and was proud of his exploits in the gang. He wanted his son to be a man like he was, not realizing that he was writing a death sentence for his son. Their mother was an ex-drug addict who cleaned herself up, and turned her life around but not enough to include God.

By the grace of God, their children refused to follow their parents' example. They wanted better for their own lives. Their parents weren't abusive but they were adamant about what they wanted their children doing and church wasn't it.

Darius went to the home to speak with them and found that they were hard to convince. The man of the house was tough looking with scars he wore proudly about his face and arms.

"I don't want my children sitting in a church learning all that turn your cheek stuff that won't do them any good out on the streets. My son needs to be a man so he can protect his sister and himself," said the dad.

"Sir with all due respect, wouldn't you rather that your son learn how to be a man from you than from the streets? It was tough back then, you lived through it, and I know you have physical and mental scars. Having gone through those things, I'm sure you wouldn't want your son to experience them as well. Don't you think it would be beneficial for him to look up to you for his instruction than some thug out there that may harm him?"

"Even so what does church have to do with it?" The father asked crossing his arms, a sure sign that he wasn't going to budge. Darius prayed silently asking the Holy Ghost to help him answer.

"Your son and daughter need to see you as head of the family as God is the head of the church. You were in a gang as a youth and learned violence and destruction. They *didn't* teach you to be a man. They *didn't* teach you to be gentle or loving. Being gentle and loving is a gift God gives us all when we become parents. What parent wants to put his child in harm's way? Gangs today are all about shootings and hurting people and drugs. There is nothing positive about it. If you allow your son to be part of that life, he may not live long enough for you to see if he had grown to be a man," Darius informed him.

"You have a point there but I still don't see how the church is going to help my boy be a man."

Again, Darius prayed for guidance. "From going to church, your son is going to learn compassion so that he won't harm anyone. He'll learn all the goodly things he will need as an adult. Someday when he has his own family, he'll know how to love them and guide them. By his example, he may even save his parents. The Bible tells us that a man is the head and the priest of his home. Right now, this house has no priest and your souls are at risk. Can you stand before God and tell him that you were the head?"

"What about my girl? What's the church going to do for her?" he seemed to be mulling over what Darius said to him.

"Well as a young lady, she will learn from her mother the things a woman needs to know. From going to church, she will learn that godly life leads to a happy life. A prayerful woman is a strong woman who will one day stand beside a strong man. They will raise strong children who will love God as they see their parents do. Really, it is a beautiful thing. We have programs in place at the church to keep your children interested in living right not only in the home, but also out in the world. As we speak, we are building a recreation center that will further keep your children off the streets. There they will find wholesome activities that are both fun and useful."

"Hey aren't you that preacher who is marrying that singer?" The father asked suddenly.

Darius gave him a self-conscious smile and nodded. "Yes I am. She is the one who is really behind the recreation center. She wants the center to benefit the community but more importantly the children in our church," Darius explained.

"Did you know that my daughter can sing? Can your fiancée give her a few pointers and help her get a career?" The father asked, this time he was friendlier.

"If your daughter can sing, she can further develop her voice in the choir. She can't sing in the choir if she isn't a member." Darius pointed out.

The father stood up suddenly. Darius, his children and his wife watched him pace and struggle with a decision. Finally, he stopped pacing to face them.

"Okay, the kids can go to church and maybe my wife and I can go sometimes but, on one condition. I yank them out if I don't see any good coming out of it."

Darius smiled and stood up too to shake his hand. The children hugged their parents then shook the pastor's hand telling him that they would be at church first thing Sunday morning. Darius walked out of the home satisfied that he might have won two more souls for Christ.

He was disturbed however, that people were beginning to equate going to Christ Tabernacle with Nina. He didn't want to become a by any means necessary leader. He wanted people to come to church because of the Word, not because of who his wife-to-be was. It seemed that Nina was becoming a very persuasive carrot. He knew it shouldn't matter what was bringing the people into the church as long as he was there to feed them the Word, but somehow knowing that Nina was the lure, felt wrong. Was he falling victim to pride? He prayed it wasn't so.

Darius drove home with a heavy heart. The church was beginning to fill up with new members almost every Sunday and he thought that God was working wonders through him. Has he let pride fill his heart, so much so that he was feeling that he was the one doing the work?

Rachel was still at his house when he arrived. He waved at her but didn't linger to speak. He went into his office and locked the door. When he reached his desk, he fell to his knees.

"Father do not let me fall into the trap pride brings. I love you and want to do your will. Help me not to boast about what I'm doing. How arrogant of me to feel that I am doing this? It is all you Father, all you. So many have fallen because of pride and have lost the vision you set before them. Do not let me fall Lord I beg you, do not let me fall!" Darius prayed. He got up and wiped the tears that slid down his cheeks. He grabbed his Bible to reaffirm the vision that God had placed in his heart for his people.

Nina walked into the house to find that Elaine had guests. It was Jennifer and Jonas. They were waiting for her it seemed. She greeted them and tried to be hospitable. She was tired and just wanted to take a shower and go to bed. She spent most of the day with the contractors and then with her lawyer, first to approve the adjustments she wanted made from when she and Darius had gone to the first walk thru. With her lawyer, she drew up contracts for the people working on the album with her. She was bone tired.

"Hey you two, what are you doing here, we didn't have an appointment did we?"

"We did and you never showed. We had a dress fitting today at four o'clock," Jennifer pointed to her watch. "When you didn't show I called Jonas and we came here to see what happened to you," she said. There was a hurt expression on her face.

Nina dropped to the nearest chair. The expression on her face was one of horror. "Oh my God, Jenny I completely forgot. I'm sorry, please forgive me," she begged.

Jennifer smiled suddenly. "Oh good I thought you blew me off because you were out with your beau or something. Anyway, we have a new appointment for the fitting. The tailor had an emergency and closed the shop early. She called while I was on the way there; I tried calling you but your phone went straight to voicemail," Jennifer explained.

"I was at the center going through another walk thru with the contractor. Then I had meetings with the musicians to draw up contracts with my lawyer. And for your information, I haven't seen Darius at all today," Nina told her friend righteously.

"Boy I wouldn't want to be in your shoes these days at all. Okay then, we stopped by to see if everything was well with you. We had a busy day as well. We have been apartment hunting and I think we may have found the one," Jennifer told Nina as they made their way to the door.

Nina turned to her and asked her to call her later with the details. Jennifer countered that she might if she could be sure that Nina was going to answer. Nina pulled out her phone and switched it back on with a flare then waved goodbye to the couple.

Walking back to the living room where she left her aunt, Nina's phone rang. Darius wanted to know why she wasn't accepting any calls.

"Hi Baby, I'm sorry I missed your call. I was in meetings all day and I just got home. Let me get myself together and I'll call you back okay?" Nina asked. She hung up after Darius agreed.

"Hi Auntie, how was your day?" Nina asked her aunt who hadn't budged from her chair since Nina walked in.

"Aren't people like you supposed to have assistants? You are running yourself ragged with all these meetings, child," Elaine accused her.

"I am not running myself ragged Auntie, and what do you mean by people like me?" she countered.

"You could've had someone else go to the center for you, that way you could've had a short day after meeting with your lawyer. Since you got back from California you haven't stopped at all," Elaine stated. She was worried about her.

"Aw Auntie you are going to make *yourself* sick worrying about me like this. I am fine and I do have sense to know when I've had enough to rest. Besides, you know all the stuff I have to do. There's Jennifer and Jonas' wedding, the center and then I have to go back to California for Theo's wedding. After that I'll start recording the gospel album," Nina informed her.

"This is what I'm talking about. You are booked solid the whole summer," said Elaine, "I just don't want to see you burnt out is all."

Nina stooped down to give kiss her aunt's smooth cheek. "Don't worry Auntie, very soon I'll go back to doing nothing just like when I first got here."

"Aren't you at least going to have dinner, I left a plate in the microwave for you," she called after Nina who was heading toward the stairs.

"It's that time of the month and you *don't* want to know what I ate today," replied Nina.

"Spare me the details I'll put your plate away. Go on up to bed, I'll see you in the morning."

"Good night Auntie," Nina yawned at her.

Nina showered quickly and slipped into bed. It was a hot night. She had the windows open but there wasn't any breeze. Picking up her phone, Nina called Darius.

"Hello my Queen," Darius answered.

"Why my Lord, you may turn my head yet. How was your day?"

"Brutal. I went to visit that family I was telling you about after work. I think I may have won the parents over. They are going to allow the kids to come to church again."

"That is awesome. So why do I hear something else in your voice?"

"It is scary how you do that. I just had a flashback to when I was a boy and wondered if my mom had eyes behind her head."

"What happened?"

"She would be facing the other way and somehow she knew what I took off the counter."

"Darius Fairchild, you know very well I was speaking of the family you went to visit," Nina was suddenly not so tired.

"Well it seems to me that you have become the carrot that attracts the people. The dad wanted to know if I was the preacher who was marrying you and when I confirmed that I was, he wanted to know if you could help his daughter start her singing career. I told him that if his daughter can sing she'd have to start in the choir first."

"Darius you know very well that the Lord works in mysterious ways. How they get into the house is irrelevant. What is relevant is what God pours into them through you. You'll find that once they are in and the Lord gets a hold of their soul, I won't be such an attraction anymore God will."

"Wow beauty and wisdom. What a treasure you are," he marveled.

"And don't you forget it. Are we doing anything tomorrow?"

"No, did you want to do something? Darius asked.

Nina yawned loudly. "Tomorrow is Saturday and I wanted to sleep in. I've had a long day and Aunt Elaine is worried that I'll burn out. So to keep her from worrying and to get the rest I do need, I thought I'd sleep in," replied Nina.

Remembering her hectic schedule while in California, Darius agreed, Nina did need to rest. "We've been back a whole week and we haven't gotten around to celebrating our engagement nor announced it yet. Then there's the fact that we haven't seen each other either. I usually have an engaged couple come up and I announce it to the congregation. I say a few words of encouragement and then I pray over their joined hands. We need to do that, it is expected," Darius insisted.

"We can do that on Sunday honey. I've been dreading going public but I guess church doesn't count as public. I wear my ring to sleep because it makes me feel closer to you but, I haven't worn it out yet."

"Good. I'll have Minister Aldridge do the honors then. I didn't even ask you what kind of day you've had. Was it as tiring as you sound?"

"Well it was. If you recall the walk thru we did at the center a couple of days ago, I went back to check on their progress and it took hours. It looked like they tore everything down again just to make those adjustments I asked for. Then I had meetings with the musicians and my lawyer to draw up contracts for them. Since this is, my project I have to make sure that everyone on board is happy and compensated. That took a few hours as well, but it is all done." Nina recited. Even her voice sounded tired Darius realized.

"Wow Cat, you really had a full day. I wish I could be there with you to rub your feet and help you relax," said Darius gently.

"Ahem, did you just call me Cat?" Nina asked suddenly perspiring.

"It just came to me all of the sudden because you sounded like a cat purring," Darius replied.

"My dad used to call me Kitten when he was happy with me and Cat when he was annoyed. Richard's wife Agatha calls me Cat too."

"So you aren't comfortable with me calling you Cat?"

"I guess I don't mind," Nina replied breathlessly.

"I have an arsenal of pet names for you but they are for when we are married," Darius half whispered.

"My Lord I think it is time for us to say good night." Nina said gently.

"May the Lord bless and keep you Cat, good night." Darius replied and hung up.

Nina slid down and closed her eyes. Darius was in a playful mood and probably didn't know how calling her Cat would affect her. The way he said it made her heart race and it made her feel like—, well he probably just didn't know.

Sunday morning Darius awoke with a start. He wrestled with his sermon all day the previous day and thought that once he had finally gotten it into his spirit he'd be able to rest. Yet this morning he was just as unsure as he was the day before. He got down on his knees to pray. He asked God to speak through him this morning and that He ministered to the people.

The feeling remained while he showered and dressed. However, the minute he stepped out onto the pulpit, he felt the Lord's anointing and he breathed a sigh of relief. There was a word for the people after all.

"This morning's sermon is taken from (James 4:6 and Matthew 18: 4.KJV) "But he giveth more grace. Wherefore he saith, God resisteth the proud, but giveth grace unto the humble". In Matthew, "Whosoever therefore shall humble himself as this little child, the same is greatest in the kingdom of heaven." Pastor Fairchild prayed then asked the congregation to take their seats.

"These past few days have been hard for me because the Lord had given me a revelation. I wanted to bring a different sermon to you today but the Holy Spirit kept leading me to those two verses I'd just read. The Word that I bring to you this morning is a lesson to both you and me. The Word that you will be *receiving* this morning probably won't have you shouting but it will *save* you. My fellow servants, the Lord has blessed us indeed. Look around you and see how much we have grown. This time last year we were a much smaller group but LOOK WHAT THE LORD HAS DONE!" he shouted suddenly.

"We have grown so much that we have to stand in the back and we have to pull up individual chairs to place them in the aisles. Were my prolific words the cause of our growth? Perhaps you believe that it was your diligence at spreading the gospel to your friends and neighbors.

Webster's dictionary defines the word pride as this: *a feeling of deep pleasure or satisfaction derived from one's own achievements.* It further defines the word humble as *having or showing a modest or low estimate of one's importance.*

The Bible tells us that if we humble ourselves as a little child that we will be greatest in the kingdom of heaven. The Bible tells us that God resists the proud but he gives grace to the humble.

Look what the Lord has done with Christ Tabernacle. Because God is doing great things in here, we have become puffed up and we have been arrogant. Why? I asked you if you thought it was my anointing to preach; I admit it I *know* that the lord has blessed me with that gift. I must realize I DID NOTHING to bring the people into the church. It was God working *through* me. It hit me the other day as I stood up here looking out over the pews. I saw a great multitude of people who weren't here last summer, and I thought to myself, wow *I* must be doing something right.

How dare I think such a thing? I am guilty of being proud of accomplishments I thought were my own. Who am I? Those of you who were mindful of your friends and neighbors, and sought to bring them the Word, you've seen the seed you sowed grow haven't you? Did you think to yourselves that if it weren't for you, sister so and so or brother so and so wouldn't be here? How *dare* you? The Lord spoke through you because God had need of your sister or brother. He used you to bring the Word, that's all. Did you think the words you spoke to them were your own? Did you think that you had that much power in you that you could change the minds of others?

Church of the living God, hear this, we are *all* servants. What we are doing is God's will. You must Thank God that He chose you to be a vessel it was never you. He worked through YOU and he worked through ME! I am ready to admit that I have been arrogant and felt proud of myself for work I thought I'd done on my own. WAKE UP CHURCH! We may lose the race if we continue this way. This is not my ministry it is the Lord's ministry.

The Bible tells us that Jesus sent the apostles two by two out into the world to teach and to bring the good news to others. *He* started the work, and left us to finish it. We didn't think it up. Jesus gave us instruction on what to do, which is our job. That is our reasonable service. Look at your neighbor and say this, "Neighbor I didn't do this, God did." The congregation repeated what he said and clapped, some stood up to praise.

Pastor Fairchild moved to step down from the pulpit and he walked up and down the center aisle. His preaching robe was drenched as he labored to bring the Word the Lord had given him. He wanted to cry because he felt humbled by what the Lord had done.

"Saints the Bible says that we must humble ourselves in his sight and he will lift us up. I have a vision for this church. I want us to grow not only in here but out there as well and if while we are growing in here we are not humble, everything will be lost. If that happened, I wouldn't blame you. I'd have to blame myself because I had not taught you humility and I had not warned you about the pitfalls of pride.

Sister Nina Bennett has been working to build a recreation center for the church and our community. Therefore, the vision is growing saints and I am confident that it will grow further. The saying, pride goeth before a fall is going to happen to us if we don't take heed now, but we aren't going to fall because the Lord has opened my eyes and yours today. The enemy is not always to blame for our pride and our lack of humility. Remember we are a sinful people who fight temptation every day. But if we continue to do his will, we have the assurance that one day soon the God of Abraham will extend his hand out to us and say well done my good and faithful servant!"

Darius walked back up to the pulpit. He wiped his face with his towel then closed his bible. The applause and the shouting that unfolded were deafening. He raised his hands high to bless the Lord, and then turned to his seat where he kneeled to pray. The ministers on the pulpit crowded around him to pray with him.

His armor bearer helped him with his robe and then Pastor Darius Fairchild walked off the pulpit to go change. Minister Aldridge stood there on the pulpit in awe of the power of God. The message the Lord had given them this morning was indeed needed and powerful enough to bring about much needed change.

He smiled and raised his hands in praise. He signaled for the praise team to come up to sing as he announced the altar call. He couldn't count the people who came up for prayer. The power of the Holy Ghost was truly working in the sanctuary he thought.

By the end of the prayer, the couple Pastor Fairchild visited about their children and two others came up for prayer and baptism. Minister Aldridge turned to look at the pastor as he returned to the pulpit. He changed to wear not his usual stylish suits but his black minister's garb and collar. He was the picture of humility, appearing as the servant he said he was.

The pastor stood up once again before the saints of Christ Tabernacle. He smiled at them radiantly and saw acceptance. He thought that he might see resentment for what he taught this morning but all he saw was acceptance.

"As you know the Lord has not only blessed the church but, he has blessed me personally in the form of Sister Nina Bennett. Last week I traveled with her to California to support her in a film in which she participated. The media leaked a story about us and so today, I wanted to set the record straight. Sister Nina, will you come up here please?" asked Pastor Fairchild.

Nina stood up and went to stand beside the pastor who came down from off the pulpit once again to stand before the congregation. Minister Aldridge stood with them. Darius pulled the engagement ring from out of his pocket and held it up high for all to see.

Some clapped and some catcalled, but everyone agreed. Pastor Fairchild placed the engagement ring on Nina's finger then he hugged her. "You know saints it isn't an easy thing I do here; this woman that God has called to walk with me is in for a hard way. If she thought the paparazzi were hard on her, wait until she becomes first lady!" he joked. Most of the congregation laughed with him. Nina blushed. "But seriously, before God and man I declare my love and devotion to this woman. I promise to love her, shelter her and be the priest of our home. Today we stand before you and ask for your blessing."

Minister Aldridge then took their hands and joined them. He prayed for them and charged them to be happy. The congregation as a whole stood up and clapped for them calling out blessings.

The family that had just joined the church was the first to congratulate the couple. Elaine and Sister Rachel and Jennifer and Jonas stood on the line that had formed to congratulate them also. Jonas' aunt sister Dorothea Jackson came to Nina to tell them how happy she was for them.

When Nina was finally able to get to her car, she was tired of smiling. She waved to Darius who promised to meet them at her aunt's and drove off.

"I knew the minute that man expressed his interest in you that he was going to marry you." Elaine said suddenly.

"Oh really, what gave him away?"

"He was lonely but he didn't sin. He waited on the Lord to give him what he needed. The whole church prayed that God would send him a woman to love. It isn't right that he was alone, especially after he had been married and lost his wife. Had he been single all along, we would have prayed that he stay that way because the Lord wanted him to be alone. Men who start their ministries single stay single because God means to use all of them. Darius came to us already engaged to be married. He wasn't meant to be alone."

"And did you think that I was going to be the one for him?" Nina asked.

Elaine shrugged. "At first I was doubtful because you were so indecisive about seeing him. You were afraid of what he does. I prayed God placed you in his path for a purpose whether it was marriage or ministry. I was praying for marriage but God gave me both. I watched you and him and seen the love grow between you. I've watched the zeal in your eyes when you fought with him about helping the church pay the mortgage. I knew then that you were the one. You had better get ready for the great work God has for you. Darius is headed for great things and he needs you by his side."

"I'm ready Auntie, I really am. I wanted to be on the sidelines because I thought that the congregation wouldn't accept me but today I saw the love and support. I don't yet know how the Lord will use me but since I already have a calling, I will use it to help Darius in his ministry," Nina told her aunt.

"Your dad would have been so proud child. I'm so glad that one of us is here to see you grow into this wonderful woman of God. You know if you really think about it, your whole career was a rehearsal for this."

Nina didn't say anything because there wasn't anything she could say. Her destiny was before her and she was happy. She wasn't even afraid anymore she realized. God had a plan for her and she was happy and ready for whatever He needed her to do.

The other night Darius called her wise and she hoped that she would be able to continue to be so to him. Even men of God needed an outside opinion every now and again. They didn't necessarily have to hear from God all the time. She realized that sometimes God would place people in your path to help you carry the burden He has given you. She was that to Darius and prayed that she never failed him.

Darius went home to change. He was taking Nina out and he didn't want to wear his clergy garb. He'd worn it this morning because he was lead to do it, he didn't quite understand why but he obeyed the Lord's voice.

It was a hot afternoon, but he pulled on a suit. He expected Nina to dress up as well. They were going to the place where it all began. They were going to the Bistro Grill Restaurant.

When Darius called for Nina she looked radiant in a black calf length scoop necked dress. The fit of it emphasized her tiny waist and he wondered if she had lost weight, but she looked beautiful and her eyes fairly glowed at him. She wore her hair up in a becoming bun.

"Are you ready," he asked in a choked up voice.

"Yes, I'm ready. I can't believe we are going back there," she answered excitedly.

"I thought it fitting we go celebrate our engagement there. I called ahead to make reservations, hopefully we won't be disturbed. I am hungry and intend to eat," Darius said.

"I think I'll have same exact foods I had the last time. Is that place going to be our place? You know the place we'll go to when we want to be sentimental?" Nina asked.

"If you want it to be, then it will be," he answered.

"I'll let you know later."

"What's that supposed to mean?"

"Nothing, I am so glad the church was so accommodating to us this morning. I love you very much Darius and I can't wait to be your wife." Nina said earnestly.

"I could answer but then we'd both be feeling uncomfortable so just know that I love you very much too," Darius said as he swung the car into the restaurant's parking lot.

Just as Nina expected, the lot was packed. They had to park across the street. Darius called ahead and naturally, since the media already were circulating the news about their engagement, the restaurant had joined the cause. The minute they crossed the street, the press surrounded them and started taking pictures and asking questions.

"I wanted to warn you that making the reservation was giving the restaurant permission to alert the press, but I didn't want to upset you. The good news is that since we are already here, if we do this today, the following days won't be so bad."

"Why didn't you tell me?" Darius asked as he blocked his face from a camera flash.

"Smile honey, and put your arms around me," Nina whispered for his ears alone.

Darius did so and the picture taking began in earnest. Nina and Darius posed for several pictures and then answered a few questions.

They wouldn't give the press a wedding date or plans on where they intended to live. Finally, they were able to enter the restaurant.

The restaurant's owner himself escorted them to the most private table he had and then bowed low to them. He clapped his hands and their waiter came to serve them.

Nina tried to order what she had the last time they had been there but she couldn't remember what she ordered. Instead, she had what Darius was having. She ordered a steak well done, wild rice, and a vegetable medley. They both had salads and iced tea to drink. Nina remembered the cheesecake was good the last time and ordered that as well.

"Baby I'm sorry I didn't think," Darius began. He felt awful that the media ruined their nice romantic evening. Even now, he could see the owner shooing people away who might have otherwise flocked to their table for autographs.

"It's all right. It would have been nice if the press hadn't mobbed us but as long as you are by side, I can handle it. I love you," Nina said in an effort to soothe him.

"I want to make it up to you. Allow me to cook you a nice romantic dinner at my house, it'll be just the two of us. I'll have romantic music playing in the background and candles everywhere. What do you think?"

Nina smiled at him and swallowed hard, "I think it will very romantic indeed. Did you know that a lot of women think it is very sexy for a man to cook for them?"

Darius reached over to take Nina's hand. He intertwined their fingers and grinned at her. "And do you think it romantic and sexy for me to cook for you Cat?"

"I think it is very sexy and very romantic for you to cook for me. I won't know what to do afterwards, jump your bones or what?" expressed Nina in a low purring voice.

"Ahem, I get your point sweetheart. I like teasing you just to see your eyes change. I never get tired of them reacting. It calls to mind what I'll see them do on our wedding night," Darius said. He knew he was on dangerous ground but he didn't care. The look on her face was intoxicating.

"Kiss me Darius" Nina demanded. Her eyes were dark and she was breathing heavy. Their table was round and once they had finished eating, he moved his chair so that they were sitting side by side. Darius leaned over to kiss her. He meant the kiss to be soft and romantic but when their lips touched, Nina pulled him closer to hold his face.

She kissed him as if they were alone. Her lips promised him things that he only dreamed. The deep purring in her throat told him that she had lost her control.

Nina broke their contact suddenly. Her eyes were so dark he couldn't tell if they were green anymore. "I love you Darius. This ring is proof that we are going to marry, I am going to be your wife, but right now, I am having a very hard time. I'm feeling things that scare me, that make me want to do things. These feelings are strong and very hard resist. Up until now, I was able to control myself, but I have no strength left," she told him. Her eyes suddenly filled with tears and he pulled her close.

He became very conscious of where they were and who might be watching or taking pictures. Their table was secluded but that didn't mean that someone couldn't take a picture. He wouldn't be able to bear it if someone took a picture of them at this most vulnerable time.

"Let's get out of here," Darius said suddenly. He signaled the waiter who came quickly. Darius told him that he wanted the check and the waiter produced it from the pocket in his apron. Darius paid and left a handsome tip then escorted his fiancée out of the restaurant.

There were a few more news vans outside. They posed for a couple more pictures and then Darius was seating Nina in the front seat of his car.

He hoped that no one was following them and he kept checking his rearview and side-view mirrors to make sure that they were not.

"Catalina I am taking you to my house because we need to talk. We will be alone but I promise you that nothing will happen. Are you okay with that?"

"I'm sorry Darius if I was a little weird back there but I thought you should know," Nina said. Her voice sounded flat.

"Okay, don't talk now. Just sit back and try to relax," Darius told her.

Because it was the weekend, the traffic was horrific. It was late when he parked the car in his drive. He debated on whether they should postpone their talk for another time but he felt that they shouldn't delay it. He held her hand as they climbed the steps up to the door. Nina was unusually subdued beside him and he worried that she might've withdrawn from him completely.

He led her directly to the living room and they sat on the loveseat.

"Catalina what's going through your mind right now?" he asked.

"I was trying to picture this romantic dinner you promised me. Are you going to have candles in here too?" Nina looked around the room trying to imagine it filled with glowing candles.

"Oh baby, I thought we were teasing each other in the restaurant. If I had known how you were feeling, I wouldn't have taken it so far. I'm so sorry."

"You don't have to be I am not a child. I've read a few romance novels in my time and I understand what I'm feeling," she told him.

"I can pray with you and it may help a little, okay?"

"Yes pray with me please," Nina murmured and they held hands.

"*Father we come before you pleading for mercy. Give us the strength we need to control our flesh. Do not let us fall to temptation in Jesus' name we pray Amen.*"

"Darius, do you still want to cook for me?"

"Of course I do, but we aren't going to let anything happen." Darius stood up then pulled Nina to her feet. He held her close for a minute and then suddenly pulled away. "Come let me take you home."

Darius drove Nina home thinking that they were going to be on their guard all the time now. He also thought that they had better find activities to do that didn't require them to be alone so much. They do well in crowds, but alone there is always the chance that either of them may say something that would make being alone together uncomfortable. *Lord I need you to speed up the year!* Darius prayed silently.

They agreed that he needn't come in so they kissed outside and left it at that. Nina climbed the stairs to her room feeling not so much ashamed as guilty. Darius wanted to have a romantic evening and so did she but she couldn't help feeling the way that she did.

They were engaged to be married and that was a wonderful thing. A promise to love each other forever was a very big deal. Had they been just a regular couple would they have been less concerned about celibacy? She knew what the bible teaches about celibacy. She also knew that some people considered an engagement the next best thing and didn't wait for the wedding night, as long as there was going to be a wedding that it was okay.

Charles Bennett came to mind and the upbringing she enjoyed. Her dad had always expected her to marry one day but he always told her that the man she married would respect her more if she were untouched. He also said that the man she married would have to be the best of the best before he would allow him to marry his daughter.

Nina smiled. Her father would have approved of Darius because he fit the bill. Darius was the best of the best. All of the sudden, Nina wasn't worried anymore. Even if Darius had not been clergy, she knew that his engrained goodness wouldn't have allowed them to sin.

She felt better and sighed with relief. Nina closed her eyes and went to sleep. Tomorrow was another day with a completely new set of mercies the lord has for her and whatever challenge came her way, she would be ready for it.

Monday morning Nina awoke to cloudy skies. She had a lot to do and didn't really want to be out in the rain. Jennifer's dress fitting was for the afternoon and then there were a thousand and one things to do at the center. It was almost finished. She started scheduling interviews to staff the center.

Jennifer was her co-director and she was not only credentialed but between jobs. They were interviewing teachers for the afterschool program Nina wanted to have available to the community later on in the week.

By the end of the day, Nina wanted to go somewhere to hide. The dress fitting went fine for her but Jennifer's dress needed a few adjustments. Jennifer had gone on a diet and lost five more pounds than she had anticipated. Now the dress just hung on her body. While she waited on the dressmaker to make the adjustments on the wedding gown, Nina chewed on aspirin. Her head hurt so bad, she felt nauseous.

"I suggest you stop skipping meals and maybe throw in a milkshake here and there. You are going to waste away by the time you get married. You are going to be this stick in this big dress, Jonas is going to grab the dress, and holler inside 'Baby you in there?'" said Nina.

"You make it sound like it is a bad thing," Jennifer said.

"Your wedding is in less than in a week and you've had the dress taken in twice already. Your body frame isn't a size six, Jen. You and Jonas are both West Indian, your culture don't take to stick figures," Nina explained.

Jennifer laughed, "You got that right. Jonas' mother comment on a picture of me he sent her. She wanted to know if I was sick. I know all about my culture Nina, but fat isn't healthy either."

"Whatever girl, I need to go home and take something for this headache. I've been getting these headaches a lot lately. I wonder if I'm coming down with something," said Nina.

"Oh no you don't, you can't get sick now. Come on let's get you home. I suggest you eat, have a cup of tea and take a couple of Tylenol for your headache. If Darius calls you, tell him that you need to rest, okay?" Jen said as they got into their cars.

"Don't worry I won't let you down Jen. Promise me that you'll eat something with lots of calories too," replied Nina.

"Deal," Jen called out from her car window and then she drove off.

Nina arrived home to find a note Elaine for her. She was out with the women's auxiliary. Seeing as how she didn't have to interact with her aunt, Nina made a sandwich for dinner. She also made a cup of tea, took the Tylenol Jennifer suggested and went to bed.

Wednesday night after bible study, Nina was talking quietly with Jennifer when Darius came to join them.

"Jennifer, Jonas tells me that you've found the perfect apartment. That is wonderful indeed," he told her.

"It is. Tomorrow we're getting the furniture delivered. I was just asking Nina if she would come help me decorate," Jennifer answered easily. Her wedding was in a few days and Nina was amazed at how calm she was.

"Do you mind if I borrowed Nina for few minutes?" Darius asked. He didn't wait for an answer and pulled Nina aside.

"She's all yours," Jen said, "See you tomorrow Nina."

Darius smiled at her and then turned coldly to Nina. "You've been avoiding me, Catalina."

"I've been busy," she replied just as coldly.

"I'd like to know why. If it is because of what happened the other night, I'm sorry but you started it. I thought you were kidding."

"I'm sorry Darius but I really don't want to discuss it right now. We can talk tomorrow." Nina said and made to leave.

"No we won't talk tomorrow, we'll talk tonight. Expect me later." He said and walked away.

Nina left the sanctuary to find Elaine waiting for her beside the car. She got in, waited for her aunt to buckle her seat belt, and drove away.

"You are going to have to talk with him sometime Nina," her aunt said.

"Are you eavesdropping Auntie?"

"No, but everyone can see that you two are at odds and not talking. His face turns to stone when he sees you and you just shut down. If this keeps up, there might not be a wedding next year."

"Then so be it. I won't have to deal with that, that arrogant— man," Nina said vehemently.

"All right, I'm staying out of it. You are on your own," declared Elaine.

"Thank you," replied Nina.

She was angry with herself for being weak. She was guilty of avoiding her fiancé but that was because she felt helpless to all the illicit thoughts overwhelming her. No amount of praying was helping. She just couldn't stop the flow of carnal thoughts or the urge to act them out. It was no wonder she was having headaches. She couldn't sleep either because her dreams were full of sensuous scenarios. She felt too embarrassed to talk with Elaine about it and she couldn't speak with Darius either because he was the source. She didn't know what to do!

It all started Sunday night when they had gone to the restaurant.

After confessing how she felt to him he had been so nice and comforting. She realized that he hadn't been in control that night either. She felt the changes in his body when he had held her close. She was surprised and tried to play it cool but there was no denying that he was just as affected as she was.

That was why she hadn't invited him in. She didn't want things to get worse. Romance novels do not describe a man's body accurately at least not the ones she's read. What would their wedding night be like if what she felt was so shocking to her?

They talked a little in California and he assured her that his charismatic presence on the pulpit didn't extend to the bedroom. She believed him then, but after the other night, she knew how wrong he was. How could she ever hope to satisfy such a virile man? Their wedding night was sure to be a disaster and he'd hate her.

Nina sat at the kitchen table with Elaine to have a cup of tea. She prayed silently that Darius would change his mind and not come by. She didn't have the strength to speak constructively with him. She didn't have the words to express adequately what she felt and she knew he wouldn't understand. This wasn't something she could discuss with her aunt or anyone. It was too embarrassing. There was no one she could talk with about this.

The doorbell chimed and it was 9:45. She hoped she could state the late hour and promise to talk with him in the morning. When Nina didn't get up to answer the door, Elaine did so murmuring the entire way about how stubborn her niece was.

"If you two don't get it together tonight I suggest you get some counseling," Nina could hear her aunt say.

"I'll take that into advisement Sister. Where is she?" Darius asked further.

"She's in the kitchen. If you need me I'll be upstairs so don't hesitate to call me."

"Sister Elaine, we may get a little loud but don't worry," he warned her.

Darius entered the kitchen to find Nina with her head down on her arms. She had her eyes closed but he knew that she wasn't asleep.

"We need to straighten this out tonight Catalina, and I for one am not leaving here until we come to an understanding. Heck I don't even know why we aren't speaking. Can you tell me what I've done?" He thought it was best to assume blame. To a woman's mind, it was usually the man's fault.

Nina opened her eyes to look up at him. He looked baffled but he didn't fool her, he could put up a good front too.

"I don't think we can discuss this Darius. Something happened the other night and I just can't talk about it with you. You'd accuse me of being silly and childish," Nina confessed.

Darius sat down and he still looked baffled when Nina looked at him again.

"What in the world are you talking about?" he asked.

Nina stood up and walked away from him to the living room. Naturally, he wouldn't think there was anything to worry about if she talked it over with him.

Darius got up to follow her. Was that had fear in her eyes, was she afraid of him? This was truly unnerving to think that she was afraid of him. Were his kisses too strong? Did he accidentally touch her inappropriately and not know it? He'd had a few hairy moments himself that night he couldn't be sure.

"Catalina you must tell me why you are afraid of me. We can't go on if I scare you, you know that don't you?" He approached her slowly. Darius took her hand in his. He lifted it up to his lips and kissed her palm. Nina pulled her hand away quickly and swallowed hard.

She threw her arms around him and held him tight. "Darius I love you but right now I'm having trouble with you touching me," Nina whispered and pulled away quickly.

"My God I did touch you inappropriately didn't I? Honey I don't remember doing it, I'm sorry." Darius caught hold of her hand.

"No Darius you didn't touch me. Please go home," Nina pleaded.

"If I didn't touch you what did I do? You have to tell me."

Nina was getting angry and scared, "I don't have to tell you anything Darius. Just go home," Nina insisted.

"I told you that I wasn't going until we resolved this issue."

Nina had never felt this desperate before and she didn't know how to control herself. Instead, she was going to do the only thing she could do. *She* was going to leave.

She walked over to the bottom of the stairs and called for her aunt.

Elaine came down as fast as she could. She stood on the bottom step regarding them. "Have you two cleared things up?" she asked them.

Nina cleared her throat. "Auntie, Darius and I are having a disagreement. I've asked him to leave but he won't so I'm going to leave. I won't talk with him anymore and you can't make me either. I suggest you sit him down and explain why he cannot force me to talk with him." Nina said calmly. She grabbed her purse she'd hung on the banister and walked out of the house.

Darius sat on the bottom step next to Elaine who had also sat down. "There is something seriously wrong with that woman. She is suddenly afraid of me but she won't tell me what I'd done."

"Darius I think there is just too much Hollywood in that child. She is so dramatic and moody. She wants me to explain why you can't force her to speak with you, but she neglected to tell me why you can't," said Elaine.

Secure in the knowledge that he hadn't done anything wrong, Darius told Elaine what had transpired between him and Nina.

"I love her Elaine, I really do. Where do you think she's gone?"

"She needs to talk with a woman her own age so I think she's gone to talk with Jennifer. Don't worry she'll be okay. Go home; I'll give you a ring when she gets back."

Darius nodded sadly and got up. He waved weakly at her and left.

Elaine locked the door and went back up to her room. Nina was such a strange child these days. She knew that her niece was becoming intimidated. She also thought that whatever was spooking her would pass. Engaged couples in the Lord often felt tested and tempted. Nina wasn't afraid of standing in a full stadium to entertain people but one man who only wants to love her scared her. Oh well, it will keep for another day she thought as she got into bed.

Nina drove straight to Sister Rachel's house. She called ahead to warn her friend that she was coming. She made Jen promise that she wouldn't let her mother in on their little talk. Jennifer was waiting for her at the door. Nina parked her car and walked into the house.

Sister Rachael and her daughter lived in another part of Cambria Heights and their house was similar to Elaine's but theirs was bigger. Their décor was West Indian with native paintings and wall hangings.

Jen bypassed the living room and took Nina upstairs to her bedroom.

"Okay girlfriend, this had better be good. What's going on with you and Darius? He looks miserable and so do you."

"Jen how long did you and he date?" Nina asked her friend.

"We had four dates, why?"

"He didn't kiss you and hold you close did he?"

"We kissed once and that was when we both realized that it wasn't going to work. What's going on?" Jen asked.

Nina recounted their dinner at the restaurant and about how they were teasing each other. She told her friend how all of the sudden she had carnal thoughts and how she wanted to act on them. Jennifer laughed at that. She laughed so hard, Nina began to think that it was a bad idea to come see her friend in the first place.

"Jen it wasn't funny then and it isn't now. I need to ask you a question. Have you and Jonas ever experienced that?"

"We have had a few moments but nothing like you've described. Jonas and I have been celibate and will remain so until our wedding night. I'll tell you one thing and you mustn't tell anyone. Promise me that it will be our secret."

Nina crossed her heart, promised, and got more comfortable on Jennifer's bed. Her bedroom was all lively colors. She could tell that she had started dismantling the room because there were a few bare spots on the walls.

"Jonas and I aren't virgins. I can't tell you his story but I can tell you mine. Before I received the Lord, I was in a relationship that was physical and I thought that he and I were going to get married but it ended badly.

I was 19 and stupid at the time. But Jonas is the best thing that has happened to me."

"What is sex like? I mean I know the mechanics of it but for a woman what is it like?" asked Nina.

"For one thing he was my first so it wasn't pleasant. I'll never forget it because it wasn't what you read in the romance novels. It wasn't romantic and he didn't know any better and wasn't gentle, but after that it was nice." At Nina's horrified expression, Jen shook her head. "Okay, imagine what you've been feeling and multiply that by a million. Then imagine knowing that the only person in the entire world who could make everything right again is him and when your bodies join it is the most wonderful feeling in the world." Jennifer told her. She had a faraway expression on face.

"Okay I get it sex is nice but were you ever afraid of his body?" Nina looked her friend in the eye not caring that she was blushing.

"Oh I get it now. Did he get excited and his body changed?"

"Yes, the other night. It wasn't the first time but this time was different. I think he was aware of how excited he had gotten but ignored it. Jennifer this has nothing to do with *any* sense of pride of his physique. It's more like, what am I going to do? I could *never* in a million years deal with, with —you know."

"You know I used to wonder about him when he's up there preaching. He exudes so much power that a girl can't help but wonder about that."

Nina's eyes were round as saucers, "Oh my God I thought I was the only one who thought that. We talked about it a little when we were away but not much. He assured me that he wasn't a brute, that he would be gentle with me when we married, but after the other night I don't care how gentle he can be, I just know that he won't be happy with me."

Jennifer laughed again. "Girl that man loves you and he's not a novice. He'll be so gentle the discomfort will be minimal. Just you wait and see." Jennifer said.

"Jen you are not grasping what I'm trying to say. I understand that he loves me and I understand that he will be gentle. What I can't fathom is how my body is going to accommodate him. He'll hate me and our wedding night will be ruined."

"Girl you are so lucky!" Jennifer gushed. She sobered up then patted

Nina on the arm. "I'm sorry, I'm getting married and my every other thought has been my wedding night. Look, try not to worry too much about it. Men and women have been joining since time began and you'll find that you and he will love each other without fear."

"So apart from the initial discomfort, it gets better right?" Nina asked again. She stood up to leave.

"*Loads* better." Jen laughed again because Nina blushed crimson this time.

"Jen I promised to keep your secret, I need you to keep this conversation between us as well. Okay?"

"My lips are sealed. I can't believe you grew up in Hollywood Nina. Didn't you and your friends talk about sex?"

"We did but my friends were all sexually active and they were all about how many guys they'd had. I was too shy to let on that I'd never done it."

"You are definitely not what anyone expected. Go home and stop worrying," she told her at the door.

"Good night." Nina said at the door.

Jennifer watched Nina get into her car before she closed the door. She shook her head as she climbed the stairs back to her room. She didn't know how she ever was going to look at pastor and not think about his attributes. She giggled once more. Nina was something else.

Nina drove to Darius' house. She took a deep breath and got out quickly to ring the doorbell. Darius must've been downstairs because he opened the door almost immediately. They stood there nearly a full minute before either of them spoke.

"I'm sorry I'm such a baby," Nina began.

"I'm sorry I scared you," Darius countered.

"May I come in?"

"Only if you want to," answered Darius pulling her in.

"I want to apologize for my behavior and maybe explain."

Darius led her to the living room and he sat in the single chair.

Nina couldn't sit down. She dropped her purse on the couch and paced.

"Okay, the other night when we came here and talked about what I was feeling I realized that you were feeling the same way too. When you kissed me and pulled me close, I felt how much your body had changed. It was a lot more than I expected, more than I've experienced before and I freaked out."

"Are you telling me that this is about, about, — my body?" Darius asked uncomfortably.

"Before you ridicule me, I want you to know that although I hadn't been with a man it doesn't mean that I don't know what I'm talking about."

"I can't change my body but I want you to know that I would never hurt you. I can't believe we are having this conversation. When did my body become an issue?"

Nina blushed crimson but she looked him straight on, "The other night you had gotten aroused more than I've ever felt you be before. You were so much more than before and it surprised me. I started thinking about how virile you must be and that I wouldn't be any good. I know we talked about it before but I didn't take all of that into account. You're just a little more than I'd imagined." Nina couldn't look at him now. She was so embarrassed to be talking about this with him.

"Men and women come in different sizes and shapes. I am taller than you are but we have no problems kissing do we? The bible says that we are fearfully and wonderfully made. You'll find that on our wedding night, knowing that we are both free of restraints, your desire for me will be more intense.—,"

"You don't have to give me a biology lesson Darius," Nina said interrupting him. "I know that my body will change so as to accommodate you much like when a woman is giving birth to a child, her body changes to let it out. It is the same principle but I also know that my body is of the small variety," Nina demonstrated with her hand.

"Do you believe that I would not love you anymore if we had a difficulty in that department?" asked Darius.

Nina went to him then and sat in his lap. "Darius I know that you probably feel that I am being silly but I love you and I want more than anything to have a wonderful life with you. I want you to be happy with all of me," she explained.

"Nina, do you have any medical problems that would make what you said a problem?" Darius asked cupping her chin so he could see her face.

"No, but I seriously doubt I'll be able to——, you know." Nina blushed again and hid her face in the crook of his neck.

"Listen to me woman we aren't going to have any problems in that category so I suggest we stop wasting time on it and move on to something that is going to be difficult for us, like house hunting," Darius said. He was more than willing to change the subject.

When Nina hadn't answered for several minutes, Darius looked down to find that she was practically asleep. He held her close for a few minutes and then shook her awake.

"Come on babe, I'll take you home," he said softly.

"No don't want to go home." Nina protested settling herself more comfortably.

"Do you want to sleep in my bed with me?" Darius asked playfully.

Nina sat up to glare at him. She got up from off his lap and grabbed her purse. "When we have children you are not allowed to discipline them, you have a mean streak in you."

"Do you want me to drive you home in my car and then pick you up for breakfast so you can retrieve yours in the morning?"

"No. Come let me out." Nina said in a no nonsense fashion.

Darius walked her to the door. "Good night Catalina."

Nina turned to him and smiled deviously. She suddenly pulled his head down to hers to kiss him. She held nothing back and pulled away only when she had gotten the desired effect from him.

"Good night big boy," she said and walked out.

"You are not allowed to discipline our children either," he called out after her.

CHAPTER EIGHTEEN

Jennifer looked picture perfect in her off-white satin and lace gown. Her bouquet was made of orchids and had the sanctuary decorated with them as well.

Nina's maid of honor gown was of the palest peach. Her hair was beautiful with tiny peach flowers pinned in it. She performed her duties with all the seriousness it deserved.

Darius wore a special preaching robe in white with gold filigree embroidery. He performed the ceremony with all seriousness until it came time for Jonas and Jennifer to exchange their vows. Clearly nervous, Darius had them laughing with little anecdotes. When he pronounced them as man and wife, Nina had tears in her eyes.

The reception was at a hall in Westchester, New York. Darius couldn't attend as he has another function to officiate at immediately following the church ceremony. As maid of honor, Nina was obligated to stay for the whole thing. The hall was beautiful and the guests were many. It seemed that all of Jonas' family made the trip from the Caribbean to witness him getting married, which made Sister Dorothea very happy.

Rachel was radiant in her mother of the bride gown and Nina wasn't surprised to see tears in her eyes as well. She supposed that Rachel would miss her daughter, as she would be living all alone now.

When Nina was finally able to leave, she pulled her dear friend aside, gave her a big hug, and told her to be happy. "When you get back from your honeymoon I'm going to need you to help me plan my wedding, so don't go getting pregnant just yet."

"Did you guys set a date?" asked the new bride.

"June of next year, but there's so much to do. You guys had been planning your wedding even before you got engaged."

"Jonas and I don't plan on having any children yet so don't you worry," Jen assured her.

"You look so beautiful girlfriend. I really wish you all the happiness in the world."

"Thank you, bye!"

Nina watched as the bridesmaids carried Jen away for more pictures. She turned to leave the reception hall and bumped into Darius coming in.

"Where did you come from? Didn't you have that presentation to do?" she asked.

"I did, but I chose not to stay for the reception so now I am free. I thought you'd appreciate the ride home. You look exquisite, Cat." Darius said appreciatively.

"Thank you and you look good enough to eat," she replied as she admired his champagne colored suit.

"Just imagine that we have one more of these to get through and the center's opening ceremony, before we can even begin to think about our own wedding," Darius said.

"You are a most unusual man you know that? I don't think I've heard a man talk about his own wedding as much as you do."

"That's because I know what I'm getting. Just out of curiosity, how were you getting home? Your aunt left long ago and most of the people from the church are gone too. I double checked before coming up here," he informed her.

"Oh well um, the limo driver and I had developed this rapport you see, and it was understood that he was taking me home tonight," Nina said with a straight face.

Once they got outside, they encountered the limo parked just a few feet away and the driver got out to wave Nina over. Darius turned incredulous eyes to her. "You were *serious?*"

"Relax dude," Nina flashed him a smile. "He's giving a bunch of us a ride back to Queens. Come with me while I tell them I won't need the ride anymore."

Nina dragged him along and sure enough, there were three other women sitting in the limo.

"Hey ladies I won't need the ride after all. My knight in shining armor came for me. This is Pastor Fairchild my fiancée," Nina told them.

"Hello ladies, nice to meet you," Darius greeted them. With the women eying him up and down, he became self-conscious and backed away.

The limo driver came around to close the door and waved at Nina once more as he got into the driver's seat. The couple waved as they took off.

"You are so cute when you are jealous. Kiss me sir knight," requested Nina playfully.

Darius bowed down low and then kissed her clear to her toes.

"The Lord's mercy endures forever, Amen." Nina murmured softly.

"Amen," Darius repeated. "Come on the car is this way." He led Nina to the car and handed her in.

The drive back to Queens was about an hour's drive from the hall. Nina leaned back and slid off her shoes. "Darius I asked Jen to help me with some of the wedding stuff, so when she gets back from her honeymoon, we'll get together to map out the whole thing. My lawyer called to ask if I would need a pre-nuptial agreement. I told him that I didn't think so but you know how lawyers can be," Nina said quietly. She'd been trying to find an opportune time to discuss the matter with Darius; she wasn't sure how he'd take it. Personally, she didn't feel the need for one.

"Even if we didn't make it as a couple, I could never lay claim to your money Nina, no matter what the law says. You do whatever you think is right."

"Fine, I'll tell him no. Where do you want to go on our honeymoon?"

Darius smiled brilliantly at her, "I hear that if you go to Aruba, you could make love on the beach and no one would bat an eye lash. The place was made for lovers," he said.

Nina shook her head, the mental picture of sand everywhere wasn't her idea of romance. "How about we make love in Cancun Mexico in a beautiful hotel suite instead?"

"I hear the water is undrinkable, but I could undress you in the Bahamas," he suggested.

Nina shook her head again. "How about we take a 14-day honeymoon cruise? We can make love to the rocking of the ship. And when the ship docks in those exotic places we can go shopping and have fun," Nina countered.

"That's a good one, write that one down," he agreed enthusiastically.

They'd been playing this game for close to a week now. It was fun and risqué but under control.

The Charles Bennett Recreation Center opened its doors on August 14, 2010. Nina had been behind the scenes booking choirs to sing and bands. She had a catering service provide the food. She didn't want Christ Tabernacle to do anything because it was a celebration for all of them as well.

Darius was the master of ceremonies and although Nina tried to stay in the background, he called her up to say a few words. Nina came up with the sound of applause ringing in her ears. She was nervous but smiled at the crowd.

"Good morning. Wow, this is a great day for all of us here in this community and for the Christ Tabernacle family. I would like to thank my Lord and Savior Jesus Christ who is the author of my life. Without him, none of this would be possible. I would also like to thank all those who worked hard to make this center a reality. From the contractors, artisans, all the way down to the City of New York who made us legal and gave us permission to close the block off for our celebration.

I am grateful that I was able to name this place after my father, the late great Charles Bennett. He would have been very proud to be part of this celebration. Now without further ado, I declare that this center is open. Have fun everybody!" Nina shouted.

Nina chose Elaine to cut the big red ribbon in front of the doors and then they were inside. The place looked just like she envisioned. Marble tiles and wood paneling for the entrance. There were four offices, two on either side of the entrance. Straight ahead from the entrance was the auditorium where the choirs and bands were going to perform. It had a capacity for 600 and then there were the games room downstairs. The kids had a choice of playing pool, pinball, Ping-Pong and other arcade games. The learning center was opposite the games room with desks and seven computers. Behind the center, lay the pool and parking lot. Except for the learning center and the offices, the whole place was open to the public.

The face painting station was a hit with the little kids. She was glad she thought of it. It was ten in the morning and the place was packed. The pool would be open around noon and the food had already started to arrive.

She hired the last of the permanent staff the week before and many of the youth from the church applied for jobs. Those who qualified were hired and she gave temporary jobs to those that weren't for the day.

By the end of the day, Nina was tired and wobbly on her feet. Elaine left an hour earlier and Darius volunteered to drive several of the children home whose parents weren't able to make the opening. She was waiting for him to return for her.

In all the excitement, she hadn't eaten. Although someone had placed a plate of food in her hand, Nina kept putting it down as she was called away to handle minor crises one after another. Finally, she hadn't eaten much.

She knew that her blood glucose level was low and the lightheadedness she felt meant that it was at the danger level. As soon as she reached home, she would eat something and have some juice, she thought.

When Darius finally returned for her and she got in the car quickly. "I know that it is only 8pm but, I am beat. The opening was a great success don't you think?" Nina asked over-brightly.

"It was great and I am very proud of you. You pulled it off," Darius replied. "I want you to sleep in Cat," he said further as he took in her tired features.

"I think I will, I have been working all week and I was up late last night making sure that everything would go well today," she agreed.

Darius pulled in front of her house and walked around to help Nina out of the car but she got out quickly to race up the steps before he could get near. Darius eyed her suspiciously.

She unlocked the door and rushed in with Darius trailing behind her.

Elaine called out that she was in the living room and they headed there.

"Is everything over?" she asked them.

"Yes it is and everyone had fun," Nina answered. She went to stand beside the sofa holding the back of it in a death grip.

"What's the matter child you look white as a ghost," her aunt declared.

Nina hadn't time to reply as she fell forward in a dead faint. Darius caught her and laid her down gently. "She hasn't eaten all day and her blood sugar is low," supplied Darius.

Elaine got up to get a wet cloth for her forehead. A few minutes later, Nina came to. Both Elaine and Darius glared down at her.

"Didn't you eat any of the food I fixed you earlier?" she asked disapprovingly.

Nina tried to sit up but Darius pushed her back down. "That was you?" she asked weakly.

Elaine wasn't amused. "Did you eat?" she asked again.

"Well I tried to, but I kept being interrupted until I lost track of where I set the plate. I could sure eat something now," Nina answered quite subdued.

"She needs something sweet first, like orange juice with extra sugar." Darius told Elaine who was already heading for the kitchen.

He knelt down shaking his head at her, "Baby you can't keep pushing yourself to do everything. You hired people to help with the activities, why didn't you delegate it to them. Suppose you'd been alone or driving?" he asked.

"Well I wasn't and I've learned a valuable lesson?" she tried for cute.

"No! You will not let this happen again is that understood?" Darius asked in a deceptively calm tone.

Elaine returned with a tray. She placed a tall glass of orange juice in her hand and handed Darius a heaping plate of fried chicken, potato salad, and macaroni and cheese for her.

"Now you eat that and see if you don't feel better," she cooed.

Darius allowed her to sit up and under their watchful supervision; Nina drank the orange juice and ate almost all of the food on the plate.

She was sick to her stomach but she couldn't tell them that. Elaine took the tray back to the kitchen and Nina leaned back against the cushions willing the nausea away.

"I don't like it when you are angry with me," she told him when she could speak.

"I don't like it either Cat," he murmured. "You get so engrossed in whatever you're doing you forget to take care of yourself."

"But I'm okay now. I admit that it was careless not to eat but I didn't do it on purpose. If I promise not to let it happen again, will you stop being angry with me?"

Darius took her hand and kissed her knuckles, "I was more scared than angry baby. I imagined all manner of things; I don't want anything to happen to you." Images of Rebecca flashed through this mind scaring him further.

"I'm sorry I worried you. I'm feeling better now and I have you and Aunt Elaine to thank for it," Nina admitted. She felt better and the nausea was gone.

"Okay I think you should call it a night and get some rest," Aunt Elaine came back saying. She motioned for Nina to get up and Darius helped her to her feet.

"I'm not trying to cut your time together short but, Nina needs to rest," she told Darius.

At the door, Nina turned to kiss Darius good-bye and then started climbing the stairs. She turned and waved to them once more.

"And don't even think that you are going to church in the morning young lady," Elaine called after her.

Taking more authority, she ushered Darius through the front door telling him that he too had better get some rest. She told him further that she expected to receive a good word from him in the morning and shut the door.

Nina climbed into bed and for the first time in a week time fell asleep immediately. She was vaguely aware that someone had come into her room but after that, she knew no more.

The following morning she awoke and sat up only to grab her head and lay back down again. Elaine peeked in already dressed to tell her that Jennifer and her husband were picking her up and that she'd see her later.

Nina groaned her reply and waved good-bye. She fell back asleep and didn't wake up again until well past noon. Feeling refreshed she showered and got dressed. The calendar on the wall across from her bed had a big red circle on Tuesday. Nina got closer to remind herself what it was and found that she and Darius were flying to South Carolina for the Council. Bishop Elias Smalls had contacted Darius this past week to finalize their arrival plans.

The plan was to fly there on Tuesday and then from Wednesday thru Saturday Darius would be presiding over the evening services and preach Thursday evening. During the day, he would conduct leadership seminars. The bishop scheduled Nina to sing on two of the evening services and help Darius in any capacity she felt reasonable.

The weekend after that was also marked. Theo and Susannah's wedding was sure to be a memorable event. Nina had the landscapers come to give the grounds a once over even though they had been on retainer since she'd moved out. Through phone calls, Nina coordinated the arrangements with Susannah. Since Nina couldn't be in two places at once, Sue was more than happy to step in and take over. Nina gave her carte blanche to do whatever she wanted short of altering the house for her wedding.

Sue sent her weekly videos of what she had done the closer it became to the wedding date. Nina also gave her a twenty thousand dollar budget to work with and it seemed that the girl used it all. Nina felt that Theo and Jason deserved that and more.

Susannah, her mother and Theo's sister teamed up to finalize the décor plans for the house and grounds. Although she hadn't grown up with her mother, she knew that mothers and daughters seldom worked well together. She hoped Theo's sister would be the voice of reason between them.

By the time Nina had gotten her bedroom straightened out, she could hear her aunt coming in downstairs. Nina met her at the foot of the stairs. "So how was service?" she asked.

"Service was glorious. Everyone wanted to know if you were okay. I told them that you were just getting some rest as you had over done it yesterday," was Elaine's reply.

"I warmed up the food for you, so if you go change we can eat." Nina told her aunt.

"That was nice of you baby, I'll be right down." Elaine said as she climbed the stairs.

The doorbell rang just as Nina wondered if Darius was going to join them. She dropped the silverware she was setting to go answer it. She nearly knocked him over as she threw herself at him.

"I see someone is feeling a lot better today. Did you get some rest?" Darius asked as he disentangled himself from her.

"Of course I'm rested can't you tell?" she asked teasingly.

"Are you ready to eat?" Darius asked.

"I was just setting the table. Aunt Elaine went up to change and she'll be down in a minute. She tells me that the sermon was glorious this morning."

"I thought so too, Minister Aldridge did a fine job. I thought he should preach so I could conserve my energy for the council."

"I have the date marked on my calendar upstairs. Do you have your seminar lesson plans ready yet? I could help you set them up and make copies if you'd like," she offered.

"While you were busy with the center and Theo's wedding plans, I was busy making trips to Staples and Office Max. I have everything ready. However while we are there, I'm going to need your help in setting up poster boards and handing out the lessons to whoever is sitting in on the seminars. You can be my assistant," Darius told her.

"Okay. The order of services has you preaching on Thursday evening and they have me singing on the Wednesday and Friday evening services. Do you think you could have it changed to Wednesday and Thursday instead? I'd like to sing on the night you preach," she asked him.

Nina finished setting the table and her Aunt joined them. Together they brought the food to the table and Darius blessed it.

"I called Bishop Elias and he said that they have other soloists scheduled also and they wouldn't be able to attend on the nights they scheduled you. If you want to know my opinion, I think he just wants to control all of the proceedings is all. But we aren't going to let that bring us down are we?" Darius asked.

"If you ask me it bothers you a lot more than you are letting on, Darius. It's too late to make any changes now. Did I tell you that I was going to the council this year too?" Elaine asked joining in on the conversation.

"She's going to be my roomy," Nina, piped in.

"Good then she can be the buffer we need between us and the bishop. He is sure to be a nuisance I'm thinking," said Darius. He was grateful that he had the opportunity to preach at the council but the bishop rubbed him the wrong way from the beginning.

"Don't you worry about Elias, he and I go back a long way. Before he moved down south, he had a church home here in New York. He was always one of those who thought more of himself than he should," Elaine informed them.

"I think I should start feeling sorry for him now. Just don't be too hard on him. I may need him in the future to preach for us out here," Darius joked.

The rest of the afternoon, Darius and Nina mapped out their strategy for their days at the council. With Elaine along, their meal times would be pleasant and a time of diffusion from any stress derived from autograph seekers and the like. They were under no illusion that although the council was a gathering of Christians, people were sure to recognize Nina and cause disturbances.

Tuesday morning Nina and her aunt got into her SUV and drove to Darius' house to pick him up. Nina and Darius got into a heated disagreement on who was driving to the airport until Elaine insisted that if they didn't make up their minds, that she was calling a cab. Nina promptly and docilely gave up the driver's seat while her aunt took the back.

"I declare sometimes you two are more like children than full grown adults," she said shaking her head.

"Perhaps if your niece weren't so stubborn, we wouldn't be having these childish arguments," Darius complained.

"It's more like if your pastor wasn't such an arrogant male chauvinist, we wouldn't be having *any* arguments," countered Nina.

"Now I don't believe you understand my meaning, get your acts together or there will be misery the likes you have never seen before in your lives," Elaine threatened them.

Darius was the first to laugh and once he started, Nina couldn't keep it in any longer either. They laughed until Elaine reached over to slap the back of Nina's seat.

She realized that they were having some fun at her expense but she wasn't amused. "You may think you are being funny but you had better not embarrass yourselves at the council. We know too many of the people attending for your shenanigans."

"Did she say shenanigans?" Darius asked Nina.

"Yup, I didn't think people said that anymore," she confirmed. That started a whole other round of laughing which made Elaine annoyed even more. She kept her mouth shut and she wouldn't talk with them again the entire ride to the airport.

She kept her silence until she was in her assigned seat on the airplane. She asked Darius to pray for a safe flight and after they said amen, she pulled out her bible and refused to look at them.

Nina seat was between Darius and her aunt. She felt repentant and apologized to her for the teasing. Elaine didn't look up from her bible and acted as if she hadn't heard.

Nina shrugged and ducked her head to get Darius' attention. "So where were we on the list of places to honeymoon?"

"I believe we rejected Cancun because the water was nasty and you didn't like the idea that no one cared if we made love on the beach in Aruba," Darius recited.

"That's right. We liked the idea of doing it on a Caribbean cruise. What do you think of Hawaii? It's supposed to be a good place too or maybe somewhere more exotic like Paris or Greece. What do you think?" Nina asked.

"All right what exactly did you two drink this morning that I didn't?

Are you going to continue this the entire time we are on this plane?" She put her bible down to regard them sternly.

"Lighten up Elaine the flight is too short to be boring. The only excitement we've had this morning was the fans crowding around Nina at the airport. It was a good thing we booked first class otherwise you'd be sitting next, to who knows whom. We are only having some fun," Darius explained.

"I get it. I just don't like being the butt of a joke. It was funny what you two did in the car but this now isn't. You are a minister and you don't know who may be watching and listening. You need to keep what you two were just doing, to yourselves," Elaine warned.

"Yes ma'am," Darius replied. Elaine was right of course. Nina and he were adults and she was right about someone watching or listening to them.

"Nina we will continue our search for the perfect honeymoon place another time. In the meantime would you like to watch a movie?" asked Darius.

"I guess it could keep us occupied. Where's the guide?" asked Nina.

Darius searched and found it hidden between the seats in front of them. First class was not full and they had a whole quad to themselves. Darius looked through the guide and found a pleasant surprise.

"Well, well. This is a movie we could all agree on, even you Sister Elaine." Darius showed them the guide. It was Nina's movie.

For the next hour and forty-five minutes, they watched the movie. Elaine was quiet and a little weepy when her brother's likeness appeared on the screen and she chuckled at the scenes of Nina as a child. She gave the movie a thumbs-up and said that she would recommend it to all her friends at church.

When their plane landed, Darius took charge to lead them through the airport.

The bishop promised to send the church van to meet them and a few others who were arriving at the same time. They had a very brief wait time before his secretary came for them. He drove a sixteen-passenger van and twelve people got on. Another van followed with their luggage. Nina sat throughout the ride listening to demo tapes the secretary happened to have of his sister singing.

Darius kept a straight face while Elaine pretended to be interested in the scenery. Nina was polite and gentle when she told the bishop's secretary that although his sister sounded very nice on the tape, she couldn't do much for her. She did give him the information on a promoter friend of hers who routinely accepted demo tapes.

The hotel was mercifully not very far from the airport and the minute the secretary parked, Darius hurried to escort Nina and Elaine into the building. The van ferrying their luggage was 10 minutes behind them. Of course it was check-in time for the out of town participants as well so Nina had to be polite and courteous as she signed autographs and have her picture taken with guests and staff alike.

Their rooms were on the same floor and Nina entered hers quickly and shut the door. Her aunt shook her head and took pity on her.

"I suppose this happens every time you travel? Maybe Darius and I can run interference for you later today. We don't have to do anything but relax and see the sights if you are up to it." Her aunt said.

"I think I should be okay if I wear my hair up and if we don't go to any place where there's likely to be a crowd. In any case, word has probably spread about my staying here and people will be on the lookout," Nina explained.

There was a knock on the door and Elaine went to answer it. It was Darius and he entered quickly. "It seems that you aren't the only celebrity here. There's a big sign downstairs about the Winans. I don't know which one of them is performing or maybe it's the pastor. Maybe we can hide in his or her wake and get out of here later," he told them.

Nina was unpacking and turned to him smiling. "Boy, the bishop is pulling all the stops to make this event a huge success, isn't he?"

Elaine shook her head and then turned to unpack as well. "What are you two planning on doing for the rest of the afternoon? Nina worried about people mobbing her and this is the first time I've witnessed it, I don't find it pleasant at all. We probably can't sight-see comfortably and where are going to eat?"

"If you two want to go see the sights, I don't mind staying in. I could use the time to go over my solos," Nina offered.

"I'd feel awful leaving you behind. Elaine why don't you go? You are bound to come across someone you know here so maybe you could pal around with them?" Darius suggested.

"That's okay, Darius. I've been to South Carolina before. I think we should stick together. I don't know about you people but I am starving. We are in the South and I for one want to have southern food," Elaine said.

"I'm for that," Nina said brightly.

"Now that you mention it, I'm hungry too," admitted Darius.

They agreed to change out of their traveling clothes and meet by the elevators.

Nina wore her hair up and slid her sunglasses on. Although it was dinnertime, the sun had not gone down yet. They were able to reach the hotel's restaurant without being recognized. Most of the people who traveled on the van with them were also entering the restaurant. They waited twenty minutes before they could get a table.

As they followed the waiter to the table, Nina tried to be as inconspicuous as possible. She took off her sunglasses as they were indoors and with the dim lighting, she thought that she was safe. It wasn't until they were having dessert that Aunt Elaine spotted the bishop heading their way.

"I thought that you might've gone elsewhere for dinner," he said by way of greeting.

Darius stood up to shake his proffered hand and to introduce his companions to him. The bishop shook hands with the women and then turned to wave someone over to him.

"I hope you don't mind if my wife and I join you. This place is packed this evening and they were trying to give us a table in the corner," he said with a superior attitude. Then he signaled a waiter to come add place settings for him and his wife.

Elaine smiled and nodded to Nina. "Elias you haven't changed one bit. How are you doing these days?"

He looked at Elaine and frowned. "I don't believe I've had the pleasure Sister?" he began.

"Elias you and I went to school together and when you were ordained as pastor, my husband was your treasurer until you transferred out here. You remember me now don't you?" Elaine asked him sweetly.

"Elaine Hughes? My lord it has been a long time, and I must say that the years has been kind to you. I was sorry to hear that you lost your husband," he turned to his wife who took it upon herself to sit as close to Nina as she dared. "Sweetheart, this is Elaine Hughes, Pastor Darius Fairchild and his fiancée Nina Bennett."

"I am pleased to meet you. I sincerely hope you enjoy your stay here. And Miss Nina if there is anything you require, don't hesitate to have the hotel staff contact us," First Lady Smalls said in her pleasant Southern drawl.

"That is very kind of you thank you," Nina replied. It wasn't lost on her that the first lady completely ignored the others at the table.

The waiter came to take the newcomers' orders and Darius took the opportunity to ask for the check.

"I saw on the television that you recently built a recreation center Darius. I thought it was a wonderful thing to do. As religious leaders we have a duty to our communities," stated the bishop.

"Actually, it was Nina's idea. As a member of Christ Tabernacle, she insisted that the church be involved," Darius replied refusing to accept any credit.

Nina put her hand on Darius' and smiled at him. "Bishop, the recreation center is being run by the church. It is my hope that while its location is in a community that's in transition the church will have the opportunity to evangelize it. Our young people are much too important to be left to chance."

"My God, what a treasure you are. We should get together sometime soon to discuss ideas, Sister Nina. You may find that we have a lot in common when it comes to the youth," exclaimed the bishop.

The waiter returned with the check and Darius quickly paid it. "Bishop it was a pleasure chatting with you," he stood up and extended his hand to Nina. "I think we are going to call it a night and start fresh in the morning."

"Aunt Elaine would you like to stay for a while to catch up with the bishop?" Nina asked her aunt.

"Aunt Elaine?" the bishop asked looking from Nina to Elaine.

"Of course you remember my brother Charles? Nina is his daughter, I thought everyone knew that," Elaine told him.

"Well isn't this a small world. Your father and I were inseparable when we were young. We used to get into all kinds of trouble together. I consider you family now. I will be upset with you if you call me anything other than Uncle Elias," replied the bishop.

Nina blinked hard and smiled. "I will try to remember that Bishop."

Elaine stood up finally to regard the couple seated at their table.

"Elias, stop teasing my niece. You and I will have plenty of time to catch up these next couple of days. First Lady Smalls it was nice meeting you. Enjoy your dinner dear."

Darius didn't wait to see what would happen next as he pulled Nina along. Elaine wasn't too far behind them when they reached the elevator banks.

"He's going to hit you up for a hefty donation and not just to the council either. You mark my words, he is going to corner you somewhere to try to convince you what a blessing it would be if you financed a project for his church." Elaine stated. The distaste on her face for the man was clear on her features.

"Relax Auntie, I am going to sing my solos and help Darius with his seminars. I will give the council a $1000.00 donation. *Uncle Elias* and I won't be having any discussions about anything," Nina told her aunt. She realized that the bishop was certainly an opportunist.

"I don't suppose he's going to be invited to the wedding is he?" Darius joked.

"I can see him now at the reception going to all my celebrity friends handing out his card." Nina replied. "Was he like this as a young man too?"

Her aunt nodded. "Elias was always trying to make a fast buck. He and Charles were friends but not as close as he made it out to be. Charles was a serious musician and was always practicing," confirmed Elaine.

Wednesday morning after having their breakfasts in their room, Nina and her aunt went to meet Darius. The conference rooms on the lobby floor were for children's seminars and youth activities. Darius was to use the one on the third floor.

Looking at the crowd, Nina suspected that Darius' seminar was popular because she was assisting. She gave no autographs and stayed quiet. Darius conducted his lessons in a timely fashion and by the time he was done, the large group of men and women who attended was very engrossed. They maintained discussions that were both engaging and informational.

By the end, most of them forgot that Nina was sitting up front across from Darius keeping the handouts in order. She gave them out, and had them fill out a form confirming that they attended. Because they had such a large group, Nina had to run to the hotel's office to make more copies of everything.

That evening, Darius conducted the worship part of the service with joy and confidence. The bishop delivered the sermon. Nina was sure that she wasn't going to like him but found that the man had a gift. He could preach and delivered a message that was both anointed and inspirational.

Nina got up to sing her solo. She went over to the musicians to instruct them on which key she was comfortable then sat at the huge grand piano. Nina sang *Amazing Grace*. She experimented with it to give it her own flavor. The musicians kept up, the audience received it well, and she was glad.

Darius preached the following night and it was marvelous. The place was full and the message was a blessing to all. Elaine wore a huge smile on her face and looked around her, proud that her pastor had done so well.

Friday after the evening service, the bishop did try to corner Nina about a project he had. He showed her a picture of the prototype for a cathedral he wanted to build. He explained that funds were low and slow in coming in. His congregation felt burdened with the edifice they had now and had difficulty in extending themselves further.

Nina looked at the picture and commented on how beautiful it was. She also commented on his vision. Nina then dropped her smile and told him that although the bishop's vision was worthy she didn't see how even if she did give him a hand that his congregation would be able to support the bigger edifice if they were having a hard time with the one they already had. She didn't wait for his reply and walked away.

Darius was busy talking with another clergyman, but saw how Bishop Smalls cornered Nina. He watched him show Nina the same picture he had the privilege to see earlier. He breathed easier when he saw Nina's face as she walked away from the bishop.

He caught up with Elaine and Nina at the elevator bank and jumped in before the doors closed. There were other people on the elevator with them and some tried to engage Nina in conversation, but Nina was polite and refused to go any further than repeating the Christian greeting of 'Praise the Lord'.

"What happened down there?" her aunt was the first to ask when they had gained their room. Darius followed them in also.

Nina turned to face both her aunt and Darius. "Uncle Elias showed me a picture of the cathedral he wants to build. It really is a beautiful structure. He wanted me to help him finance it because his congregation was financially strapped with the church they have now. I couldn't believe how he could even ask me such a thing."

"That's Elias for you, always thinking big. So what did you tell him?" Elaine wanted to know.

"I told him that I couldn't see how his congregation was going to be able to handle such a big structure if they were having trouble with the one they already had. I mean I understand that he means well, but if he really wanted to do the Lord's will, he would do well ministering with what he has now. The time may come when the Lord will bless him with a bigger church building or even that cathedral, but his time hasn't come yet and I actually felt insulted," replied Nina.

"That's kind of the way I felt when he first approached me. I wondered if it was the Lord leading him to ask you to sing or if it was his ego wanting to puff up with a successful council. I prayed after that asking God for forgiveness for thinking that way about the man. I decided that coming out here was more for furthering the ministry than for showing off." Darius told them.

"This kind of brings that sermon you preached to mind Pastor," said Elaine. "We let our pride lead us and not acknowledge Him in our affairs. We need to pray for that man. He is anointed but he is guilty of pride and the lack of humility." Elaine said.

Darius held out his hands and the women each took one forming a circle and together they prayed for the bishop. They asked God to open his eyes before it was too late lest he lose everything. They prayed for themselves as well lest they fell too.

It was late and neither of them were tired enough to call it a night. They decided that they would venture outside for a late night snack. During their stay, they were able to eat elsewhere and have that authentic Southern cuisine Elaine wanted.

Nina found that it was greasy and heavy on the stomach. The version her aunt cooked at home was much healthier. As much as Darius loved collard greens, he found that it was too spicy and the smoked pork not as palatable as the smoked turkey Elaine and Rachel used. They stayed away from chitterlings; steak fried chicken, and smothered chicken. Nina wasn't surprised that the majority of the people who ate those foods was overweight and had a variety of health issues.

Across the street from the hotel was a choice of pizza, chicken and ice cream. Pizza won easily and they strolled leisurely to get it. It was nice out with a cooling breeze. Darius walked between the women linking arms with Nina's aunt and holding Nina's hand.

At the pizza place, they sat to eat a small cheese pie with sweet tea. Quite a few people from the council sat at the few tables around them. By now, they had been used to seeing Nina around and just waved.

Suddenly, Nina ducked her head to signal Darius. The bishop entered the restaurant and it looked like he hadn't spotted them yet, but when he did he walked over to join them.

"That was a fine song you blessed us with Sister Nina, and that sermon you preached last night blessed my soul Darius. Once all the business with the council is over, I'd like to contact you to preach at my church. I like to have anointed people around me," he said. Then he got up and went to the counter. It seemed that he ordered ahead and had just come to pick up his food. "Wife is lactose intolerant so I get to eat this all by myself," he chuckled. He waved and left the restaurant.

"I guess he got over his disappointment quickly. I didn't think he'd ever speak to me again," Nina said.

"Don't you worry he's gearing up for another try." Elaine pointed out.

"I don't know about you ladies but I think the council was a great success and that it blessed my soul. I fellowshipped, I networked and I learned. But most of all I love being in God's presence and he truly was there," stated Darius. He didn't want to discuss anything to do with the bishop anymore. Nina and Elaine both agreed with him.

They walked back to the hotel in companionable silence. Darius felt that he gained invaluable contacts and Nina was just feeling blessed to be in the company of fellow Christians who praised with sincerity. Elaine felt that she was chaperoning two people who the Lord has especially set apart. Darius and Nina hadn't really needed anyone to look over them.

CHAPTER NINETEEN

Theodore and Susannah's wedding was the society event of the year, it seemed. Nina tried to be as subtle as possible as this was Theo and Susannah's day. She didn't want her presence to steal the spotlight from off of them. She was grateful that her home was giving someone else the chance to express love.

The ceremony itself was outdoors under a huge white tent. They transformed the grounds into a paradise with flowers and statuary for the reception. Nina almost couldn't distinguish the wait staff and the Greek statues. The bride's table sat on a raised platform apart from their guests.

Susannah's family went all out it seemed. Nina estimated that the wedding was costing them at least $200,000 or more. It would've been more if she hadn't loaned them her house. Theo's family arrived and Nina was happy to chat with them. His sister and her husband sat up front on the groom's family side, while Susannah's family sat opposite them. The families appeared to be well acquainted and Nina was relieved.

Theo pulled her aside to thank her again and to tell her how nervous he was. He told her that Sue's family and his had finally sat down together to find that they had the same background. They too had emigrated from the islands to find success abroad. Her father offered him a job in one of his bottling plants. He told Nina that he was stalling on his answer. He was very happy doing what he was doing and felt that he was well capable of supporting his wife and son. Sue's dad felt that he needed a more stable source of income.

Nina patted him on the arm and told him that once his father-in-law saw how happy and well cared for his daughter was that he'd lay off, she hoped. While the wedding ceremony was gearing up to start, Nina stepped away to the house to look around. She and Darius were spending the night. She wanted to check the gate she had placed at the top of the stairs. The guests had run of the house but she insisted that the upstairs remain private and prohibited to the public.

She found the gate wide open, however. She frowned and hurried along the hallway to check the rooms. Darius' room was the first one she came to and she opened the door to check in it. It was empty so she inserted the key in the lock and locked it. Then she checked and locked her dad's old room. She also locked the other guest rooms and moved on.

Her bedroom was the last one at the end of the hall; she was surprised to find the door standing ajar. She approached cautiously to find three women and one man standing in the middle of her bedroom.

"Excuse me may I help you?" Nina asked as she entered the room.

"Oh," the man said. Clearly, they knew that they were trespassing. "We just wanted to see where you slept," he answered lamely.

"I am sure the Driscoll's told everyone that the upstairs part of the house was off limits. There is a gate at the top of the stairs for a reason. I would appreciate it if you would go back downstairs where the public is permitted," Nina said gently.

One of the women blushed and smiled sheepishly. "Miss Bennett we meant no harm. Come on guys let's go back to the wedding." Nina watched them file out and she followed them to the top of the stairs before she went back to check her bedroom.

She hadn't brought anything of value with her but, she felt violated that people were in her room and perhaps going through her things. She locked the door with the intention of reiterating that the upstairs was strictly off limits.

The ceremony was a solemn event and Susannah was a vision in white. Her gown was an original from none other than her mother. Nina found out later that Sue's mother was a successful designer who had some very influential clientele.

The reception was the longest part of the whole affair and the most extravagant. Strolling violinists serenaded the guests with classical music. The food was upper crust and Nina wasn't impressed. All around her, she saw waste. She didn't know if it was her dad or Richard's influence on how she spent her money but she couldn't help thinking that all of this was ostentatious.

She compared Sue's to Jennifer's wedding and realized that perhaps that's how the people of Christ Tabernacle saw her when she first arrived. Although she felt confident that no one thought of her that way any longer, she knew that she would never make her wedding to Darius an event.

Nina was exhausted after the festivities ended. Although she was a guest, she took it upon herself to serve as supervisor to the wait staff and cleaning crew. The men responsible for tearing down the big tent in the yard were late. Theo and Susannah took off on their honeymoon and her parents only stayed long enough to supervise that everything was back in order, and then thanked her for her generosity.

Mrs. Driscoll gave Nina her business card. She indicated that she would be interested in designing her wedding gown; Nina told her that she would think about it. Of course, Nina did not intend to do any such thing. Her wedding was going to be in New York and done with significantly less fanfare. Still she was happy for her friend. She knew that this was neither Theo nor his sister's idea, had he any say in how things went; it would have been a lot simpler.

"I don't think I'll ever forget this wedding for as long as I live. You'd think that some princess was getting married. Don't get me wrong, I probably will go all out if we have a daughter too, but this was—, I have no words," stated Darius.

Nina linked her arm through his as they walked from the front door to the living room. It took hours for the rental company to take down all their decorations. It was so late when they started that Nina insisted that they come back in the morning to finish.

"I have no words either but maybe they thought of their daughter as a princess," she said being kind. "It is obvious that Sue's family has money and I don't know if it was the mother or the daughter, but wow," Nina said.

"I want our wedding to be classy and non-abrasive. We are going to be the focus of the celebration and not the décor." Darius told her.

"What was your first wedding like?" She hadn't seen any pictures of his first wedding in any of the albums she'd seen at his house.

"It was nice and simple. Rebecca and I were just starting out and we didn't have much. I was still a youth pastor so my salary wasn't up there either. The church gave us a very nice wedding. The women's auxiliary decorated the church and the assembly hall downstairs. The reception was wonderful. We felt all the love and effort they put in and that was what that made it memorable," he replied.

"Do you want them involved this time?" she asked.

"That's entirely up to you baby. You are the one that has to be pleased with all of it. I only care about saying my vows and claiming you as my wife."

"I guess I'll cross that bridge when I come to it. Jennifer didn't have them involved and I didn't hear anything contrary about it. I guess we are a little different. I'll have Aunt Elaine ask around for me to see how they feel. I don't want them to feel that I'm looking down my nose at them or that I don't want them involved."

"Goodness baby, are you still worried about how the congregation feels or what they say about you? I thought you'd gotten over that."

"Darius I'm not marrying a deacon, I'm marrying their pastor. I'm going to be first lady to them and believe me, as a woman, you don't want women being your enemy. They can be brutal," Nina told him solemnly.

Darius merely shook his head and didn't comment. He'd learned a long time ago, that when it came to women and how they saw things, men had better stay out of it. It was safer that way.

The following morning, Darius and Nina left the house after the party rental people finished packing up their decorations. The cab ride to the airport was less comfortable than when Theo drove them and Nina felt his absence keenly, but she hoped that he and his wife were having a good time.

The airport personnel gave Nina the royal treatment at check-in and for once in her whole life, she was grateful. She and the Pastor Fairchild boarded the plane with minimal fuss.

Once the plane landed, Darius quickly gathered their luggage and headed for the parking lot. Nina's SUV was dusty but neither cared. The drive home was uneventful and when Darius parked in front of her aunt's house, Nina turned to him and smiled tiredly at him.

"I haven't been this happy to see home in a long time. I am so weary of all this traveling. The weddings are done, the center is up and running so I don't expect to set foot on another airplane for at least six months," she said.

"You and I both," he agreed.

Since they were only gone two days, Nina hadn't packed much. She told Darius that she could handle her bag and encouraged him to transfer his bag to his car and to get going. Like last time, he hadn't rested on the plane and he was tired.

This time he didn't even try to argue. He obediently took his bag from her, walked over to his car, and got in. He waved weakly as he drove away and Nina said a silent prayer that he reached home safely.

Elaine was happy to see her and wanted all the details about the wedding. She said that some of it was on television. The story was that Nina had loaned out her gorgeous mansion out to her bodyguard for his wedding. Elaine admitted to taping it because it involved her.

After Nina freshened up, she sat with her aunt to watch the story. Nina added more information as the television version was not very forthcoming. Nina told her aunt all about the garish décor and the tasteless food she had to endure. Elaine laughed so hard she had tears in her eyes.

The next few weeks, Nina relaxed during the day not doing very much. She made appearances at the center but left all the work to Jennifer. In the evenings, she met with her musicians to rehearse for the album. At first, she wasn't tired but after the second week, she began to feel it. Darius insisted that she not go to the center on the nights she rehearsed, but sometimes the schedules changed. One evening they had to cancel the rehearsal altogether because two of the musicians had other obligations. Nina hadn't minded because these things happened. She knew she had a good group of professionals and that's all that mattered.

The album didn't have a specific release date so they had all the time in the world to work on it. During one of the rehearsals however, the bassist wanted to know when they were going to record and they had loosely discussed sometime in the spring. It wasn't set in stone but it looked possible.

By late fall, she had cut rehearsals to once a week as they had all the songs for the album perfect. Nina was very proud that it was going so well. They finished the music part, it was just a matter of putting together a back-up group and then they'd be ready to record.

Jonas suggested that she use choir members but Nina had her doubts about that. It wasn't that she didn't feel that they could sing well, it was just that it would prove to be even more costly for her. She'd have to draw up contracts and such. Nina told Jonas that she would think about it and left it at that. She wasn't cheap when it came to her work, but she'd rather work with professionals first before she involved the church choir. She only hoped that Jonas hadn't raised anyone's hopes up.

Aunt Elaine finally decided to retire and Nina threw her a big party at the center. All her friends from the church and work attended. Her boss presented her with a crystal vase as a parting gift. Elaine worked 25 years for that company and she was sad to be leaving. Nina told her that perhaps she could find something to do at the center to relieve her boredom. She agreed eagerly to that.

Darius began looking for ways to expand the church building to accommodate the growing congregation. He invited architects to come look the building over to see if they raised the roof to expand the balcony, they could add more seats. He wasn't committed to it yet but very soon, they would seriously have to do something.

All that made him very happy. He had a growing flock and he hoped that he was doing a good job of providing for them. He had two new believers' classes that graduated already and he found that he needed to start another soon. The church staff was happy to do the work.

Every night he got down on his knees to first thank God and then to ask for guidance. As fast as the church was growing, some received Christ and asked for baptism but ended up going elsewhere to worship. Darius didn't hold that against them at all. Actually, he was just glad that he was the instrument that brought them to the Lord. Filling the pews was never his primary goal, but they were filling up just the same. Winning souls for Christ in these perilous times was more important to him than anything was.

Since Nina had quietly paid a big chunk of the mortgage, Christ Tabernacle hadn't needed to ask for additional offerings to make up a deficit. The trustee's board was happy and didn't bug him as much anymore. It startled Darius at how much Nina eventually paid but he didn't argue with her about it. He was learning to allow more and more members whose job it was to help carry the load and he found that he worried less as well. That ulcer his doctor worried about was healing nicely.

Jennifer turned out to be a natural as administrator and she was doing wonderful things at the center. She expanded the learning center to include job training for the youth at the church as well as those in the surrounding community. The missionary group found plenty of work to do since the center opened its doors as well.

The Charles Bennett Recreational Center brought jobs to the neighborhood and more stability as well. The crime rate that plagued the area had gone down considerably, so that the police precinct contacted the center about doing crime prevention talks and possibly holding self-defense classes there to help continue the safety of the community. Nina and Jennifer were both thrilled. Not in her wildest dreams did she think so many programs or opportunities and benefits would have come to the area because of the center. She felt truly blessed that she saw the need and been inspired to do something about it.

In early March, whilst Nina was in the midst of recording her gospel album, her lawyer contacted her about the sale of her house. She had almost given up hope that it would sell. The house had been up for sale almost two years. She turned down at least two prospective buyers because she felt that they weren't suitable. She discussed with her lawyer the kind of people she hoped would buy it.

Mr. Dullard assured her that the family wanting to buy her house was exactly the type of people she was looking for, Christian and able to care for the house like she had, and besides they were not even haggling over the price. He went on to tell her that the televangelist and his family were impressed with her ethics and trusted that the house was what it appeared to be.

It took another couple of weeks before everything was in order for the bank. Nina relaxed and let her lawyer handle the transaction while she concentrated on her wedding. Darius and she had been looking for a suitable home for themselves and found that it was very hard to find what they were looking for, or for a price they were comfortable with.

The clock was ticking and she was beginning to get nervous. Darius realized that their dream home was nowhere to be found and compromised. They would live in his house in the meantime and expand their search to outside the surrounding area for their dream home. Nina was glad that finding a home was one less thing that needed her attention and concentrated her energies fine-tuning her wedding plans.

By mid-May, Nina finally finished recording the album to focus on her wedding fully. The gown she settled for was a white off the shoulder creation by Demetrios. The long sleeved gown of taffeta and tulle was embellished with lace and beading. The attached train was at least three feet long.

The bridesmaids' gowns were blue by Mia Solano. The strapless A-line gown with a sweetheart neckline and the asymmetrical bodice was a hit with the girls. For propriety's sake, Nina insisted the girls wear the optional satin jacket.

The flower girls were going to wear baby blue gowns with an empire waist, satin princess A-line skirts with an organza floor length bow in the back.

Darius and his groomsmen were going to wear white modern tuxedoes with blue vests and ties to compliment the bridesmaids. Darius' tuxedo, vest and tie were all white.

The very last week in May, Nina began to feel butterflies in her stomach. Her aunt was busy organizing the women's auxiliary. They were going to aid the usher board as the guest list grew to gargantuan size.

The church's lower level was too small to host the reception so Darius and Nina decided to rent the very hall that Jonas and Jennifer used for their wedding. The only difference was that they were using the bigger ballroom for the reception. They were adamant on using the church for the ceremony and scheduled the honorable Bishop Thomas C. Lewis to officiate.

The media somehow found out about the wedding and turned it into a celebrity event. The press was relentless with finding ways to get statements and interviews. The couple hadn't planned to have to deal with the media at all and now had to find a way to keep them happy without ruining the sanctity of their ceremony.

On Darius' last day at work, his co-workers threw him a party that left him feeling overwhelmed. He welcomed their love and well wishes.

The women's auxiliary threw Nina a surprise bachelorette party hosted at Jennifer's apartment. Once she got over her surprise she calmed down to feel assured that since the women's auxiliary arranged it was going to be dignified. Her shock was complete when they finished eating and they urged her to open her gifts. From the eldest of the women who had to be in her early seventies, Nina received lingerie guaranteed to raise Darius' blood pressure. She received similar gifts from the other women as well.

Even Elaine got her something racy. By the time Nina opened her last gift, she was of the impression that they weren't expecting her and Darius to come out of the bedroom the entire time they were on their honeymoon. She didn't say anything, as she had been blushing non-stop from the moment she opened her first gift. No one gave her a single gift useful out of the bedroom.

"I really don't know what to say. I've already bought negligee for my honeymoon but it seems that I have no imagination. I'm taking these that you guys got me instead," she told them blushing once again.

"We got together and discussed what kind of gifts we should get you. It is apparent that you are inexperienced so we thought that we might give you a little help," Sister Winston said. The other women eagerly nodded too.

Flushing crimson yet once again, Nina smiled and nodded. "Thanks to you ladies, I won't have to do much to entice Darius."

That broke the awkward moment and they all laughed, each taking turns telling stories of their honeymoons. By the end of the evening, Nina relaxed enough to suggest that she was just a little bit worried about the wedding night. Elaine was the first to offer her advice. She told her that she shouldn't be afraid of whether she was good or not, the important thing to know was that the honeymoon period was a time of sharing and nurturing. She told Nina that she and Darius had a lifetime to explore the physical part of their marriage and that it would be all right.

On Saturday June 11, 2011, Nina awoke to bright sunshine. She worried all day the previous day because of the rain. The weather report predicted rain all night and possibly into the following day. According to the report, the rain was to go on well into mid-day on her wedding day. God was a good God and He had granted her wish. She wanted a sunny day and it looked like it was going to be.

Nina unplugged her cell phone and looked around the bedroom she had been living in for two years and felt a slight twinge of sadness. After today, she would no longer sleep in this room. She would be sleeping with her husband. That brought a smile to her face. She frowned thinking that her aunt would be alone again and although Aunt Elaine assured her that she would be fine, Nina worried for her.

She dialed Darius' number and waited for him to answer. She got out of bed to walk around the room. They moved her bedroom set to the house and exchanged the furniture in Darius' bedroom with hers. Then they transferred the furniture in the spare bedroom to this room for her aunt to use as a guest room if she chose to.

Across from the bed hung her wedding gown on a rack along with gowns belonging to some of the bridal party. She'd been staring at it for three days now and today she was finally going to wear it.

"Good morning sleepyhead. Are you ready to be married today?" Nina asked her husband-to-be.

"I don't know. Was that today? I woke up all confused. First, I was in the wrong room and in the wrong bed. Nothing looks familiar and I haven't had my coffee yet. Did you know that Rachel isn't coming in today?"

"You are a nut you know that don't you. I won't get to see you until this afternoon so I thought I'd talk with you until the house starts to fill up with women who are going to boss me around and tell me what to do."

"You poor baby, I'm going to have a houseful of men who are going to tease me and tell me what to do too. But I'd rather have them than those women hounding me," Darius sympathized.

"Richard called me last night to tell me how nervous he was. You'd think that walking me down the aisle was a world premiere or something."

"It is a big deal for a father to walk his daughter down the aisle baby. And it is an honor to walk the young woman whom he thinks of as a daughter down the aisle."

"Yeah I guess. Theo and Susannah are here too. They weren't sure if they'd be able to get a flight out yesterday but they surprised me by calling last night to ask about a good place to eat. Everyone I invited arrived last night and I feel so blessed," Nina said a little tearfully.

"We are blessed sweetheart. I have more clergy than family attending our wedding and that is something. Minister Aldridge will be preaching for the next two Sundays while we honeymoon on that beautiful ship. We'll have nothing to do but indulge ourselves for the next two weeks."

"Two weeks of shopping, eating exotic foods and sunbathing on deck. I'm sure to get a tan this summer," said Nina.

"Well maybe by the second week you'll be able to sunbathe. The first week you and I will be getting acquainted, there will be no sunbathing or getting off the ship to shop."

Nina groaned deep in her throat. "Well see now you've messed yourself up. I'm nervous all over again, so I'm going hang up. I'll see you at the church," Nina told him.

"Don't you dare hang up on me woman."

"I will if you don't behave. Talk about something else," Nina warned him.

"Okay, I'm sorry. I love you so much and I can hardly believe that you are finally going to be mine. Just think that this time tomorrow; you'll wake up next to me. I'll look over at you and know that you are mine."

"I'll be yours and you'll be mine," Nina breathed.

"The doorbell just rang, I guess I have to go," Darius told her with a huge sigh.

"'Bye I love you," Nina said and hung up. The time on her cell phone said that it was nine in the morning. If she lay back down, she could take a nap to rest for her long day she thought. She got back in the bed then threw the covers over her head.

Two hours later, the house was full of bridesmaids, flower girls and their mothers. Jennifer was her maid-of-honor and in charge of helping her get dressed. She was sterner than any director she had ever worked with. After letting Nina shower, Jennifer took Nina downstairs where she insisted that she eat something. Aunt Elaine took over to prepare her a light breakfast of fruit and juice. No one allowed her any coffee and Nina was getting a headache until someone suggested she have caffeinated tea instead.

The tea sufficed but Nina still missed the coffee taste and aroma. Then it was time for her make-up. Jennifer again was in charge and when she was done, she stepped back to allow Nina to see herself in the mirror. Nina smiled at the beautiful woman staring back at her.

"Gee Jen when did you become a make-up artist? Even my old make-up artist in California couldn't get me to look like this," said Nina in awe.

"I didn't have to do anything special, this is all you," insisted Jen.

Nina looked at her reflection again and shook her head. "No something is different. You don't have to tell me your secret," argued Nina.

Jennifer gently turned Nina's head to face the mirror once again. "Your eyes are shiny and your cheeks are rosy. You are glowing because you are in love and this is your wedding day. I *really* didn't have to do much. Now as far as your hair goes, that hairdresser you have is a genius. Darius is going to drop dead when he sees you."

Nina smiled at her friend in the mirror. While she was doing her make-up, Nina made her admit to telling the women of her concerns for her wedding night. Jen confessed but explained that she didn't tell them everything just the part where she felt nervous and scared.

"The day is turning out to be gorgeous. We could probably take a few pictures outside before going to the church," Jen commented.

"Why don't you go check to see if everyone else is ready before I get dressed? It is getting too hot to be in this gown if no one else is ready," suggested Nina.

Jennifer agreed and left to go see what the other women were doing. She returned a few minutes later to say that the photographer had arrived and was waiting. The bridal party was downstairs with him.

Nina stood up from the dressing table then went to stand in the middle of the room looking at the gown. Her heart started beating very hard and she became dizzy for a minute until she realized that was holding her breath.

"You are going to make yourself sick Nina, try to relax," Jen suggested. She'd been watching her friend fight these little anxiety attacks all morning.

"I recall telling you the same thing last year, so don't you go get high and mighty with me," Nina said glaring at her friend.

"And snippy too, girl you better get a grip soon," replied Jen pointing a finger at her friend.

"Perhaps I wouldn't be so snippy if I had some coffee up in here," Nina said mimicking Jen's tone.

"Okay, I promise to get you a small cup if you relax and let me do my job, is that a deal?" Jennifer put her hand out.

Nina placed her hand in her friend's and they shook hands. "Deal, get it now before I have a nervous breakdown."

Jen left the room once again shaking her head and mumbling to herself. Nina was sure acting the Diva today she thought, but she did sneak down into the kitchen to pour a small cup of coffee for her friend.

Nina took the cup from Jen gingerly. First, she inhaled the robust aroma and then she took a sip. She closed her eyes to savor the buzz they deprived her of all morning. Ten minutes later, Nina was calmer and relaxed. She told Jennifer that even though she knew the coffee was decaf, she still enjoyed it.

"Boy we can't fool you. Your aunt said that sometime during the morning you would be insisting on a cup so she made a pot of decaf just in case."

"I know everyone feels that I should be calm but coffee doesn't make me hyper, it evens me out. I'm anxious because I'm getting married today and I'm nervous," Nina replied gesturing with her hands.

"I know girl, I know exactly how you feel. In a couple of hours however, everything is going to be *just* fine." Jennifer smiled deviously at her reflection then winked at Nina.

When the limousines arrived, Nina and her entourage were just finishing with the pictures outside the house. The press that gathered was happy to be able to get as many shots as they wanted. The television crew tried to get statements but Nina only smiled and waved.

Finally, the women were able to pile into the three limos that took up much of the parking spaces on the block. Nina had seven bridesmaids and seven flower girls, one bible bearer and a set of miniature bride and groom.

Jennifer fussed over Nina's veil, which had combs that seemed too feeble to attach to Nina's hair. Somehow, the hairdresser had given Nina soft curly tendrils on either side of her head and loose curls, which fell down her back in different lengths. At the crown of her head was a high bun with ivory beads pinned in it.

At the church, there was another group of photographers and media waiting to get shots of her and the wedding party. Nina decided that she was going to ignore them and concentrate on matters that were more important. She was getting married.

Richard met her in one of the front rooms and he couldn't stop smiling at her. "You look lovely Nina. Your dad would've been so proud of you and I am honored to walk you down the aisle," he said with a little tremor in his voice.

"Richard I don't think I've ever seen you nervous. I'm afraid I can't help you because I'm nervous myself," Nina admitted.

"Don't worry it'll be over soon. Then you can relax on the cruise."

"Darius said it should be twenty minutes tops and then it is just a matter of sitting through the speeches from the best man and picture taking at the reception. So I figure that it'll be more like an hour here and two and a half at the reception if we can get away early."

"No matter, let's just concentrate on now," Richard reached into his jacket and pulled out an envelope. "Agatha insisted that I give this to you now instead of later. Is there a pocket in your gown?" he asked searching her gown.

Nina shook her head. She raised a small beaded handbag. "I have this."

Richard smiled, "Perfect." He folded the envelope in half and helped Nina put it in her bag.

"Richard you really didn't have to give me anything. Having you stand in for Dad was gift enough," Nina told her old friend. Her eyes were filling up with tears and she fought to keep them in. "Jennifer will kill me if she sees me crying," she said weakly as she fanned her face.

There was a knock on the door and Nina took a deep breath then linked her arm with Richard's arm. The procession was slow going but when it was finally their turn she squeezed Richard's arm and held on tightly.

She kept her gaze straight, afraid to look at anyone on either side of the aisle. The church looked lovely and there were so many flashes that she couldn't look anywhere but straight ahead anyway.

Partway to the front of the church Darius began walking to meet them. When he was standing directly in front of her, she released Richard's arm, waited for the customary kiss on the cheek, and then watched both men shake hands. Darius took her arm and linked it with his and together they continued to the front of the church.

The ceremony lasted longer than usual and that was because the Bishop's sermon was a little longer than was expected. Finally, it was time for them to exchange vows. Darius' voice was clear and strong but Nina couldn't keep the tremors out of hers. By the time she had completed her vows, there were tears spilling onto her cheeks. Their hands shook when they exchanged rings.

"By the power of our Savior Jesus Christ and the state of New York City, I now pronounce you husband and wife," Bishop Lewis announced, "you may kiss your bride."

Nina could hear the commotion as people rushed up as close as they dared to get a picture. Darius made a big production of lifting her veil and when he had laid it back, he smiled tenderly at her.

"You are my beloved," he said for her ears alone and then he kissed her.

Nina slid her arms around his shoulders and kissed him for all she was worth. It didn't last very long but it was sufficient to please their audience who clapped loudly. Darius smiled and winked at her and together they turned to face everyone.

The walk down the aisle was less scary, Nina was able to look at her friends, and smile and she even waved. The camera flashes were still bright but she didn't care, she was happy because she was finally Mrs. Darius Fairchild.

EPILOGUE

Nina got out of the SUV and slammed the door shut. She rushed to her aunt's front door to ring the bell. Elaine opened the door quickly and stepped back to allow her niece in. She never got tired of seeing her. She was so cute and round. Nina was in her ninth month of pregnancy.

"Shouldn't you be home with your feet up?" Aunt Elaine asked. Her voice was gruff but Nina could tell the she was pleased to see her.

"You'd think that wouldn't you?" Darius said at the door behind his wife. "She went behind my back to hire painters to come paint the nursery. When I got home I found her huffing and puffing unable to breathe," Darius reported looking disgusted.

Nina turned to glare at her husband, "If you'd taken the time to ask I would've told you that I had been up and down the stairs and that was why you found me out of breath," she countered. She turned on her heel and headed for the kitchen. She was drinking a glass of water when they reached her.

"Nina you know that you can't be doing so much. Wasn't Rachel there with you?" Elaine asked looking at her watch.

"Rachel left early, she had an appointment. I am not a child and I wasn't overdoing it. I merely went up to check on the painters, took some items out of the room, and came back down. Your nephew is just being his arrogant and overprotective self, that's all," Nina, said glaring at her husband again.

Darius threw his hands up in exasperation. "You see? Elaine she's driving me crazy. You'd think that after two years of marriage I'd be able to handle her, but no she does stuff like this and I can't take it."

Nina absentmindedly rubbed her belly where their child just kicked and brushed past him. She sat gingerly on the edge of the sofa and shook her hair out of her eyes. Shortly after their wedding, she decided that she was going to grow her locks out and get it cut. Now she sported shoulder length curly red hair.

Darius was the first to reach her and stood beside her. "Baby I'm sorry but I worry about you. I wouldn't worry so much if you'd just take it easy. The doctor wants you to rest these last couple of weeks because once the baby comes you won't get much."

"I'm not trying to be difficult honey; I just want everything to be prefect for our baby. In a matter of weeks we are going to have this little person who's going to be totally dependent on us and nothing is ready yet."

"The furniture is being delivered the end of this week and since you've gone and got the room painted, everything *is* ready," Darius pointed out.

They found their dream home shortly after they learned that Nina was expecting. It was an old mansion on Long Island. The commute to and from the church wasn't bad on a Sunday but during the week it was horrendous depending on the time of day. The house needed some repair but otherwise perfect for their needs. Because of the condition of the house, they were able to buy it for considerably less than it was worth.

Nina hired an architect to remake the house into their dream home and the architect did it in six months. They got everything they'd talk about so long ago and more. The previous owners were musicians so the studio was already in place as well as the swimming pool and basketball court. The house had four bedrooms and the master bedroom had a beautiful fireplace in it. The connecting bath had a Jacuzzi tube big enough for two.

They moved in two months earlier and been buying and placing furniture ever since. The nursery was the last room to furnish and decorate. They wanted it perfect for their child. There in was the problem. They couldn't agree on anything from what color the nursery should be to the furniture they should get. Finally, Darius gave up and left it up to his wife to decide how the room should look and to furnish it.

Elaine sat opposite her niece and nephew-in-law and watched them.

Together those two had accomplished so much in so little a time for the church. Christ Tabernacle's membership had grown so much that they expanded the building. By some miracle, the house next door, which was a corner house, went up for sale. The church had no trouble buying it. They were able to enlarge the church building to accommodate six hundred more people.

The recreation center was doing fantastic as well. Most of the youths in the church worked there after school tutoring or helping with the twice a week senior care services. Jennifer thought that it would be a good idea during the winter to have the seniors host activities at the center. So twice a week they met for exercise club or social club.

Nina's gospel album was a great success and she received an award for new gospel artist of the year. She was planning on another when she found out that she was going to be a mother. Her husband suggested that she wait and she agreed.

Darius no longer held an outside job. He worked full-time for the church. He was either going to the hospital to visit his members, to their homes, or at the center counseling or coaching basketball to the youths. He belonged to most of the community affairs councils. He was ministering as he always dreamed he would. All of this was possible because Nina had come into their lives. Now, she was a blessing that was driving everyone crazy.

"How long before the painters are finished," asked Elaine?

"They were done by the time I got home," Darius told her.

"So you are here to let the fumes clear out correct?"

"Yes Auntie. The painters assured me that the fumes were at a minimum but Mr. Worrypants here insisted on reading the label on the paint can to make sure," reported Nina.

"The paint can cautions pregnant women to be careful so that's what we are doing. We left all the windows in the room open to air it out," replied Mr. Worrypants.

"So now that we are all calm, would you like to stay for dinner," asked Elaine?

"I thought you'd never ask, I'm starving," Nina accepted excitedly.

Darius turned to help her up and smiled at Elaine. "Besides arguing with me, her other pastime is eating. I sure hope you lose some of that weight baby, I want my sexy wife back," Darius teased Nina.

"Not a chance. If I recall it was being sexy that got me in this condition in the first place. I think I like being plump," Nina declared. Suddenly, she scrunched her face up in pain.

"Are you still getting those false labor pains Catalina?" Darius asked putting his arms around her. She was getting those pains quite often lately and although their obstetrician assured them that they were just a preparation mechanism for the real thing, he worried.

"Yeah, but I'll be fine once I eat and get some rest," Nina assured him with a weak smile. She too was getting nervous and worried that she wouldn't be able to tell the real thing when it did happen. These contractions were painful.

"Are you sure?" Aunt Elaine asked not entirely convinced.

Nina straightened up to smile at them. She was feeling better and she was hungry. "I'm fine, did I smell fried chicken?"

"She's all right," Darius said with a relieved expression on his face.

Nina ate three pieces of chicken and two big pieces of cornbread on top of the rice and peas her aunt prepared. Elaine couldn't believe how much her niece had eaten. She had to have gained close to forty pounds she mused, but she looked radiant and happy.

They spent another hour relaxing where Elaine and Darius took turns feeling the baby kick and trying to coax Nina into telling them what the baby's sex was. Nina insisted on surprising everyone. She decorated the nursery with a theme instead of a color. The background color was a muted yellow and mango color and she put up generic nursery themed decals on the walls.

All the clothes she bought were neutral so that either a boy or girl could wear them for the first six months. The car seat cover was white. The sleigh crib was a dark mahogany as well as the changing table and bureau. The carpet was the same color as the walls. All of which gave Darius no clue as to what their child was going to be.

He then tried a different tactic. He asked to name their child and Nina told him that he could pick out a name for each sex. She explained that when the baby was born he'd know which name to put on the birth certificate. Darius chose Darius Charles Fairchild in honor of the father-in-law that he never met for a boy and Elizabeth Grace Fairchild for a girl.

Nina agreed and her aunt felt touched that her brother had a namesake. Still she gave no indication whatsoever that she favored one name over the other. She just wouldn't budge. Finally, they left for home promising Elaine that they would pick her up for church on Sunday.

When they arrived home, Nina didn't argue with her husband about waiting for morning to see the nursery. She had a glass of juice and allowed him to escort her upstairs to their bedroom.

Nina and Darius worked hard in decorating their home. She sent for all of the furniture she had in storage from California and once they arrived, they divided them between the house in Queens and their new home in Long Island. Darius became comfortable with Nina spending money; she never made him feel less manly because she had more than he had. He loved that about her.

In the award room of their new home, she displayed her awards and some of her father's. Aunt Elaine kept the rest of them for herself. The family portrait that once graced her home in California now hung prominently in her aunt's home. Nina had a copy made for herself, which she kept in the award room.

The kitchen was the only room in the entire house that she insisted on doing completely over, and once it was done Darius found that it was similar to the old house in California. As for his home office, Darius had total control. It was his domain to do what he will; he had it done in blue and white.

The couple arranged for Elaine to move in for a few weeks once the baby was born to help. Nina was well capable of keeping her own house but gave in when her pregnancy progressed. The tasks that she found easy became complicated. Darius put his foot down when she was going up and down the stairs to do laundry after her feet started to swell. Because of the commute, Sister Rachel was only able to come in a couple of days a week so help was minimal.

Nina got in bed and sighed softly. Her feet hurt and were swollen. Although she teased Darius about her weight, she secretly worried that she wouldn't be able to shed the pounds after the birth. She was mature enough to know that her husband wouldn't really care about her weight but she was a woman after all and one of the things she did like about her body was that it was toned and shapely.

All that would change if she didn't lose the weight but she was going to give it her best effort. If she did everything to lose weight and it didn't work then she wouldn't worry about it. Life had so much more to offer her than for her to waste time obsessing about weight. She'd been looking at her old albums and seen the pictures of her parents. Her mother was still shapely after having had her and that was comforting.

The following morning, Darius left later than usual for the church. He had several appointments and rescheduled two of them for another time. He didn't want to leave Nina alone. He trusted her to rest but she was due in two weeks and he felt that he should stay close. Living so far away made it a constant worry for him. He pictured his stubborn wife trying to drive to the hospital herself if he wasn't around when the time came. They took the prenatal classes the hospital offered and he felt confident that they would do all right in the delivery room, but getting there was the only problem.

Wednesday morning Rachel arrived a few minutes before Darius left and she brought Jennifer with her. He waved at the women as he pulled out of the driveway.

"Hello mama, how are you feeling?" Jennifer asked.

"Heavy if you must know," Nina began. She turned to Rachel and smiled. "Rachel I had some toast and a glass of milk. Help yourself if you want anything." She clasped Jen's hand and pulled her along to the living room.

"Girl I don't know how you keep this place so clean. It must take you days to get it all done and I bet that by the time you got it done it's time to do it again," commented Jen looking around in awe.

"It's not that hard. There are days I don't do anything. The summer months are the busy ones because the dust piles up. If anything it is just the bathrooms, bedroom and kitchen that need constant attention," Nina assured her.

"Your aunt insisted that I come spend the day with you so here I am," Jennifer answered her unspoken question.

"I thought so. She and Darius are treating me like I'm this fragile piece of china and it is driving me batty." Nina waved her arms like a bird.

"It isn't every day that he becomes a father and this is your first child too. I know how independent you are but honey you are married now and you have to share. And seriously would it hurt to let the man take care of you?"

"You're one to talk. You're only four months along and I bet you feel great and want to continue doing the things you've been doing, but I've seen Jonas and your mother hovering over you. I'm not trying to be difficult it's just that I don't feel that I can't do anything. I know to rest when I get tired. And believe me Darius doesn't let me get away with anything," said Nina shaking her head.

"Even so take everybody's advice and relax and enjoy being you for whatever amount of time you have left. Put your feet up and just be still," Jen advised.

"Okay. Today I am not going to do anything. I'll wait for Darius to come home before I do anything in the nursery. The furniture doesn't arrive for a few days yet."

At the mention of the nursery, Jennifer's eyes lit up and she asked to see it. Nina led the way and once they were in the room, Jennifer let out a little squeal.

"Oh Nina it is beautiful. It is so bright and colorful. I've never seen a nursery look like this before, it reminds me of the islands. Jonas and I honeymooned in Barbados. The islands are so full of color that just looking around made me happy."

"That's what I thought when I first started. Darius and I went to the Bahamas and I loved the colors too. The people smiled a lot and everything was so vibrant. I wanted to do one of the rooms like this but it didn't feel right. For a nursery, it feels right. You really like it?" asked Nina.

"Oh yes I do. You know that it doesn't matter what you have, boy or girl your child is going to be the happiest little being. Aren't you excited?"

"I am but a little scared too. Darius worries that he won't be here when I go into labor and I just worry about the whole process," admitted Nina.

"Girl I don't think there is anything you can't do. Look at all the things you've done since you came here. You've built a recreation center that's doing *fantastic* things in our community and you've done a movie about your parents that's been a hit for how long? Don't even get me started on that album of yours. Giving birth is going to be a snap for you," Jennifer said snapping her fingers.

"You make it sound like I did all those things by myself. If God wasn't with me, I shudder to think where I'd be today. I just keep praying that He gives me an easy birth. Darius and I have been to the classes and we watched a movie of an actual birth. I couldn't get it out of my head for weeks. Anyway there is nothing I can do about it, the child has to be born regardless of how I feel about it," Nina shrugged.

"That's true. Come on let's go back downstairs. This is the first time I've been here since you've redone the place and I want a tour."

Nina took her friend around her house. She showed her the rooms upstairs before they went down to the lower levels, after which Nina took her out back to sit poolside. Rachel brought them some fruit juice and instructed them to relax.

They spent the rest of the day just relaxing and enjoying each other's company. By the time Darius returned, Nina was very relaxed and less fussy. Rachel and her daughter had dinner with the expecting couple before they left.

Darius showered and changed into a pair of shorts. It was hot and as much as he wanted to turn the air conditioning on, he knew that Nina would soon become uncomfortable. Instead, they sat poolside enjoying the quiet and the occasional breeze.

"Darius my hospital stay is only a day and a half and you'll have to place the furniture when it comes. I think I'm in labor," Nina told her husband quietly.

While pregnant, it was their custom for her to sit spoon fashion while he rubbed her belly. His hand froze as he took in what she said.

"Are you sure Baby?" he asked. His voice shook.

"I'm sure," Nina replied calmly.

Darius got up and helped his wife to her feet. On the way through the house, Nina had a contraction harder than the ones she had been experiencing. She stopped to do her breathing exercises. With Jennifer's help, she showered earlier. She packed her overnight bag weeks earlier and it was in the SUV along with the infant car seat. On the way to the hospital, Nina called her aunt to let her know that they were on their way.

The hospital admitted Nina even though she wasn't in full labor. She started her labor later the following day.

Nina gave birth to Elizabeth Grace Fairchild on Friday July 11, 2013 at 3 am. She weighed in at 7 pounds, 8 ounces. Nina was so relieved that it was over that she didn't have time to feel happy. It wasn't a difficult birth by usual standards, but she was in labor for over fifteen hours. The doctor wanted to do a cesarean section because the baby had not descended into the birth canal after all that time. Nina insisted that they wait and asked that everyone leave the room. She asked her husband to place his hands on her belly and to pray with her.

Darius prayed earnestly. He prayed for the child to descend into the birth canal and for his wife's strength to be renewed. Nina was tired and developed dark circles under her eyes. After the prayer, she had a series of strong contractions and the baby began to descend and soon crowned for birth.

"God's good mercy endureth forever," Nina whispered tiredly.

"Amen. I'm so proud of you. Our daughter is beautiful." Darius whispered back.

It was a couple of hours before anyone could see Nina, but the baby was the center of attraction in the nursery. When she opened her eyes, Darius wasn't surprised to see the hazel eyes that stared unseeingly at everyone.

The following Sunday, Darius walked up to the pulpit and asked the church to help him praise the Lord for the blessings he had received. Then he asked that they opened their Bibles to Matthew 7:7-11 (KJV).

"Saints the Scriptures speak about prayer and faith. When Jesus walked the Earth, he taught us about faith and about prayer. One day while he was teaching, he taught the disciples how to pray. Everything you can think of is in that prayer that He taught us. Yet sometimes you have to get out of the box and speak even more plainly. That was how Jesus prayed, how he operated.

When the man who was demon possessed came up against him, the demon immediately recognized who he was and he was afraid even while he was being defiant. Jesus spoke with authority and commanded the demon to leave. That's the kind of faith we need, and that's the kind of authority we need also. Miracles still happen today because of the power of faith-filled prayer that is chock full of authority. You can still pray and have your prayer answered. You can still command the enemy to leave your children alone or to unstop a loved one's hearing so that he may hear the Master's call.

Brothers and sisters faith is not hard to achieve if you really believe. Praying and believing that God will answer your prayer is faith. Praying for something and then forgetting it is faith-filled prayer. Some of us come up here and pray for the same thing repeatedly. If you had prayed with authority and believed that God heard and answered your prayer, you wouldn't have to come up here to pray for the same thing yet again.

Last week my wife went into labor. She suffered for a long time and the doctors were ready to operate. Although she was in pain, she believed that the God of Abraham would deliver her. She asked that the room be cleared and then asked me to pray with her. Saints, she gave birth shortly thereafter. That was an act of faith! Faced with the possibility of surgery, she knew that if she asked God to intercede for her that He would.

We need to have faith like that saints. Christ didn't die in vain and he didn't teach us in vain. He gave us the authority to go to the Father for our needs. Don't let the enemy cloud your thinking saints. We have power to overcome anything. Faith is our weapon and our shield. The Word says that He will open up the windows of heaven for you and pour you out a blessing so great that you won't have room enough for it. I don't know about you but I want that kind of blessing. That blessing doesn't just go for those who obediently pay their tithes; it goes for all of us who come to him in faith. So stand up on your feet and test out your faith. Pray to your Father!"

Filled with the Holy Ghost, Darius stepped down to lay hands on those the Lord led him. After service Darius didn't linger, he had finally learned to share his load and to have his assistant ministers handle the many requests that he would routinely hear out and try to accommodate. He went home to his wife and daughter all the while praising God for being His Beloved.

ABOUT THE AUTHOR

Lisa Arnoux-Brown is a widow, a mother of five, and a grandmother of six. Although a native of New York, she's lived in Massachusetts, where she began her writing career and is the proud author of four of the In the Line of Duty series. Lisa is now embarking on a new journey to write Christian books. Her first labor of love, Beloved, took prayer and express attention to her Christian surroundings. She has worked as a dialysis technician for the past twelve years, work she continues to find rewarding.

ABOUT THE AUTHOR